CW01024289

BUDGE'S EGYPT
A CLASSIC 19TH-CENTURY
TRAVEL GUIDE

E. A. Wallis Budge

DOVER PUBLICATIONS, INC.
Mineola, New York

Published in Canada by General Publishing Company, Ltd., 30 Lesmill Road, Don Mills, Toronto, Ontario.

Bibliographical Note

This Dover edition, first published in 2001, is an unabridged republication of the work originally published by Thos. Cook & Son, London, in 1890 under the title *The Nile: Notes for Travellers in Egypt*. The original foldout map appears here as a double-page spread (pp. xvi–xvii).

Library of Congress Cataloging-in-Publication Data

Budge, E. A. Wallis (Ernest Alfred Wallis), Sir, 1857–1934.
  [Nile]
  Budge's Egypt : a classic 19th-century travel guide / E.A. Wallis Budge.—Dover ed.
    p. cm.
  Originally published: The Nile. London : T. Cook & Son, 1890.
  Includes bibliographical references and index.
  ISBN 0-486-41721-2 (pbk.)
    1. Egypt—Guidebooks. 2. Nile River—Guidebooks. I. Title.

DT45 .B9 2001
916.204'55—dc21

2001028453

Manufactured in the United States of America
Dover Publications, Inc., 31 East 2nd Street, Mineola, N.Y. 11501

INTRODUCTION.

———•———

Having for some years felt the insufficiency of the information given by Dragomans to travellers on the Nile, and finding with one or two striking exceptions how limited is their knowledge of facts relating to the history of the antiquities in Upper Egypt, Messrs. Thos. Cook and Son have arranged with Mr. E. A. Wallis Budge to compile the following pages, which they have much pleasure in presenting to every passenger under their Nile arrangements on their Tourist Steamers and Dhahabiyyehs. In this way passengers will no longer be liable to be misled (unintentionally) by Dragomans, but will be able at their leisure to prepare themselves for what they have to see, and thus by an agreeable study add to the interest with which their visits to the various places are made.

PREFACE.

The short descriptions of the principal Egyptian monuments on each side of the Nile between Cairo and the Second Cataract (Wâdi Ḥalfah), printed in the following pages, are not in any way intended to form a "Guide to Egypt": they are drawn up for the use of those travellers who have a very few weeks to spend in Egypt, and who wish to carry in their memories some of the more important facts connected with the fast-perishing remains of one of the most interesting and ancient civilizations that has been developed on the face of the earth. The existing guide books are generally too voluminous and diffuse for such travellers; and are, moreover, in many respects inaccurate. Experience has shown that the greater number of travellers in that country are more interested in history and matters connected with Egyptian civilization from B.C. 4400 to B.C. 450, than with Egypt under the rule of the Assyrians and Persians, Greeks and Romans, Arabs and Turks. It is for this reason that no attempt has been made to describe, otherwise than in the briefest possible manner, its history under these foreign rulers, and only such facts connected with them as are absolutely necessary for a right understanding of its monuments have been inserted. In addition to such descriptions, a few chapters have been added on the history of the country during the rule of the Pharaohs, its people, the religion and method of writing. At the end of the book a fairly full list of the most important Egyptian kings is appended, and in order to make this list as useful as possible, a transliteration of each name is printed beneath it, together with the ordinary form of the name. The list of three hundred hieroglyphic characters and their phonetic values, printed on pp. 61–68, will, it is hoped, be useful to those who may like to spell out the royal names on tombs and temples and the commoner words which occur in the inscriptions. For those who wish to study independently the various branches of Egyptology, a list of the more readily obtained books is given in the "Programme" issued yearly by Thos. Cook and Son.

In transcribing Arabic names of places the most authoritative forms have been followed, but such well-known names as "Luxor," in Arabic *El-Uḳṣûr* or *El-ḳuṣûr*, and "Cairo," in Arabic *Ḳâhira*, have not been altered. Similarly, the ordinary well-known forms of the Egyptian proper names "Rameses," "Thothmes," "Amenophis," "Amāsis," "Psammetichus," "Hophra" or "Apries," etc., etc., have been used in preference to the more correct transcriptions " Rā-messu," " Tehuti-mes," " Åmen-hetep," " Åāh-mes," " Psemthek," " Uah-åb-Rā."

The dates assigned to the Egyptian kings are those of Dr. H. Brugsch, who bases his calculations on the assumption that the average duration of a generation was thirty-three years. Hence it will be readily understood that the date assigned to Rameses II. (B.C. 1333), for instance, is only approximately correct.

E. A. WALLIS BUDGE.

September, 1890

CONTENTS.

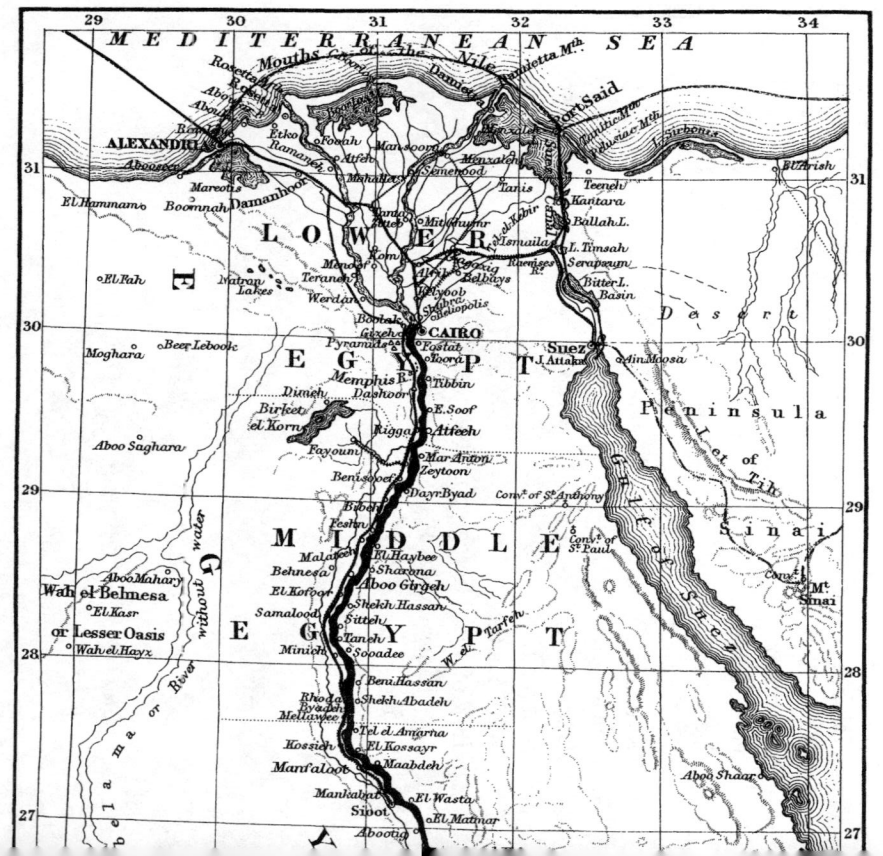

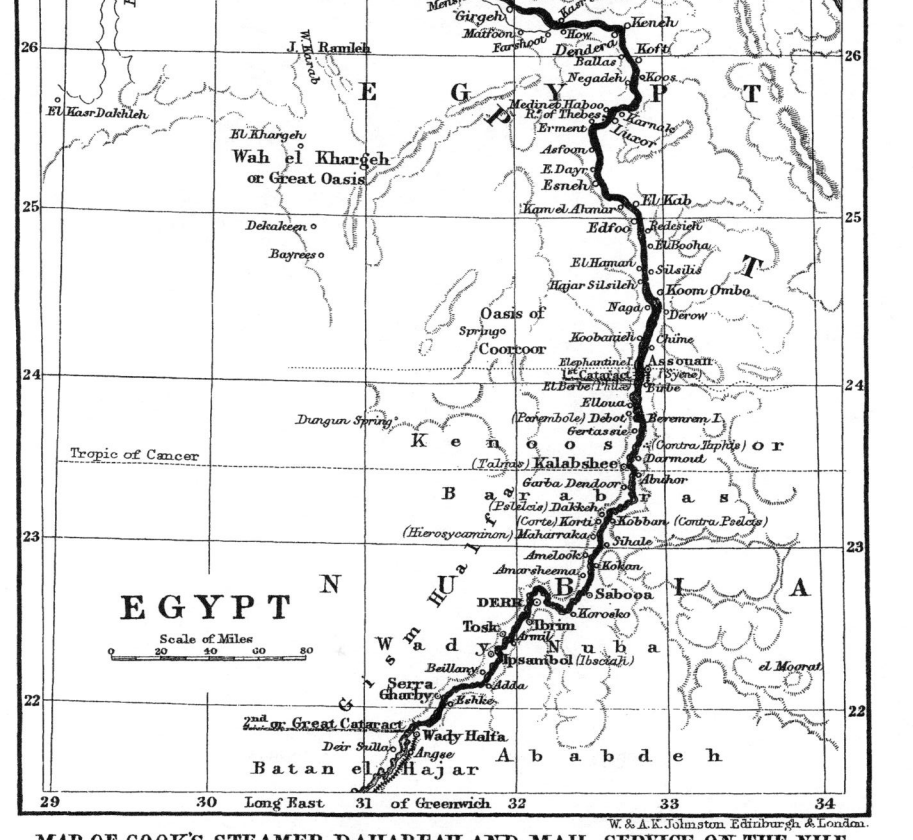

MAP OF COOK'S STEAMER, DAHABEAH, AND MAIL SERVICE ON THE NILE.

NOTES FOR TRAVELLERS IN EGYPT.

EGYPTIAN HISTORY.

THE history of Egypt is the oldest history known to us. It is true that the earliest of the Babylonian kings whose names are known lived very little later than the earliest kings of Egypt, nevertheless our knowledge of the early Egyptian is greater than of the early Babylonian kings. A large portion of Egyptian history can be constructed from the native records of the Egyptians, and it is now possible to correct and modify many of the statements upon this subject made by Herodotus, Diodorus Siculus and other classical authors. The native and other documents from which Egyptian history is obtained are :—

I. Lists of Kings found in the **Turin Papyrus,** the **Tablet of Abydos,** the **Tablet of Sakkârah,** and the **Tablet of Karnak.** The Turin papyrus contained a complete list of kings beginning with the god-kings and continuing down to the end of the rule of the Hyksos, about B.C. 1700. The name of each king during this period, together with the length of his reign in years, months and days, was given, and it would have been, beyond all doubt, the most valuable of all documents for the chronology of the oldest period of Egyptian history, if scholars had been able to make use of it in the perfect condition in which it was

discovered. When it arrived in Turin, however, it was
found to be broken into more than one hundred and fifty
fragments. So far back as 1824, Champollion recognized
the true value of the fragments, and placed some of them
in their chronological order. Its evidence is of the greatest
importance for the history of the XIIIth and XIVth dynasties, because in this section the papyrus is tolerably perfect ;
for the earlier dynasties it is of very little use.

On the monuments each Egyptian king has usually two
names, the prenomen and the nomen ; each of these
is contained in a cartouche.* Thus the prenomen of

Thothmes III. is (cartouche) Rā-men-cheper, and his

nomen is (cartouche) Teḥuti-mes. Rā-men-cheper means
something like " Rā (the Sun-god) establishes becoming
or existence ;" Teḥuti-mes means "born of Thoth," or
"Thoth's son." These names are quite distinct from
his titles. Before the prenomen comes the title

suten net, " King of the North and South,"† and after it

comes se Rā, "son of the Sun," preceding the
nomen. Each prenomen has a meaning, but it is at times
difficult to render it exactly in English. Every king styled
himself king of "the North and South," and "son of the
Sun." The first title is sometimes varied by " Beautiful

---

* Cartouche is the name which is usually given to the oval ⊂⊃, in
which the name of a royal person is enclosed.

† *I.e.,* "the universe." " Whatever the Sun passed over or through
was divided into two, and grammatically took the dual form ; as
chuta, the horizon where the Sun rises or sets, *àbtà,* the East,
àmentà, the West." Renouf, *Proc. Soc. Bib. Arch.,* 1890,
p. 356.

god, lord of the two earths."* In the earliest times the kings were named after some attribute possessed by them ; thus Menà, the first king of Egypt, is the "firm" or "established." In the Turin papyrus only the prenomens of the kings are given, but its statements are confirmed and amplified by the other lists.

The **Tablet of Abydos**† was discovered by Dümichen in the temple of Osiris at Abydos, during M. Mariette's excavations there in 1864. This list gives us the names of seventy-five kings, beginning with Menà or Menes, and ending with Seti I., the father of Rameses II.; it is not a complete list, and it would seem as if the scribe who drew up the list only inserted such names as he considered worthy of living for ever. The **Tablet of Sakkârah** was discovered at Sakkârah by Mariette, in the grave of a dignitary who lived during the reign of Rameses II. In spite of a break in it, and some orthographical errors, it is a valuable list; it gives the names of forty-seven kings, and it agrees very closely with the Abydos list. It is a curious fact that it begins with the name of Mer-ba-pen, the sixth king of the Ist dynasty. The **Tablet of Karnak** was discovered at Karnak by Burton, and was taken to Paris by Prisse. It

---

* Some kings had a large number of titles. Thus Thothmes III. is styled "Horus, mighty bull, diademed with law, the lord, maker of things, Rā-men-cheper," etc., etc. He is also called :

"King of the North and South, mighty in all lands"; "God, exalted one of the white crown, beloved of Rā"; "Golden **Horus,** mighty of valour, smiter of the Nine Bows," etc.

† See page 184.

was drawn up in the time of Thothmes III., and contains the names of sixty-one of his ancestors. They are not arranged in any chronological order, but the tablet is of the highest historical importance, for it records the names of some of the rulers from the XIIIth to the XVIIth dynasties, and gives the names of those of the XIth dynasty more completely than any other list.

II. Annals of Egyptian Kings inscribed upon the walls of temples, obelisks, and buildings. The narrative of such inscriptions is very simple, and practically such records merely represent itineraries in which the names of conquered and tributary lands and people are given ; incidentally facts of interest are noted down. As the day and month and regnal years of the king by whom these expeditions were undertaken are generally given, these inscriptions throw much light on history. The lists of tribute are also useful, for they show what the products of the various countries were. The poetical version* of the history of the famous battle of Rameses II. against the Cheta by the poet Pen-ta-urt is a pleasant variety of historical narrative. The inscription on the stele† of Piānchi, the Ethiopian conqueror of Egypt, is decidedly remarkable for the minute details of his fights, the speeches made by himself and his conquered foes, and the mention of many facts‡ which are not commonly noticed by Egyptian annalists. The vigour and poetical nature of the narrative are also very striking.

* See the notice of the official Egyptian account on page 253.

† Preserved at Gîzeh.

‡ For example, it is stated that when Piānchi had taken possession of the storehouses and treasury of Nimrod his foe, he went afterwards into the stables, and found that the horses there had been kept short of food. Bursting into a rage he turned to Nimrod and said, "By my life, by my darling Rā, who revives my nostrils with life, to have kept my horses hungry is more heinous in my sight than any other offence which thou hast committed against me." Mariette, *Monuments Divers*, pl. 2, ll. 65, 66.

III. Historical Stelæ and Papyri, which briefly relate in chronological order the various expeditions undertaken by the king for whom they were made. Egyptian kings occasionally caused summaries of their principal conquests and of the chief events of their reign to be drawn up ; examples of these are (*a*) the stele of Thothmes III.,* and (*b*) the last section of the great **Harris Papyrus,** in which Rameses III. reviews all the good works which he has brought to a successful issue to the glory of the gods of Egypt and for the benefit of her inhabitants. This wonderful papyrus measures 135 feet by 18 inches, and was found in a box in the temple at Medînet Habu, built by Rameses III. ; it is now in the British Museum.

IV. Decrees, Scarabs, Statues of Kings and Private Persons are fruitful sources of information about historical, religious, and chronological subjects.

V. Biblical notices about Egypt and allusions to events of Egyptian history.

VI. The Cuneiform Inscriptions. Within the last two years a number of tablets inscribed in cuneiform have been found at Tell el-Amarna. The inscriptions relate to a period of Egyptian history which falls in the sixteenth century B.C., and they are letters from the kings of Babylon, Nineveh, and other cities of Mesopotamia and of Phœnicia relating to marriages, offensive and defensive alliances, military matters, etc., etc., and reports on the rebellions and wars which took place at that time, addressed to Amenophis III. and to his son Chut-en-âten or Amenophis IV. The Babylonian king who writes is called Kurigalzu. Thothmes III. had carried his victorious arms into Mesopotamia, and one of his successors, Amenophis III., delighted to go there and shoot the lions with which the country abounded. During one of these hunting expeditions he fell in love with the daughter of Tushratta, the king of

* Preserved at Gîzeh.

Mitanni, and married her, and he brought her to Egypt, accompanied by 317 of her attendants. It will be some time before these inscriptions are fully made out, but the examination of them has already been carried sufficiently far to show that they will throw some valuable light upon the social condition of Egypt and of the countries which were subject to her at that time. Some of the tablets are written with cuneiform characters in a language which is at present unknown; and some of them have dockets in hieratic which state from what country they were brought. The discovery of these tablets shows that there must have been people at the court of Amenophis III. who understood the cuneiform characters, and that the officers in command over towns in Phœnicia subject to the rule of Egypt could, when occasion required, write their despatches in cuneiform. The greater part of these tablets are now in the Museums of London and Berlin, some are at the Gîzeh Museum, and some are in private hands.

The Assyrian kings Sennacherib, Esarhaddon, and Assurbanipal marched against Egypt; Tirhakah defeated Sennacherib at Eltekeh, but was defeated by Esarhaddon, the son of Sennacherib, who drove him back into Ethiopia. Esarhaddon's son, Assurbanipal, also attacked Tirhakah and defeated him. Thebes was captured, and Egypt was divided into twenty-two provinces, over some of which Assyrian viceroys were placed. A fragment of a Babylonian tablet states that Nebuchadnezzar II. marched into Egypt.

VII. The Greek and Roman writers upon Egypt are many; and of these the best known are Herodotus, Manetho, and Diodorus Siculus. **Herodotus** devotes the whole of the second and the beginning of the third book of his work to a history of Egypt and the Egyptians, and his is the oldest Greek treatise on the subject known to us. In spite of the attacks made upon his work during the last few years, the evidence of the hieroglyphic inscriptions which are being deciphered year after year shows that on the whole his work is trustworthy. A work more valuable than that of Herodotus is the Egyptian history of **Manetho** (still living in B.C. 271) of Sebennytus, who is said by Plutarch to have been a contemporary of Ptolemy I.; his work, however, was written during the reign of Ptolemy II. Philadelphus (B.C. 286–247). According to words put into his mouth, he was chief priest and scribe in one of the temples of Egypt, and he appears to have been perfectly acquainted with the ancient Egyptian language and literature. He had also had the benefit of a Greek education, and was therefore peculiarly fitted to draw up in Greek for Ptolemy Philadelphus a history of Egypt and her religion. The remains of the great Egyptian history of Manetho are preserved in the polemical treatise of Josephus against Apion, in which a series of passages of Egyptian history from the XVth to the XIXth dynasties is given, and in the list of the dynasties, together with the number of years of the reign of each king, given by Africanus and Eusebius on his authority. At the beginning of his work Manetho gives a list of gods and demi-gods who ruled over Egypt before Menes, the first human king of Egypt; the thirty dynasties known to us he divides into three sections:— I–XI, XII–XIX, and XX–XXX. **Diodorus Siculus,** who visited Egypt B.C. 57, wrote a history of the country, its people and its religion, based chiefly upon the works of Herodotus and Hekatæus. He was not so able a writer nor so accurate an observer as Herodotus, and his work contains many blunders. Other important ancient writers on Egypt are Strabo,* Chaeremon,† Josephus,‡ Plutarch§ and Horapollo.‖

According to Manetho, there reigned over Egypt before Menà, or Menes, the first human king of that country, a

---

* About A.D. 15.   † About A.D. 50.   ‡ About A.D. 75.
§ About A.D. 100.   ‖ About A.D. 400.

number of beings called Shesu Ḥeru, or "followers of Horus"; of their deeds and history nothing is known. Some have believed that during their rule Egypt was divided into two parts, each ruled by its own king; and others have thought that the whole of Upper and Lower Egypt was divided into a large series of small, independent principalities, which were united under one head in the person of Menes. There is, however, no support to be obtained from the inscriptions for either of these theories. The kings of Egypt following after the mythical period are divided into thirty dynasties. For the sake of convenience, Egyptian history is divided into three periods:—I, the **Ancient Empire,** which includes the first eleven dynasties; II, the **Middle Empire,** which includes the next nine dynasties (XIIth–XXth); and, III, the **New Empire,** which includes the remaining ten dynasties, one of which was of Persian kings. The rule of the Saïte kings was followed by that of the **Persians, Ptolemies** and **Romans.** The rule of the Muḥammedans, which began A.D. 641, ended A.D. 1517, when the country was conquered by the Turks; since this time Egypt has been nominally a pashalik of Turkey.

The date assigned to the first dynasty is variously given by different scholars: by Champollion-Figeac it is B.C. 5867, by Böckh 5702, by Bunsen 3623, by Lepsius 3892, by Lieblein 3893, by Mariette 5004, and by Brugsch 4400. As far as can be seen, there is much to be said in favour of that given by Brugsch, and his dates are adopted throughout in this book.

HISTORICAL SUMMARY.

ANCIENT EMPIRE.

Dynasty I, from This, or Thinis.

B.C.

4400. Menà, the first human king of Egypt, founded Memphis, having turned aside the course of the Nile, and established a temple service there.

4366. Tetà, wrote a book on anatomy, and continued buildings at Memphis.

4266. Ḥesep-ti. Some papyri state that the 64th Chapter of the Book of the Dead was written in his time.

Dynasty II, from Memphis.

4133. Bet'au, in whose reign an earthquake swallowed up many people at Bubastis.

4100. Kakau, in whose days the worship of Apis at Memphis, and that of Mnevis at Heliopolis, was continued.

4066. Ba-en-neter, in whose days, according to John of Antioch, the Nile flowed with honey for eleven days. During the reign of this king the succession of females to the throne of Egypt was declared valid.

4000. Senṭ. The sepulchral stele of one of this king's priests is preserved at Oxford.

Dynasty III, from Memphis.

——. Nefer-ka-Seker, in whose reign an eclipse appears to be mentioned.

Dynasty IV, from Memphis.

B.C.

3766. Seneferu. Important contemporaneous monuments of this king exist. During his reign the copper mines of Wâdi Ma'arah were worked.

3733. Chufu (Cheops), who fought with the people of Sinai; he built the first pyramid of Gîzeh.

3666. Châ-f-Râ (Chephren), the builder of the second pyramid at Gîzeh.

3633. Men-kau-Râ (Mycerinus), the builder of the third pyramid at Gîzeh. The fragments of his coffin are in the British Museum. Some copies of the Book of the Dead say that the 64th chapter of that work was compiled during the reign of this king.

Dynasty V, from Elephantine.

3366. Ṭeṭ-ka-Râ. The Precepts of Ptaḥ-ḥetep were written during the reign of this king.

3333. Unâs, whose pyramid at Saḳḳârah was explored in 1881.

Dynasty VI, from Memphis.

3266. Tetâ, the builder of a pyramid at Saḳḳârah.

3233. Pepi-meri-Râ, the builder of a pyramid at Saḳḳârah.

3200. Mer-en-Râ.

3166. Nefer-ka-Râ.

3133 (?). Nit-àqert (Nitocris), "the beautiful woman with rosy cheeks."

3100. { *Dynasties VII and VIII, from Memphis.*
      { *Dynasties IX and X, from Heracleopolis.*

Nefer-ka.

Nefer-Seḥ . . . .

Àb.

Nefer-kau-Râ.

Charthi.

B.C.

3033. Nefer-ka-Rā.
3000. Nefer-ka-Rā-Nebi.
2966. Tet-ka-Rā-.....
2933. Nefer-ka-Rā-Chentu.
2900. Mer-en-Heru.
2866. Se-nefer-ka-Rā.
2833. Ka-en-Rā.
2800. Nefer-ka-Rā-Tererl.
2766. Nefer-ka-Rā-Heru.
2733. Nefer-ka-Rā Pepi Seneb.
2700. Nefer-ka-Rā-Ānnu.
2633. Nefer-kau-Rā.
2600. Nefer-kau-Heru.
2533. Nefer-ȧri-ka-Rā.*

Dynasty XI, from Diospolis, or Thebes.

From the time of Nitocris to Ȧmenemḥāt I. Egyptian
history is nearly a blank. The names of a large
number of kings who ruled during this period are
known, but they cannot, at present, be arranged in
exact chronological order.

2500. Se-ānch-ka-Rā. This king is known to us through an
inscription at Hamamât, which states that he sent
an expedition to the land of Punt; this shows
that at that early date an active trade must have
been carried on across the Arabian desert between
Egypt and Arabia. The other kings of the XIth
dynasty bore the names of Ȧntef-āa, Ȧn-ȧntef,
Ȧmentuf, Ȧn-āa, and Mentu-ḥetep. Se-ānch-ka-Rā
appears to have been the immediate predecessor of
the XIIth dynasty.

* These names are obtained from the TABLET OF ABYDOS.

MIDDLE EMPIRE.

Dynasty XII, from Diospolis, or Thebes.

B.C.

2466. Åmenemḥāt I. ascended the throne of Egypt after hard fighting; he conquered the Uaua, a Libyan tribe that lived near Korosko in Nubia, and wrote a series of instructions for his son Usertsen I. The story of Senehet was written during this reign.

2433. Usertsen I. made war against the tribes of Ethiopia; he erected granite obelisks and built largely at Heliopolis.

2400. Åmenemḥāt II.   Chnemu-ḥetep, son of Neḥerå, whose tomb is at Beni-hasân, lived during the reign of this king.

2366. Usertsen II.

2333. Usertsen III.

2300. Åmenemḥāt III.   During this king's reign special attention was paid to the rise of the Nile, and canals were dug and sluices made for irrigating the country; in this reign the famous Lake Moeris, in the district called by the Arabs El-Fayûm,* was built. The rise of the Nile was marked on the rocks at Semneh, about thirty-five miles above the second cataract, and the inscriptions are visible to this day.

2266. Åmenemḥāt IV.

2233. *Dynasties XIII–XVII.   The Hyksos Period.*

According to Manetho these dynasties were as follows :—

Dynasty XIII, from Thebes, 60 kings in 453 years.

,,	XIV,	,,	Choïs,†	76	,,	,, 484 ,,
,,	XV,	Hyksos,		6	,,	,, 260 ,,
,,	XVI,	,,		10	,,	,, 251 ,,
,,	XVII,	from Thebes,		10	,,	,, 10 ,,

---

* From the Coptic ϤΙΟⲖⲖ, "the lake."   † A town in the Delta.

Unfortunately there are no monuments whereby we can correct or modify these figures. The Hyksos appear to have made their way from the countries in and to the west of Mesopotamia into Egypt. They joined with their countrymen, who had already settled in the Delta, and were able to defeat the native kings; it is thought that their rule lasted 500 years, and that Joseph arrived in Egypt towards the end of this period. The principal Hyksos kings of the XVIth dynasty are Āpepi I. and Āpepi II.; Nubti and the native Egyptian princes ruled under them. Under Se-qenen-Rā, a Theban ruler of the XVIIth dynasty, a war broke out between the Egyptians and the Hyksos, which continued for many years, and resulted in the expulsion of the foreign rulers.

Dynasty XVIII, from Thebes.

B.C.

1700. Åḥmes, who re-established the independence of Egypt.

1666. Åmen-ḥetep (Amenophis) I.

1633. Teḥuti-mes (Thothmes) I.

1600.   ,,   ,,   II.

1600. { Ḥāt-shepset, sister of Thothmes II. She sent an expedition to Punt.

Teḥuti-mes (Thothmes) III. made victorious expeditions into Mesopotamia. He was one of the greatest kings that ever ruled over Egypt.

1566. Åmen-ḥetep II.

1533. Teḥuti-mes IV.

1500. Åmen-ḥetep III. warred successfully in the lands to the south of Egypt and in Asia. He made it a custom to go into Mesopotamia to shoot lions, and, while there he married the daughter of Tushratta, the king of Mitanni. The correspondence and despatches from kings of Babylon, Mesopotamia, and Phœnicia have recently been found at Tell el-Amarna, and large portions of them are now preserved in the Museums of London and Berlin.

Âmen-ḥetep IV. or Chu-en-Âten ("brilliance, or glory of the solar disk"), the founder of the city Chu-âten, the ruins of which are called Tell el-Amarna, and of the heresy of the disk-worshippers. He was succeeded by a few kings who held the same religious opinions as himself.

Dynasty XIX, from Thebes.

B.C.

1400. Rameses I.

1366. Seti I. conquered the rebellious tribes in Western Asia, built the Memnonium at Abydos. He was famous as a builder, and attended with great care to the material welfare of his kingdom. He is said to have built a canal from the Nile to the Red Sea.

1333. Rameses II. undertook many warlike expeditions, and brought Nubia, Abyssinia, and Mesopotamia under the rule of Egypt. He was a great builder, and a liberal patron of the arts and sciences; learned men like Pentaurt were attached to his court. He is famous as one of the oppressors of the Israelites.

1300. Seti Meneptaḥ II. is thought to have been the Pharaoh of the Exodus.

NEW EMPIRE.

Dynasty XX, from Thebes.

1200. Rameses III. was famous for his buildings, and for the splendid gifts which he made to the temples of Thebes, Abydos and Heliopolis. His reign represented an era of great commercial prosperity.

1166–1133. Rameses IV.–XII.

Dynasty XXI, from Tanis and Thebes.

	I. Tanis.	II. Thebes.
B.C. 1100– 1000.	Se-Mentu. Pasebchānu I. Âmen-em-âpt. Pasebchānu II.	Ḥer-Ḥeru. Pi-ānchi. Pai-net'em I–III.

Dynasty XXII, from Bubastis (Tell-Basṭa).

966. Shashanq (Shishak) I. (see 1 Kings, xiv. 25–28 ;
2 Chron., xii. 2–13) besieged Jerusalem.

933. Uasarken I.
900. Takeleth I.
866. Uasarken II.
833. Shashanq II.
     Takeleth II.
     Shashanq III.
800. Pamai
     Shashanq IV.

These kings appear to have been of Semitic origin ; their names are Semitic, as, for example, Uasarken = Babylonian *Sarginu* (Sargon) ; Takeleth = *Tukulti* (Tiglath).

Dynasty XXIII, from Tanis.

766. Peṭā-Bast.
     Uasarken III.

Dynasty XXIV, from Saïs (Sâ el-Ḥager).

733. Bak-en-ren-f (Bocchoris).

Dynasty XXV, from Ethiopia.

700. Shabaka (Sabaco).
     Shabataka.

693. Taharqa (Tirhakah, 2 Kings, xix. 9) is famous for
     having conquered Sennacherib and delivered Heze-
     kiah ; he was, however, defeated by Esarhaddon
     and Assurbanipal, the son and grandson respec-
     tively of Sennacherib. Tirhakah's son-in-law,
     Urdamanah, was also defeated by the Assyrians.

Dynasty XXVI, from Saïs.

B.C.

666. Psemthek I. (Psammetichus) allowed Greeks to settle in the Delta, and employed Greek soldiers to fight for him.

612. Nekau II. (Necho) defeated Josiah, king of Judah, and was defeated by Nebuchadnezzar II. son of Nabopolassar, king of Babylon.

596. Psammetichus II.

591. Uaḥ-âb-Râ (Hophrah of the Bible, Gr. Apries) marched to the help of Zedekiah, king of Judah, who was defeated by Nebuchadnezzar II. His army rebelled against him, and he was dethroned ; Amāsis, a general in his army, then succeeded to the throne.

572. Âḥmes II. favoured the Greeks, and granted them many privileges ; in his reign Naucratis became a great city.

528. Psammetichus III. was defeated at Pelusium by Cambyses the Persian, and taken prisoner ; he was afterwards slain for rebelling against the Persians.

Dynasty XXVII, from Persia.

527. Cambyses marched against the Ethiopians and the inhabitants of the Oases.

521. Darius Hystaspes endeavoured to open up the ancient routes of commerce ; he established a coinage, and adopted a conciliatory and tolerant system of government, and favoured all attempts to promote the welfare of Egypt.

486. Xerxes I.

465. Artaxerxes I., during whose reign the Egyptians revolted, headed by Amyrtæus.

B.C.

425. Darius Nothus, during whose reign the Egyptians revolted successfully, and a second Amyrtæus became king of Egypt.

405. Artaxerxes II.

Dynasty XXVIII, from Saïs.

Åmen-ruṭ (Amyrtæus), reigned six years.

Dynasty XXIX, from Mendes.

399. Naifãauruṭ I.

393. Haḳar.

380. P-se-mut.

379. Naifãauruṭ II.

Dynasty XXX, from Sebennytus.

378. Necht-Ḥeru-ḥeb (Nectanebus I.) defeated the Persians at Mendes.

360. T'e-ḥer surrendered to the Persians.

358. Necht-neb-f (Nectanebus II.) devoted himself to the pursuit of magic, and neglected his empire; when Artaxerxes III. (Ochus) marched against him, he fled from his kingdom, and the Persians again ruled Egypt.

PERSIANS.

340. Artaxerxes III. (Ochus).

338. Arses.

336. Darius III. (Codomannus) conquered by Alexander the Great at Issus.

MACEDONIANS.

332. Alexander the Great founded Alexandria. He showed his toleration of the Egyptian religion, by sacrificing to the god Åmen of Libya.

PTOLEMIES.

B.C.

305. Ptolemy I. Soter, son of Lagus, became king of
    Egypt after Alexander's death. He founded the
    famous Alexandrian Library, and encouraged
    learned Greeks to make Alexandria their home;
    he died B.C. 284.

286. Ptolemy II. Philadelphus built the Pharos, founded
    Berenice and Arsinoë, caused Manetho's Egyptian
    history to be compiled, and the Greek version
    of the Old Testament (Septuagint) to be made.

247. Ptolemy III. Euergetes I. The stele of Canopus *
    was set up in the ninth year of his reign; he
    obtained possession of all Syria, and was a patron
    of the arts and sciences.

222. Ptolemy IV. Philopator defeated Antiochus, and
    founded the temple at Edfu.

205. Ptolemy V. Epiphanes. During his reign the help
    of the Romans against Antiochus was asked for by
    the Egyptians. Coelesyria and Palestine were lost
    to Egypt. He was poisoned B.C. 182, and his son
    Ptolemy VI. Eupator, died in that same year. The
    Rosetta Stone was set up in the eighth year of the
    reign of this king.

182. Ptolemy VII. Philometor was taken prisoner at
    Pelusium by Antiochus IV., B.C. 171, and died
    B.C. 146. He reigned alone at first, then con-
    jointly (B.C. 170—165) with Ptolemy IX. Euergetes
    II. (also called Physcon), and finally having gone to

---

* This important stele, preserved at Gîzeh, is inscribed in hiero
glyphics, Greek and demotic with a decree made at Canopus by the
priesthood, assembled there from all parts of Egypt, in honour of
Ptolemy III. It mentions the great benefits which he had conferred
upon Egypt, and states what festivals are to be celebrated in his
honour and in that of Berenice, etc., and concludes with a resolution
ordering that a copy of this inscription in hieroglyphics, Greek and
demotic shall be placed in every large temple of Egypt. Two other
copies of this work are known.

Rome on account of his quarrel with Physcon, he reigned sole monarch of Egypt (B.C. 165). Physcon was overthrown B.C. 132, reigned again B.C. 125, and died B.C. 117.

B.C.

170. Ptolemy VIII. is murdered by Physcon.

117. Ptolemy X. Soter II. Philometor II. (Lathyrus), reigns jointly with Cleopatra III. Ptolemy X. is banished (B.C. 106), his brother Ptolemy XI. Alexander I. is made co-regent, but afterwards banished (B.C. 89) and slain (B.C. 87); Ptolemy X. is recalled, and dies B.C. 81.

81. Ptolemy XII. Alexander II. is slain.

81. Ptolemy XIII. Neos Dionysos (Auletes), ascends the throne; dies B.C. 52.

52. Ptolemy XIV. Dionysos II. and Cleopatra VII. are, according to the will of Ptolemy XIII. to marry each other; the Roman senate to be their guardian. Ptolemy XIV. banishes Cleopatra, and is a party to the murder of Pompey, their guardian, who visits Egypt after his defeat at Pharsalia. Cæsar arrives in Egypt to support Cleopatra (B.C. 48); Ptolemy XIV., is drowned; Ptolemy XV., brother of Cleopatra VII., appointed her co-regent by Cæsar (B.C. 47); he is murdered at her wish, and her son by Cæsar, Ptolemy XVI., Cæsarion, is named co-regent (B.C. 45).

42. Antony orders Cleopatra to appear before him, and is seduced by her charms; he kills himself, and Cleopatra dies by the bite of an asp. Egypt becomes a Roman province B.C. 30.

ROMANS.

27. Cæsar Augustus becomes master of the Roman Empire. Cornelius Gallus is the first prefect of

Egypt.   Under the third prefect, Aelius Gallus, Candace, queen of the Ethiopians, invades Egypt, A.D. but is defeated.

14. Tiberius.   In his reign Germanicus visited Egypt.

37. Caligula.   In his reign a persecution of the Jews took place.

41. Claudius.

55. Nero.   In his reign Christianity was first preached in Egypt by Saint Mark.   The Blemmyes made raids upon the southern frontier of Egypt.

69. Vespasian.   Jerusalem destroyed A.D. 70.

82. Domitian causes temples to Isis and Serapis to be built at Rome.

98. Trajan.   The Nile and Red Sea Canal (Amnis Trajânus) re-opened.

117. Hadrian.   Visited Egypt twice.

161. Marcus Aurelius caused the famous *Itinerary* to be made.

180. Commodus.

193. Septimus Severus.

211. Caracalla visited Egypt, and caused a large number of young men to be massacred at Alexandria.

217. Macrinus.

218. Elagabalus.

249. Decius.   Christians persecuted.

253. Valerianus.   Christians persecuted.

260. Gallienus.   Persecution of Christians stayed.   Zenobia, Queen of Palmyra, invades Egypt A.D. 268.

270. Aurelian.   Zenobia becomes Queen of Egypt for a short time, but is dethroned A.D. 273.

276. Probus.

284. Diocletian.   "Pompey's Pillar" erected A.D. 302; persecution of Christians A.D. 304.   The Copts date the era of the Martyrs from the day of Diocletian's accession to the throne (August 29).

A.D.

324. Constantine the Great, the Christian Emperor, in whose reign, A.D. 325, the Council of Nicæa was held. At this council it was decided that Christ and His Father were of one and the *same* nature, as taught by Athanasius; and the doctrine of Arius,* that Christ and God were only *similar* in nature, was decreed heretical.

337. Constantius. George of Cappadocia, an Arian, is made Bishop of Alexandria.

379. Theodosius I., the Great, proclaims Christianity the religion of his empire. The Arians and followers of the ancient Egyptian religion were persecuted.

THE BYZANTINES.

395. Arcadius, Emperor of the East. The Anthropomorphites,† who affirmed that God was of human form, destroyed the greater number of their opponents.

408. Theodosius II. In his reign the doctrines of Nestorius were condemned by Cyril of Alexandria. Nestorius, from the two natures of Christ, inferred also two persons, a human and a divine. "In the Syrian school, Nestorius had been taught (A.D. 429–431) to abhor the confusion of the two natures,

---

* "He was a most expert logician, but perverted his talents to evil purposes, and had the audacity to preach what no one before him had ever suggested, namely, that the Son of God was made out of that which had no prior existence ; that there was a period of time in which He existed not ; that, as possessing free will, He was capable of virtue, or of vice ; and that He was created and made."—Sozomen, *Eccles. Hist.*, Bk. I., ch. 15. For the statement of the views of Arius by his opponent Alexander, Bishop of Alexandria, see his letter addressed to the Catholic Church generally, in Socrates, *Eccles. Hist.*, Bk. I., ch. 6.

† The leader of this persecution was Theophilus, Bishop of Alexandria, who, before he discovered that the majority of the Egyptian monks were Anthropomorphites, was himself opposed to this body.

and nicely to discriminate the humanity of his *master* Christ from the Divinity of the *Lord* Jesus. The Blessed Virgin he revered as the mother of Christ, but his ears were offended with the rash and recent title of mother of God, which had been insensibly adopted since the origin of the Arian controversy. From the pulpit of Constantinople, a friend of the patriarch,* and afterwards the patriarch himself, repeatedly preached against the use, or the abuse, of a word unknown to the apostles, unauthorized by the church, and which could only tend to alarm the timorous, to mislead the simple, to amuse the profane, and to justify, by a seeming resemblance, the old genealogy of Olympus. In his calmer moments Nestorius confessed, that it might be tolerated or excused by the union of the two natures, and the communication of their *idioms* (*i.e.*, a transfer of properties of each nature to the other—of infinity to man, passibility to God, etc.): but he was exasperated, by contradiction, to disclaim the worship of a newborn, an infant Deity, to draw his inadequate similes from the conjugal or civil partnerships of life, and to describe the manhood of Christ, as the robe, the instrument, the tabernacle of his Godhead."— Gibbon, *Decline and Fall*, chap. 47.

A.D. 450. Marcianus. The Monophysite doctrine of Eutyches was condemned at the Council of Chalcedon, A.D. 451. Eutyches, from the one person of Christ, inferred also one nature, viz., the Divine—the human having been absorbed into it. Silco invaded Egypt with his Nubian followers.

* Anastasius of Antioch, who said, " Let no one call Mary *Theotokos;* for Mary was but a woman ; and it is impossible that God should be born of a woman."—Socrates, *Eccles. Hist.*, Bk. VII., chap. xxxii.

A.D.

474. Zeno. He issued the *Henoticon*, an edict which, while affirming the Incarnation, made no attempt to decide the difficult question whether Christ possessed a single or a double nature.

481. Anastasius.

527. Justinian. The Monophysites separated from the Melchites and chose their own patriarch; they were afterwards called Copts, القبط.*

610. Heraclius. The Persians under Chosroes hold Egypt for ten years; they are expelled by Heraclius A.D. 629.

MUHAMMEDANS.

638. 'Amr ibn el-'Âsi conquers Egypt.

644. 'Othmân.

750. Merwân II., the last of the 'Omayyade dynasty, was put to death in Egypt.

750–870. The 'Abbasides rule over Egypt.

786. Harûn er-Rashîd.

813. Mâmûn visited Egypt, and opened the Great Pyramid.

870. Ahmed ibn-Tulûn governs Egypt.

884. Khamarûyeh enlarges Fostât.

969–1171. The Fâtimites govern Egypt, with Masr el-Kâhira † (Cairo) as their residence.

975. Azîz, son of Mu'izz, great grandson of 'Obêdallâh.

996. Hâkim, son of 'Azîz, founder of the Druses. This remarkable prince wished to be considered as God incarnate.

* The name given to the native Christians of Egypt by the Arabs, from ⲔⲨⲚⲦⲀⲒⲞⲤ for Αἰγύπτιος.

† القاهرة.

A.D.

1020. Zâhir, son of Hâkim.

1036. Abu Tamîm el-Mustansir.

1094. Musta'li, son of el-Mustansir, captured Jerusalem (A.D. 1096), but was defeated by the Crusaders under Godfrey de Bouillon.

1160. 'Adîd Ledînallâh, the last of the Fâtimites.

1171. Salâheddîn (Saladin) defeated the Crusaders at Hittîn, and recaptured Jerusalem.

1193. Melik el'-Adîl.

1218. Melik el-Kâmil, the builder of Mansûrah.

1240. Melik es-Sâleh, the usurper, captured Jerusalem, Damascus, and Ascalon. Louis IX., of France, attacked and captured Damietta, but was made prisoner at Mansûrah, with all his army.

1250–1380. The Bahrite Mamelukes.

1260. Bêbars.

1277. Kalaûn.

1291. El-Ashraf Khalîl captured Acre.

1346. Hasan.

1382–1517. Burgite or Circassian Mamelukes.

1382. Barkûk.

1422. Bursbey.

1468. Kait Bey.

1501. El-Ghûri.

1517. Tûmân Bey is deposed by Selim I. of Constantinople, and Egypt becomes a Turkish Pashalik.

1771. 'Ali Bey sultân of Egypt.

1798. Napoleon Bonaparte stormed Alexandria ; battle of the Pyramids ; and French fleet destroyed off Abukîr by the English.

1801. French compelled by the English to evacuate Egypt.

1805. Muhammad 'Ali appointed Pasha of Egypt.

1811. Assassination of the Mamelukes by him.

1831. Declares his independence.

A.D.

1848. Ibrâhîm Pasha.

1849. Death of Muḥammad ʿAli. ʿAbbâs Pasha was strangled at Benha.

1854. Saʿîd Pasha. The railway from Alexandria was completed, and the making of the Suez Canal begun in his reign. He founded the Bûlâk Museum, and encouraged excavations on the sites of the ancient cities of Egypt.

1863. Ismaʿîl, son of Ibrâhîm Pasha, and grandson of Muḥammad ʿAli, was born in 1830. He was made Khedive in 1867. He caused railways, docks, and canals to be made, systems of telegraphs and postage to be established; he built sugar factories, and endeavoured to advance the material welfare of Egypt. The Suez Canal was opened during his reign (1869). He greatly extended the boundaries of Egypt, and obtained possession of Suakin (Sauâkin), Masowa (Masauʿa), and two ports in the Gulf of Aden, a part of the Somâli coast, a large part of the frontier of Abyssinia, and the Province of Dârfûr. The tribute paid by him to the Porte amounted to nearly £700,000. During his reign the national debt of Egypt became so great, that a Commission was appointed to enquire what steps should be taken in the matter. In 1879, as a result of pressure put upon the Porte, Ismaʿîl was dethroned, and Tewfik, his eldest son, was appointed to succeed him.

1882. Massacre of Europeans in June; bombardment of Alexandria by the English fleet in July; occupation of Egypt by English troops; defeat of ʿArabi Pasha.

1885. Murder of Gordon, and the abandonment of the Sudân.

1886–1890. English troops continue to occupy Egypt.

DATES ASSIGNED TO THE EGYPTIAN DYNASTIES BY EGYPTOLOGISTS.

Dynasty.	Champollion-Figeac.	Lepsius (in 1858).	Brugsch (in 1877).	Mariette.
I.	B.C. 5,867	3,892	4,400	5,004
II.	5,615	3,639	4,133	4,751
III.	5,318	3,338	3,966	4,449
IV.	5,121	3,124	3,733	4,235
V.	4,673	2,840	3,566	3,951
VI.	4,425	2,744	3,300	3,703
VII.	4,222	2,592	3,100	3,500
VIII.	4,147	2,522	——	3,500
IX.	4,047	2,674	——	3,358
X.	3,947	2,565	——	3,249
XI.	3,762	2,423	——	3,064
XII.	3,703	2,380	2,466	2,851
XIII.	3,417	2,136	2,235	——
XIV.	3,004	2,267	——	2,398
XV.	2,520	2,101	——	2,214
XVI.	2,270	1,842	——	——
XVII.	2,082	1,684	——	——
XVIII.	1,822	1,591	1,700	1,703
XIX.	1,473	1,443	1,400	1,462
XX.	1,279	1,209	1,200	1,288
XXI.	1,101	1,091	1,100	1,110
XXII.	971	961	966	980
XXIII.	851	787	766	810
XXIV.	762	729	733	721
XXV.	718	716	700	715
XXVI.	674	685	666	665
XXVII.	524	525	527	527
XXVIII.	404	525	——	406
XXIX.	398	399	399	399
XXX.	377	378	378	378
XXXI.	339	340	340	340

THE COUNTRY OF EGYPT.

The Ancient Egyptians called Egypt 〔△⊗ *Baq* or ⊗ *Baqet;* ☰ ◠‖◠⊗ *Ta-merá;* and ☰◠⊗ *Kamt.* Baq seems to refer to Egypt as the olive-producing country, and Ta-merá as the land of the inundation; the name by which it is most commonly called in the inscriptions is Kam, *i.e.,* " Black," from the darkness of its soil. It was also called the " land of the sycamore," and the land of " the eye of Horus " (*i.e.,* the Sun). It was divided by the Egyptians into two parts : I. Upper Egypt ☰⊗ *Ta-res* or ☰⊗ *Ta-qemá,* " the southern land ;" and II. Lower Egypt ☰, *Ta-meh,* " the northern land." The kings of Egypt styled themselves *suten net,* " king of the North and South," and *neb taui,* " lord of two earths." *

The country was divided into nomes, the number of which is variously given ; the list given by some of the classical authorities contains thirty-six, but judging by the monuments the number was nearer forty. The nome (*hesp*) was divided into four parts ; 1, the capital town (*nut*); 2, the cultivated land ; 3, the marshes, which could only at times be used for purposes of cultivation ; and 4, the canals, which had to be kept clear and provided with sluices, etc.,

---

* As ruler of the two countries, each king wore the crown ⚜, which was make up of ⚜, the *teśer,* or red crown, representing the northern part of Egypt, and ⚜, the *het',* or white crown, representing the southern part of Egypt.

for irrigation purposes. During the rule of the Greeks Egypt was divided into three parts : Upper, Central, and Lower Egypt ; Central Egypt consisted of seven nomes, and was called Heptanomis.

LIST OF NOMES OF EGYPT—UPPER EGYPT.

Nome.	Capital.	Divinity.
1. Ta-Kens.	Ābu(Elephantine),in later times Nubt (Ombos).	Chnemu.
2. Tes-Ḥeru.	Ṭeb (Apollinopolis magna, Arab. Uṭfu or Edfu).	Ḥeru - Beḫu-tet.
3. Ten.	Necheb(Eileithyia),in later times Sene (Latopolis), Esneh.	Necheb.
4. Uast.	Uast (Thebes), in later times Hermonthis.	Āmen-Rā.
5. Ḥerui.	Kebti (Coptos).	Āmsu.
6. Āa-ti.	Taenterer (Denderah).	Hathor (Ḥet Ḥert).
7. Sechem.	Ḥa (Diospolis parva).	Hathor.
8. Åbṭ.	Åbṭu (Abydos), in earlier times Teni (This).	Anḥur.
9. Amsu.	Åpu (Panopolis).	Åmsu.
10. Uat′et.	Ṭebu (Aphroditopolis).	Hathor.
11. Set.	Shasḥetep (Hypsele).	Chnemu.
12. Ṭuf.	Nen-ent-bak(Antaeopolis).	Horus.
13. Atefchent.	Saiut (Lycopolis, Arab. Sîûṭ).	Åp-uat.
14. Atef-peḥ.	Kesi (Cusae).	Hathor.
15. Un.	Chemennu (Hermopolis).	Thoth.
16. Meḥ-maḥet.	Ḥebennu (Hipponon).	Horus.
17.	Kasa (Cynonpolis).	Anubis.
18. Sapet.	Ḥa-suten(Alabastronpolis).	Anubis.
19. Uab.	Pa-mat′et (Oxyrhynchos).	Set.

Nome.	Capital.	Divinity.
20. Am-chent.	Chenensu (Heracleopolis magna).	Ḥeru-shefi.
21. Am-peḥ.	Se-men Ḥeru.	Chnemu.
22. Maten.	Ṭep-àḥet (Aphroditopolis).	Hathor.

LOWER EGYPT.

1. Anub-ḥet'.	Men-nefer (Memphis).	Ptaḥ.
2. Aā.	Sechem (Letopolis).	Ḥeru-ur.
3. Àment.	Nenten-Ḥapi (Apis).	Ḥathor-nub.
4. Sepi-res.	T'eka (Canopus).	Àmen-Rā.
5. Sepi-emḥet.	Sa (Sais).	Neit.
6. Kaset	Chesun (Choïs).	Àmen-Rā.
7. . . . Àment.	Sent-Nefer (Metelis).	Ḥu.
8. . . . Àbṭet.	T'ukot (Sethroë).	Atmu.
9. At'i.	Pa-Àusar (Busiris).	Osiris.
10. Kakem.	Ḥataḥeràb (Athribis).	Ḥeru-chenti-chati.
11. Kaḥebes.	Kaḥebes (Kabasos).	Isis.
12. Kat'eb.	T'eb-neter (Sebennythos).	Anḥur.
13. Ḥakaṭ.	Ànnu (Heliopolis).	Rā.
14. Chent-àbeṭ.	T'an (Tanis).	Horus.
15. Teḥuti.	Pa-Teḥuti (Hermopolis).	Thoth.
16. Char.	Pabaneb-ṭeṭ (Mendes).	Ba-neb-ṭeṭ
17. Sam-beḥutet.	Pa-chen-en-Àmen (Diospolis).	Àmen-Rā.
18. Amchent.	Pa-Bast (Bubastis).	Bast.
19. Am-peḥ.	Pa Uat' (Buto).	Uat'.
20. Sept.	Kesem (Phakussa).	Sept.

Egypt proper terminates at Aswân (Syene); the territory south of that town for a certain distance on each side of the river Nile is called Nubia. The races who lived there in very early times caused the Egyptians much trouble, and we know from the tomb-inscriptions at Aswân that expeditions were sent against these peoples by the

Egyptians as far back as the XIIth dynasty. The area of the land in Egypt proper available for cultivation is about 11,500 square miles; the Delta contains about 6,500 miles, and the Nile Valley with the Fayûm 5,000 miles. The Oases of the Libyan Desert and the Peninsula of Sinai are considered as parts of Egypt. Lower and Upper Egypt are each divided into seven Provinces, the names of which are as follows:—

Lower Egypt.	Upper Egypt.
Behêreh (capital, Damanhur).	Beni-Suêf (capital, Beni-suêf).
Kalyûb (capital, Benha).	
Sherkîyeh (capital, Zakâzîk).	Minyeh (capital, Minyeh).
Dakhalîyeh (capital, Man-sûra).	Sîût (capital, Asyût).
	Girgeh (capital, Suhag).
Menûf.	Keneh (capital, Keneh).
Gharbîyeh (capital Tanta).	Esneh (capital, Esneh).
Gîzeh.	Wâdi Halfah.

Large towns like Alexandria, Port Sa'îd, Suez, Cairo, Damietta, and Isma'îlîya are governed by native rulers.

In ancient days the population of Egypt proper is said to have been from seven and a-half to nine millions; at the present time it is probably well over eight millions. The population of the provinces south of Egypt, and which originally belonged to her, has never been accurately ascertained. The country on each side of the Bahr el-Abyad is very thickly peopled; it is generally thought that the population of this and the other provinces which belonged to Egypt in the time of Isma'îl amounts to about ten millions.

THE ANCIENT EGYPTIANS.

The Egyptians, whom the sculptures and monuments make known to us as being among the most ancient inhabitants of the country, belong, beyond all doubt, to the Caucasian race, and they seem to have migrated thither from the East. The original home of the invaders was, apparently, Asia, and they made their way across Mesopotamia and Arabia, and across the Isthmus of Suez into Egypt. It has been suggested that they sailed across the Indian Ocean and up the Red Sea, on the western shore of which they landed. It is, however, very doubtful if a people who lived in the middle of a huge land like central Asia, would have enough experience to make and handle ships sufficiently large to cross such seas. No period can be fixed for the arrival of the new-comers from the East into Egypt ; we are, however, justified in assuming that it took place before B.C. 5000.

When the people from the East had made their way into Egypt, they found there an aboriginal race with a dark skin and complexion. The Egyptians generally called their land ✍🏺 Kamt, *i.e.*, "black"; and if the dark, rich colour of the cultivated land of Egypt be considered, the appropriateness of the term will be at once evident. The hieroglyphic which is read *Kam*, is the skin of a crocodile, and we know from Horapollo (ed. Cory, p. 87), that this sign was used to express anything of a dark colour.* The name " Ham " is given to Egypt by the

---

* " To denote *darkness*, they represent the TAIL OF A CROCODILE, for by no other means does the crocodile inflict death and destruction on any animal which it may have caught than by first striking it with its tail, and rendering it incapable of motion."

Bible; this word may be compared with the Coptic ⲔⲎⲗⲗⲉ, ⲔⲎⲗⲗⲓ or ϪⲎⲗⲗⲓ. The children of Ham are said to be Cush, Mizraim, Put, and Canaan. The second of these, Miṣraim, is the name given to Egypt by the Hebrews. The dual form of the word, which means "the double Miṣor," probably has reference to the "two lands" (in Egypt. ⸗), over which the Egyptian kings, in their inscriptions, proclaimed their rule. The descendants of Cush are represented on the monuments by the inhabitants of Nubia and the negro tribes which live to the south of that country. In the earliest times the descendants of Cush appear to have had the same religion as the Egyptians. The Put of the Bible is thought by some to be represented by the land of Punt, or spice-land, of the monuments. The people of Punt appear to have dwelt on both sides of the Red Sea to the south of Egypt and on the Somâli coast, and as far back as B.C. 2500 a large trade was carried on between them and the Egyptians; it is thought that the Egyptians regarded them as kinsmen. The aboriginal inhabitants of Phœnicia were probably the kinsfolk of the descendants of Miṣraim, called by the Bible Canaanites. Diodorus and some other classical authorities tell us that Egypt was colonized from Ethiopia; for this view, however, there is no support. The civilization, religion, arts of building, etc., of the Ethiopians are all of Egyptian origin, and in this, as in so many other points relating to the history of Egypt, the Greeks were either misinformed, or they misunderstood what they were told.

An examination of the painted representations of the Egyptians by native artists, shows us that the pure Egyptian was of slender make, with broad shoulders, long hands and feet, and sinewy legs and arms. His forehead was high, his chin square, his eyes large, his cheeks full, his mouth wide, his lips full, and his nose short and rounded. His jaws did not protrude, and his hair is smooth and fine. The evidence of the pictures on the tombs is supported and confirmed by the skulls and bones of mummies which anthropologists have examined and measured during the last few years ; hence all attempts to prove that the Egyptian is of negro origin are overthrown at the outset by facts which cannot be controverted. In cases where the Egyptians intermarried with people of Semitic origin, we find aquiline noses.* One of the most remarkable things connected with the Egyptians of to-day is the fact that a very large number of them have reproduced, without the slightest alteration, many of the personal features of their ancestors who lived seven thousand years ago. The traveller is often accompanied on a visit to a tomb of the Ancient Empire by a modern Egyptian who, in his attitudes, form, and face, is a veritable reproduction of the hereditary nobleman who built the tomb which he is examining. It may be that no invading race has ever found itself physically able to reproduce persistently its own characteristics for any important length of time, or it may be that the absorption of such races by intermarriage with the natives, together with the influence

* A very good example of this is seen in the black granite head of the statue of Osorkon II., presented to the British Museum (No. 1063) by the Committee of the Egypt Exploration Fund. The lower part of the nose is broken away, but enough of the upper part remains to show what was its original angle. It was confidently asserted that this head belonged to a statue of a Hyksos king, but the assertion was not supported by any trustworthy evidence. The face and features are those of a man whose ancestors were Semites and Egyptians, and men with similar countenances are to be seen in the desert to the south-east of Palestine to this day. A clinching proof that the statue is not that of a Hyksos king was brought forward by Prof. Lanzone of Turin, who, in the earlier part of this year, showed Mr. Renouf a small statue of Osorkon II., having precisely the same face and features. The XXIInd dynasty, to which this king belonged, were Semites, as their names show, and they were always regarded by the Egyptians as foreigners, and ∿, the determinative of a man from a foreign country, was placed after each of their names.

of the climate, has made such characteristics disappear; the fact, however, remains, that the physical type of the Egyptian fellâḥ is exactly what it was in the earliest dynasties. The invasions of the Babylonians, Hyksos, Ethiopians (including negro races), Assyrians, Persians, Greeks, Romans, Arabs, and Turks, have had no permanent effect either on their physical or mental characteristics. The Egyptian has seen the civilizations of all these nations rise up, progress flourish, decay, and pass away; he has been influenced from time to time by their religious views and learning; he has been the servant of each of them in turn, and has paid tribute to them all; he has, nevertheless, survived all of them save one. It will, of course, be understood that the inhabitants of the towns form a class quite distinct from the Egyptians of the country; the townsfolk represent a mixture of many nationalities, and their character and features change according to the exigencies of the time and circumstances in which they live, and the influence of the ruling power.

THE MODERN EGYPTIANS.

The total population of Egypt proper may be fixed roughly at 8,000,000, of whom about 130,000 are foreigners.

Sir Francis Grenfell is of opinion that the population of Egypt is now nearer *nine* than eight millions. In a country where an increase in population always means an increase in taxation, it is quite impossible to obtain an accurate census. As far back as the time of David* the idea of "numbering the people" has been unpopular in the East.

It is exceedingly difficult to obtain an exact idea of what the population of Egypt actually was in Pharaonic times, for the inscriptions tell us nothing. Herodotus gives us no information on this matter, but Diodorus tells us that it amounted to 7,000,000 in ancient times. The priests at Thebes informed Germanicus in A.D. 19 that in the times of Rameses II. the country contained 700,000 † fighting men; it will also be remembered that the Bible states that the "children of Israel journeyed from Rameses to Succoth, about six hundred thousand on foot that were men, beside children. And a mixed multitude went up also with them." Exodus xii. 37, 38. In the time of Vespasian 7,500,000 persons paid poll-tax; we may assume that about 500,000 were exempt, and therefore there must have been at least 8,000,000 of people in Egypt, without reckoning slaves. (Mommsen, *Provinces of Rome*, Vol. II., p. 258.) It is probable, however, that the population of Egypt under the

---

* "And Satan stood up against Israel, and moved David to number Israel." 1 Chronicles xxi. 1.

† "Septigenta milia aetate militari." Tacitus, *Annals*, Bk. ii., 60.

rule of the Pharaohs has been greatly exaggerated, chiefly because no accurate data were at hand whereby errors might be corrected. During the occupation of the country by the French in 1798–1801 it was said to be 2,500,000; Sir Gardner Wilkinson, however, set it down at as low a figure as 1,500,000. In 1821 the population numbered 2,514,000, and in 1846 it had risen to 4,456,186. The last census was ordered by Khedival decree on December 2, 1881, and it was completed in May 3, 1882. According to the official statement published in the *Recensement Général de l'Égypte*, at Cairo, in 1884, it amounted in 1882 to 6,806,381 persons, of whom 3,216,847 were men, and 3,252,869 were women. Of the 6,806,381 persons, 6,708,185 were inhabitants of the country, and 98,196 were nomads. It showed that there were in the total 245,779 Beduîn and 90,886 foreigners; the number was made up in the following manner :—

Cairo, 374,838; Alexandria, 231,396; Damietta, 43,616; Rosetta, 19,378; Port Sa'îd, 21,296, and Suez, 11,175. Of the provinces Behêreh contained 398,856; Sherkîyeh, 464,655; Dakhalîyeh, 586,033; Gharbîyeh, 929,488; Kalyûb, 271,488; Menûf, 646,013; Asyût, 562,137; Beni-Suêf, 219,573; Fayûm, 228,709; Gîzeh, 283,083; Minyeh, 314,818; Esneh, 237,961; Girgeh, 521,413; Keneh 406,858. The dwellers in the Oases* and the Peninsula of Sinai were not reckoned in the total given above. The annual increase in the population was estimated at 56,202, but at this rate the population of Egypt would only number a little over 7,000,000.

---

* The Egyptian Oases are five : Wâh el-Khârgeh, 90 miles from Thebes; Wâh ed-Dakhaliyeh, or Oasis Minor with warm springs, to the west of the city of Oxyrhynchos; Farâfra, about 80 miles north of Oasis Minor; Sîwa, where there was a temple to Jupiter Ammon, to the south-west of Alexandria; and Wâh el-Bahriyeh, to the north of Wâh el-Khârgeh.

The population of Egypt to-day comprises the Fellâhîn, Copts, Beduîn, Jews, Turks, Negroes, Nubians and people from Abyssinia, Armenians and Europeans.

The **Fellâhîn** amount to about four-fifths of the entire population of Egypt, and are chiefly employed in agricultural pursuits. In physical type they greatly resemble the ancient Egyptians as depicted on the monuments. Their complexion is dark ; they have straight eyebrows, high cheek bones, flat noses with low bridges, slightly protruding jaws, broad shoulders, large mouths and full lips. The colour of their skin becomes darker as the south is approached. The whole of the cultivation of Egypt is in the hands of the fellâhîn.

The **Copts** are also direct descendants from the ancient Egyptians, and inhabit chiefly the cities of Upper Egypt. such as Asyût and Aḥmîm. The name Copt is derived from قبط Kubt, the Arabic form of the Coptic form of the Greek name for Egyptian, Αἰγύπτιος ; it may be mentioned, in passing, that Αἴγυπτος, Egypt, is thought by some to be derived from an ancient Egyptian name for Memphis, Ḥet-ka-Ptaḥ, " The house of the genius of Ptaḥ." The number of Copts in Egypt to-day is estimated at about 350,000, and the greater number of them are engaged in the trades of goldsmiths, clothworkers, etc. ; a respectable body of clerks and accountants in the postal, telegraph and government offices in Egypt, is drawn from their community. They are clever with their fingers, and are capable of rapid education up to a certain point; beyond this they rarely go. Physically, they are of a finer type than the fellâhîn ; their heads are longer and their features are more European.

The Copts are famous in ecclesiastical history for having embraced with extraordinary zeal and rapidity the doctrines of Christianity as preached by St. Mark at Alexandria. Before the end of the third century A.D., Egypt was filled with hundreds of thousands of ascetics, monks, recluses and solitaries who had thrown over their own weird and confused religious beliefs and embraced Christianity; they then retired to the mountains and deserts of their country to dedicate their lives to the service of the Christians' God. The Egyptians, their ancestors, who lived sixteen hundred years before Christ, had already arrived at the conception of a god who was one in his person, but who manifested himself in the world under many forms and many names. The Greeks and the Romans, who successively held Egypt, caused many changes to come over the native religion of the country which they governed; and since the conflicting myths and theories taught to the people of Egypt under their rule had bewildered their minds and confused their beliefs, they gladly accepted the simple teaching of Christ's Apostle as a veritable gift of God. Their religious belief took the form of that of Eutyches (died after 451), who sacrificed the "distinction of the two natures in Christ to the unity of the person to such an extent as to make the incarnation an absorption of the human nature by the divine, or a deification of human nature, even of the body." In other words, they believed that Christ had but one composite nature, and for this reason they were called Monophysites; in their liturgies they stated that God had been crucified. They formed a part of the Alexandrian Church until the Council of Chalcedon, A.D. 451, when it was laid down that Christ had a *double* nature—human and divine, but after this date they separated themselves from it, and were accounted heretics by it, because they obstinately refused to give up their belief in the *one* divine nature of Christ which embraced and included the human. To the sect of Monophysites or Eutychians the Copts still belong. The orthodox church of Alexandria and its heretical offshoot continued to discuss with anger and tumult the subtle points of their different opinions, until the fifth Œcumenical Council, held at Constantinople A.D. 553, made some concessions to the Monophysite party. Shortly after, however, new dissensions arose which so weakened the orthodox church that the Monophysite party hailed with gladness the arrival of the arms of Muḥammad the Prophet, and joined its forces with his that they might destroy the power of their theological opponents. After 'Amr had made himself master of Egypt (A.D. 640), he appointed the Copts to positions of dignity and wealth ; finding, however, that they were unworthy of his confidence, they were reduced, and finally persecuted with vigour. From the time of Cyril, Patriarch of Alexandria, A.D. 1235 onwards, but little is known of the history of the Coptic Church. The Copt of to-day usually troubles himself little about theological matters ; in certain cases, however, he affirms with considerable firmness the doctrine of the "one nature."

The knowledge of the Coptic language is, generally speaking, extinct ; it is exceedingly doubtful if three Coptic scholars, in the Western sense of the word, exist even among the priests. The language spoken by them is Arabic, and though copies of parts of the Bible are found in churches and private houses, they are usually accompanied by an Arabic version of the Coptic text, which is more usually read than the Coptic. The Bible, in all or part, was translated from Greek into Coptic in the third century of our era ; some, however, think that the translation was not made until the eighth century. The versions of the principal books of the Old and the whole of the New Testament, together with lives of saints, monks and martyrs, form the greater part of Coptic literature. The Coptic language is, at base, a dialect of ancient Egyptian ; many of the nouns and verbs found in the hieroglyphic texts remain unchanged in Coptic, and a large number of others can, by making proper allowance for phonetic decay and dialectic differences, be identified without difficulty. The Copts used the Greek alphabet to write down their language, but found it neces-

sary to borrow six* signs from the demotic forms of
ancient Egyptian characters to express the sounds which
they found unrepresented in Greek.   The dialect of Upper
Egypt is called "Sahidic"† or Theban, and that of Lower
Egypt "Memphitic." ‡   During the last few years the study
of Coptic has revived among European scholars, but this is
partly owing to the fact that the importance of a knowledge
of the language, as a preliminary to the study of hieroglyphics,
has been at length recognized.   The Roman Propagandist
Tuki§ published during the last century some valuable works;
in spite, however, of the activity of scholars and the enterprise of publishers, it still costs nearly £5 to purchase a
copy of as much of the Memphitic Coptic version of the
Bible as has come down to us.

The **Beduîn** are represented by the various Arabic-
speaking and Muḥammedan tribes, who live in the deserts
which lie on each side of the Nile; they amount in number
to about 250,000.   The Bisharîn, Hadendoa, and Ababdeh
tribes, who speak a language (called 'to bedyhawîyeh') which
is like ancient Egyptian in some respects, and who live in

---

* These signs are: ϣ = 𓈙 *sh*;   ϥ = 𓆑 *f*;

   ϩ = 𓎛 *ch*;   ϧ = 𓐍 *ḥ*;

   ϫ = 𓏤 *ǧ*;   ϭ = 𓎼 *č*.

† This is the older and richer dialect of Coptic, it was spoken from
Minyeh to Aswân.

‡ More correctly called Boheiric, from the province of Boheirâ in the
Delta; the name Bashmuric has been wrongly applied to this dialect,
but as it appears to have been exclusively the language of Memphis, it
may be styled "Middle Egyptian."   The dialect of Bushmûr on the
Lake of Menzaleh appears to have become extinct about A.D. 900, and
to have left no traces of itself behind.   See Stern, *Kopt. Gram.*, p. 1.

§ Among more recent scholars may be named Wilkins, Zoega,
Tattam, Ideler, Schwartze, Revillout, Hyvernat, Amélineau, Stern,
Guidi, Lagarde, etc.

the most southern part of Upper Egypt, Nubia, and Abyssinia, are included among this number. Among these three tribes the institutions of Muḥammed are not observed with any great strictness. When the Beduîn settle down to village or town life, they appear to lose all the bravery and fine qualities of independent manhood which characterize them when they live in their home, the desert.

The inhabitants of Cairo, Alexandria, and other large towns form a class of people quite distinct from the other inhabitants of Egypt; in Alexandria there is a very large Greek element, and in Cairo the number of Turks is very great. In the bazaars of Cairo one may see the offspring of marriages between members of nearly every European nation and Egyptian or Nubian women, the colour of their skins varying from a dark brick-red to nearly white. The shopkeepers are fully alive to their opportunities of making money, and would, beyond doubt, become rich but for their natural indolence and belief in fate. Whatever they appear or however much they may mask their belief in the Muḥam-medan religion, it must never be forgotten that they have the greatest dislike to every religion but their own. The love of gain alone causes them to submit to the remarks made upon them by Europeans, and to submit to their entrance and sojourning among them.

The **Nubians** or Berbers, as they are sometimes called, inhabit the tract of land which extends from Aswân or Syene to the fourth cataract. The word Nubia appears to be derived from *nub*, 'gold,' because Nubia was a gold-producing country. The word Berber is considered to mean 'barbarian' by some, and to be also of Egyptian origin. They speak a language which is allied to some of the North African tongues, and rarely speak Arabic well. The Nubians found in Egypt are generally doorkeepers and domestic servants, who can usually be depended upon for their honesty and obedience.

The **Negroes** form a large part of the non-native population of Egypt, and are employed by natives to perform hard work, or are held by them as slaves. They are Muḥammedans by religion, and come from the countries known by the name of Sudân. Negro women make good and faithful servants.

The Syrian Christians who have settled down in Egypt are generally known by the name of **Levantines.** They are shrewd business men, and the facility and rapidity with which they learn European languages places them in positions of trust and emolument.

The **Turks** form a comparatively small portion of the population of Egypt, but many civil and military appointments are, or were, in their hands. Many of them are the children of Circassian slaves. The merchants are famous for their civility to foreigners and their keen eye to business.

The **Armenians** and **Jews** form a small but important part of the inhabitants in the large towns of Egypt. The former are famous for their linguistic attainments and wealth ; the latter have blue eyes, fair hair and skin, and busy themselves in mercantile pursuits and the business of bankers and money-changing.

The European population in Egypt consists of Greeks about 65,000, Italians 30,000, French 14,000, English 9,000, Germans, Austrians, Russians, etc., etc., about 10,000. The greater part of the business of Alexandria is in the hands of the Greek merchants ; many of whom are famous for their wealth. It is said that the Greek community contributes most largely to the crime in the country, but when their numbers are taken into consideration, it will be seen that this is an exaggeration. The enterprise and good business habits of the Greeks in Alexandria have made it the great city that it is. The French, Austrian, German, and English nations are likewise represented there, and in Cairo, by several first-rate business houses. The destructive fanaticism peculiar to the Muḥammedan mind, so common in the far east parts of Mesopotamia, seems to be non-existent in Egypt ; such fanaticism as exists is, no doubt, kept in check by the presence of Europeans, and all the different peoples live side by side in a most peaceable manner. The great benefit derived by Egypt from the immigration of Europeans during the last few years, is evident from the increased material prosperity of the country, and the administration of equitable laws which has obtained.

THE NILE.

The river Nile is one of the longest rivers in the world; its Egyptian name was Ḥāpi, 𓎛𓂝𓏤𓈗𓈘, and the Arabs call it *baḥr*, or 'sea.' It is formed by the junction, at 15° 34' N. lat., and 30° 30' 58" E. long., of two great arms, the *Baḥr el-Azraḳ, i.e.*, the 'turbid,' or Blue Nile, from the S.E., and the *Baḥr el-Abyaḍ, i.e.*, the 'clear,' or White Nile, from the S.W.* The eastern branch rises in Goyam, in Abyssinia, at an elevation of about 10,000 feet above the level of the sea. Flowing through the lake of Dembea it passes round the eastern frontier of Goyam, till, when nearing the 10th degree N. lat., it takes a north-west direction, which it preserves until it reaches Kharṭûm; here it unites with the Baḥr el-Abyaḍ, the other great arm, which flows from the S.W. The Baḥr el-Abyaḍ, or White Nile, is so called because of the fine whitish clay which colours its waters. It is broader and deeper than the eastern arm, and it brings down a much larger volume of water; the ancients appear to have regarded it as the true Nile. There can, however, be no doubt that the Baḥr el-Azraḳ has the best right to be considered the true Nile, for during the violent and rapid course which it takes from the Abyssinian mountains, it carries down with it all the rich mud which, during the lapse of ages, has been spread

---

* The White Nile rises in the mountainous districts a few degrees north of the Equator, and the principal streams which flow into it are those of the Sobât, Giraffe, and Gazelle rivers. It is not navigable, and its banks are so low that its whitish slimy deposit often extends to a distance of two miles from the stream. For about a hundred miles south of Kharṭûm the river is little more than a marsh.

over the land on each side of its course and formed the
land of Egypt. In truth, then, Egypt is the gift of the
Baḥr el-Azraḳ. The course of the Baḥr el-Abyaḍ was
traced by Linant in 1827 for about 160 miles from its confluence with the Baḥr el-Azraḳ. At the point of confluence
it measures about 600 yards across, a little farther up it is
from three to four miles wide, and during the inundation the
distance from side to side is twenty-one miles. In an ordinary
season it is about 24 feet deep.

The source of the Nile was not discovered by Bruce,
but by Captains Grant and Speke and Sir Samuel Baker.
Its parents are the Albert Nyanza and Victoria Nyanza
Lakes. The fountain-head of the Nile, Victoria Nyanza,
is a huge basin, far below the level of the country round
about, into which several streams empty themselves. About
200 miles below Khartûm the united river receives, on
the east side, the waters of the Atbara, which rises in the
mountains of Abyssinia, and from this point onwards to its
embouchure, a distance of about 1,750 miles, the Nile
receives no affluent whatever. From Khartûm to Cairo the
Nile falls about 400 yards; its width is about 1,100 yards
in its widest part. The course of the Nile has been
explored to a length of about 3,500 miles. At Abu Ḥammed
the river turns suddenly to the south-west, and flows in this
direction until it reaches Donḳola, where it again curves
to the north. The river enters Nubia, flowing over a ledge
of granite rocks which form the third cataract. Under the
22nd parallel N. lat. is the second cataract, which ends
a few miles above Wâdi Ḥalfah, and about 180 miles lower
down is the first cataract, which ends at Aswân, or Syene,
a little above the island of Elephantine. After entering
Egypt, the Nile flows in a steady stream, always to the
north, and deposits the mud which is the life of Egypt.
The breadth of the Nile valley varies from four to ten
miles in Nubia, and from fifteen to thirty in Egypt. The

width of the strips of cultivated land on each bank of
the river in Egypt together is never more than eight or
nine miles.

In ancient days the Nile poured its waters into the
sea by seven mouths ; those of Damietta and Rosetta*
are now, however, the only two which remain. The Delta
is, in its widest part, about ninety miles across from east
to west, and the distance of the apex from the sea is
also about ninety miles. Many attempts have been made
to ascertain the age of Egypt by estimating the annual
alluvial deposit ; the results, however, cannot be implicitly
relied on.

The **inundation** is caused by the descent of the rain
which falls on the Abyssinian mountains. The indications
of the rise of the river may be seen at the cataracts as
early as the end of May, and a steady increase goes on until
the middle of July, when the increase of water becomes very
great. The Nile continues to rise until the middle of September, when it remains stationary for a period of about
three weeks, sometimes a little less. In October it rises
again, and attains its highest level. From this period it
begins to subside, and, though it rises yet once more, and
reaches occasionally its former highest point, it sinks steadily
until the month of June, when it is again at its lowest level.

The modern ceremony of ' Cutting the Dam ' of the river
takes place generally in the second or third week of August
at Fum el-Khalîg, at Cairo. In ancient days the ceremony
of cutting the canals was accompanied with great festivities,
and great attention was paid to the height of the river
in various parts of Egypt, that the cutting might take place
at the most favourable time. We learn, on the authority
of Seneca, that offerings of gold and other gifts were thrown

---

* The seven mouths were called the Pelusiac, Tanitic, Mendesian,
Phatnitic, Sebennytic, Bolbitic, and the Canopic.

into the Nile at Philæ by the priests to propitiate the divinity of the river.

If the height of the inundation is about forty-one feet the best results from agricultural labour are obtained; a couple of feet of water, more or less, is always attended with disastrous results either in the Delta or Upper Egypt. The dykes, or embankments, which kept the waters of the Nile in check, and regulated their distribution over the lands, were, in Pharaonic days, maintained in a state of efficiency by public funds, and, in the time of the Romans, any person found destroying a dyke was either condemned to hard labour in the public works or mines, or to be branded and sent to the Oasis. If we accept the state ments of Strabo, we may believe that the ancient system of irrigation was so perfect that the varying height of the inundation caused but little inconvenience to the inhabi- tants of Egypt, as far as the results of agricultural labours were concerned, though an unusually high Nile would, of course, wash away whole villages and drown much cattle. If the statements made by ancient writers be com- pared, it will be seen that the actual height of the in- undation is the same now as it always was, and that it maintains the same proportion with the land it irrigates. According to Sir Gardner Wilkinson (*Ancient Egypt*, II., 431), the cubit measures of the Nilometers ought, after certain periods, to be raised proportionately if we wish to arrive at great accuracy in the measurement of the waters. The level of the land, which always keeps pace with that of the river, increases at the rate of six inches in a hundred years in some places, and in others less. The proof of this is that the highest scale in the Nilometer at the island of Elephantine, which served to measure the inundation in the reigns of the early Roman emperors, is now far below the level of the ordinary high Nile; and the obelisk of Heliopolis, the colossi at Thebes, and other similarly situated monuments, are now washed by the waters of the inundation and imbedded to a certain height in a stratum of alluvial soil which has been deposited around their base. The land about Elephantine and at Thebes has been raised about nine feet in 1,700 years. The usual rise of the river at Cairo is twenty-five feet, at Thebes thirty-eight feet, and at Aswân forty-nine feet. The average rate of the current is about three miles per hour. As the river bed rises higher and higher the amount of land covered by the waters of the inundation grows more and more. It is estimated that, if all the land thus watered were thoroughly cultivated, Egypt would, for its size, be one of the richest countries in the world.* The ancient Egyptians fully recognized how very much they owed to the Nile, and, in their hymns, they thank the Nile-god in appropriate and grateful terms. Statues of the god are painted green and red, which colours are supposed to represent 1. the colour of the river in June, when it is a bright green, before the inundation; and 2. the ruddy hue which its waters have when charged with the red mud brought down from the Abyssinian mountains.

---

* It is greatly to be hoped that Sir Colin Scott Moncrieff will be enabled to increase the scope of the valuable work which he has done in the Irrigation Department, and to gradually carry out the works necessary to bring into cultivation those districts which are now a wilderness.

EGYPTIAN WRITING.

The system of writing employed by the earliest inhabitants of the Valley of the Nile known to us was entirely pictorial, and had much in common with the pictorial writing of the Chinese and the ancient people who migrated into Babylonia from the East. There appears to be no inscription in which pictorial characters are used entirely, for the earliest inscriptions now known to us contain alphabetic characters. Inscriptions upon statues, coffins, tombs, temples, etc., in which figures or representations of objects are employed, are usually termed 'Hieroglyphic' (from the Greek ἱερογλυφικός); for writing on papyri a cursive form of hieroglyphic called 'Hieratic' (from the Greek ἱερατικός), was employed by the priests, who, at times, also used hieroglyphic; a third kind of writing, consisting of purely conventional modifications of hieratic characters, which preserve little of the original form, was employed for social and business purposes; it is called demotic (from the Greek δημοτικός). The following will show the different forms of the characters in the three styles of writing—

I. HIERATIC.

II. Hieroglyphic Transcript of No. I.

III. Demotic.

IV. Hieroglyphic Transcript of No. III.

No. I is copied from the Prisse * papyrus (Maxims of Ptaḥ-ḥetep, p. V, l. 1), and is transcribed and translated as follows :—

àb   temu   àn   seχa - nef   sef
.... the heart fails, not remembers he yesterday.
qes   men-f   en   āuu   bu nefer χeper em-
The body suffers it in [its] entirety, happiness becomes
bu [bàn]

wretchedness.†

No. III is copied from the demotic version inscribed on the stele of Canopus (see p. 18), and No. IV. is the corresponding passage in the hieroglyphic version of the

---

* This papyrus is the oldest in the world, and was written about B.C. 2500 ; it was presented to the Bibliothèque Nationale by Prisse, who acquired it at Thebes.

† Ptaḥ-ḥetep is lamenting the troubles of old age, and the complete passage runs : " The understanding perisheth, an old man remembers not yesterday.   The body becometh altogether pain ; happiness turneth into wretchedness ; and taste vanishes away."

Decree. The transliteration of the Demotic, according to Hess (*Roman von Stne Ha-m-us*, p. 80), is :—*p-ḥon nuter* ..... *ua n-n-ueb' ent sâtp er-p-ma ueb er-ube p-gi-n-er mnḥ n-n-nuter'*, "a prophet, or one of the priests who are selected for the sanctuary to perform the dressing of the gods." The transliteration of the hieroglyphic text is: *ḥen neter erpu uā àmⵀ ābu setep er āb-ur àu smā er māret neteru em sati-sen.*

The earliest hieroglyphic inscription is that found on the stele of Senṭ preserved at Oxford ; it dates from the second dynasty. The oldest hieratic inscription is that contained in the famous Prisse papyrus which records the advice of Ptaḥ-ḥetep to his son. It dates from the XIth or XIIth dynasty. The demotic writing appears to have come into use about B.C. 900. Hieroglyphics were used until the third century after Christ, and hieratic and demotic for at least a century later. The inscriptions on the Rosetta and Canopus stelæ are written in hieroglyphic, demotic, and Greek characters. The Egyptians inscribed, wrote, or painted inscriptions upon almost every kind of substance, but the material most used by them for their histories, and religious and other works was papyrus. Sections from the stem of the papyrus plant were carefully cut, and the layers were taken off, pressed flat, and several of them gummed one over the other transversely ; thus almost any length of papyrus for writing upon could be made. The longest known is the great Harris papyrus, No. 1 ; it measures 135 feet by 18 inches. The scribe wrote upon the papyrus with reeds, and the inks were principally made of vegetable colour. Black and red are the commonest colours used, but some papyri are painted with as many as eleven or thirteen. The scribe's palette was a rectangular piece of wood varying from six to thirteen inches long by two, or two and a half, inches wide. In the middle was a hollow for holding the reeds, and at one end were the circular or oval cavities in which the colours were placed.

At the beginning of the Greek rule over Egypt, the knowledge of the use of the ancient Egyptian language began to decline, and the language of Greece began to modify and eventually to supersede that of Egypt. When we consider that Ptolemy I. Soter, succeeded in attracting to Alexandria a large number of the greatest Greek scholars of the day, such as Euclid the mathematician, Stilpo of Megara, Theodorus of Cyrene and Diodorus Cronus, the philosophers, Zenodotus the grammarian, Philetas the poet, from Cos, and many others, this is not to be wondered at. The founding of the great Alexandrian Library and Museum, and the endowment of these institutions for the support of a number of the most eminent Greek philosophers and scholars, was an act of far-sighted policy on the part of Ptolemy I., whose aim was to make the learning and language of the Greeks to become dominant in Egypt. Little by little the principal posts in the Government were monopolised by the Greeks, and little by little the Egyptians became servants and slaves to their intellectually superior masters. In respect to their language, " the Egyptians were not prohibited from making use, so far as it seemed requisite according to ritual or otherwise appropriate, of the native language and of its time-hallowed written signs ; in this old home, moreover, of the use of writing in ordinary intercourse the native language, alone familiar to the great public, and the usual writing must necessarily have been allowed not merely in the case of private contracts, but even as regards tax-receipts and similar documents. But this was a concession, and the ruling Hellenism strove to enlarge its domain." Mommsen, *The Provinces of the Roman Empire*, Vol. II., p. 243. It is true that Ptolemy II. Philadelphus, employed the famous Manetho (*i.e.,* , Mer-en-Teḥuti, 'beloved of Thoth') to draw up a history of Egypt, and an account of the ancient Egyptian religion from the papyri and other native records; but it is also true that during the reigns of these two Ptolemies that the Egyptians were firmly kept in obscurity, and that the ancient priest-college of Heliopolis was suppressed. A century or two after the Christian era, Greek had obtained such a hold upon the inhabitants of Egypt that the Egyptian Christians, the followers and disciples of St. Mark, were obliged to use the Greek alphabet to write down the Egyptian, that is to say Coptic translation of the books of the Old and New Testaments. The letters ϣ, *sh*, ϥ, *f*, ϧ, χ, ϩ, *h*, ϭ, *č*, ϫ, *ǧ*, were added from the demotic forms of hieratic characters to represent sounds which were unknown in the Greek language. During the Greek rule over Egypt many of the hieroglyphic characters had new phonetic values given to them; by this time the knowledge of hieroglyphic writing had practically died out.

The history of the decipherment of hieroglyphics is of great interest, but no thorough account of it can be given here; only the most important facts connected with it can be mentioned. During the XVIth–XVIIIth centuries many attempts were made by scholars to interpret the hieroglyphic inscriptions then known to the world, but they resulted in nothing useful. The fact is they did not understand the nature of the problem to be solved, and they failed to perceive the use of the same hieroglyphic character as a phonetic or determinative in the same inscription. In 1799, a French officer discovered at Bolbitane or Rosetta a basalt slab inscribed in the hieroglyphic, demotic, and Greek characters; it was shortly after captured by the English army, and taken to London, where it was carefully examined by Dr. Thomas Young.*

* Thomas Young was born at Milverton, in Somersetshire, on the 13th of June, 1773; both his parents were Quakers. At the age of fourteen he is said to have been versed in Greek, Latin, French,

The Society of Antiquaries published a fac-simile of the inscription, which was distributed among scholars, and Silvestre de Sacy and Akerblad made some useful dis coveries about certain parts of the demotic version of the inscription. Dr. Young was enabled, ten years after, to make translations of the three inscriptions, and the results of his studies were published in 1821. In 1822 M. Champollion * (Le Jeune) published a translation of the same inscriptions, and was enabled to make out something like an alphabet. There appears to be no doubt that he was greatly helped by the publications and labours of Young, who had succeeded in grouping certain words in demotic, and in assigning ac curate values to some of the Egyptian characters used in writing the names of the Greek rulers of Egypt. Young made many mistakes, but some of his work was of value. Champollion, to whom the credit of definitely settling the phonetic values of several signs really belongs, had been carefully grounded in the Coptic language, and was there-fore enabled with little difficulty to recognize the hiero-glyphic forms of the words which were familiar to him in Coptic; Young had no such advantage. Champollion's system was subjected to many attacks, but little by little it gained ground, and the labours of other scholars have

Italian, Hebrew, Persian and Arabic. He took his degree of M.D. in July, 1796, in 1802 he was appointed professor of natural philosophy at the Royal Institution, and in 1810 he was elected physician to St. George's Hospital. He was not, however, a popular physician. He died on the 10th of May, 1829.

* Jean François le Jeune Champollion was born at Figeac, depart-ment Du Lot, in 1796. He was educated at Grenoble, and afterwards at Paris, where he devoted himself to the study of Coptic. In the year 1824 he was ordered by Charles X. to visit all the important collections of Egyptian antiquities in Europe. On his return he was appointed Director of the Louvre. In 1828 he was sent on a scientific mission to Egypt, and was afterwards made professor of Egyptian antiquities at the Collège de France. He died in 1831.

proved that he was right. The other early workers in the field of hieroglyphics were Dr. Samuel Birch in England; Dr. Lepsius in Germany, and MM. Rosellini and Salvolini in Italy. The study of hieroglyphics has become comparatively general, and each year sees books of texts published, learned papers on Egyptian grammar written, and translations made into the various European languages.

In hieroglyphic inscriptions the signs are used in two ways: I, IDEOGRAPHIC, II, PHONETIC. In the ideographic system a word is expressed by a picture or *ideograph* thus: *māu*, 'water'; in the phonetic system the same word is written ___ⓒ *m* + *ā* + *u*, no regard being paid to the fact that represents an owl, ___ a hand and forearm, and ⓒ a rope. Similarly *emsuḥ* is a 'crocodile' in the ideographic system, but phonetically it is written *m* + *s* + *u* + *ḥ*. The ideographic system is probably older than the phonetic.

PHONETIC signs are: I, ALPHABETIC, as *m*, *s*, *u*; or II, SYLLABIC, as *mer*, *χeper*, *ḥetep*. The sign *χeper* can be written 1, ; 2, ; 3, ; 4, ; the sign *nefer* can be written 1, ; 2, ; 3, ; 4, ; 5, . The scribes took pains to represent the exact value of these syllabic signs in order that no mistake might be made.

The IDEOGRAPHIC signs are also used as determinatives, and are placed after words written phonetically to determine their meaning. For example, *nem* means 'to sleep,' 'to walk,' 'to go back,' 'to become infirm,' 'tongue' and 'again'; without a determinative the meaning of this word in a sentence would be easily mistaken. DETERMINATIVES are of two kinds: I, *ideographic*, and II, *generic*. Thus after ⟨𓄿⟩ *màu*, 'cat,' a cat, ⟨𓃠⟩, was written; this is an *ideographic* determinative. After ⟨𓈌⟩ *ḳerḥ*, 'darkness,' the night sky with a star in it, ⟨𓇶⟩, was written; this is a *generic* determinative. A word has frequently more than one determinative; for example, in the word ⟨𓃀𓄿𓎛⟩ *bāḥ*, 'to overflow,' ⟨𓄿⟩ is a determinative of the sound *bāḥ*; ⟨𓈖⟩ is a determinative of water, ⟨𓈈⟩ of a lake or collection of water, and ⟨𓈐⟩ of ground. The list of hieroglyphic signs with their phonetic values given on pp. 61–68 will be of use in reading kings' names, etc.; for convenience however the hieroglyphic alphabet is added here. The system of transliteration of Egyptian characters used in this book is that most generally adopted.

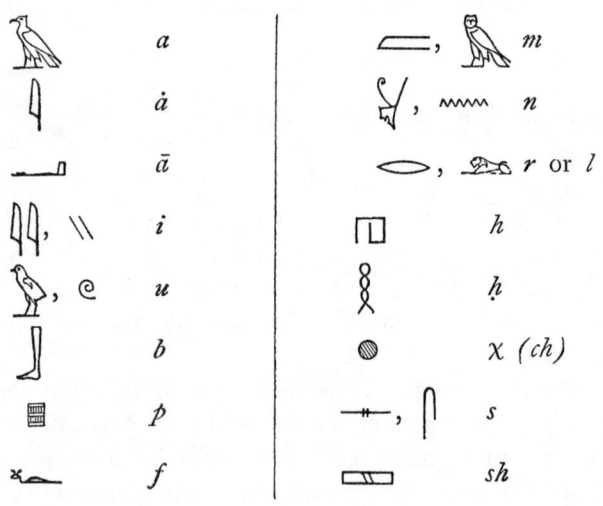

𓄿	*a*		⟨𓅓⟩	*m*
𓇋	*ȧ*		⟨𓈖⟩	*n*
𓂝	*ā*		⟨𓂋⟩	*r* or *l*
𓏭, \\	*i*		𓉔	*h*
𓅱, ℮	*u*		𓎛	*ḥ*
𓃀	*b*		⊙	*χ (ch)*
𓊪	*p*		—, 𓊨	*s*
𓆑	*f*		▭	*sh*

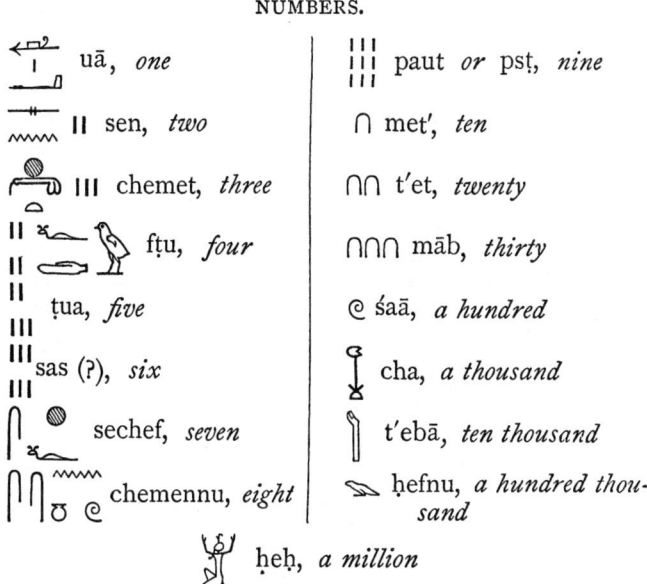

⏝ *k* | ⌒ *t*

△ *q* | ⊂⊃ *ṭ*

⬠ *ḳ* | ❱, ⊨ *θ (th)*

❱ *t'* (like *ch* in child)

The number of hieroglyphic characters is about two thousand.

NUMBERS.

uā, *one* | ‖‖‖ paut *or* psṭ, *nine*

‖ sen, *two* | ∩ met', *ten*

‖‖ chemet, *three* | ∩∩ t'et, *twenty*

fṭu, *four* | ∩∩∩ māb, *thirty*

ṭua, *five* | ℮ śaā, *a hundred*

sas (?), *six* | cha, *a thousand*

sechef, *seven* | t'ebā, *ten thousand*

chemennu, *eight* | ḥefnu, *a hundred thousand*

ḥeḥ, *a million*

The forms of the numbers 40, 50, 60, 70, 80 and 90 are not known exactly.

Hieroglyphic inscriptions are usually to be read in the opposite direction to which the characters face; there is however no hard and fast rule in this matter. On the papyri they are read in various directions, and there are instances in which the ancient copyist mistook the end of a chapter for its beginning, and copied the whole of it in the reverse order.   Some inscriptions are to be read in perpendicular lines.

The following transliterated and translated extract from the first page of the "Tale of the Two Brothers" will explain the foregoing statements.

I.

àr   ementuf   χertu   sen   sen

There were once on a time brothers two [the children]

en   uā   muθet   en   uā   àtf

of   one   mother   and of   one   father;

Ànpu   ren   pa   āa   àu   Batau

Anubis   was the name   of the   elder,   was   Bata

ren   pa   śeràu   χer   àr

the name   of the   younger.   Now   as regards

Ànpu   su   χeri   pa   χeri   ḥemṭ

Anpu,   he   possessed   a house   and had   a wife,

2.   àu   paif   sen   śeràu   emmā-f

and was   his   brother   younger   [living] with him

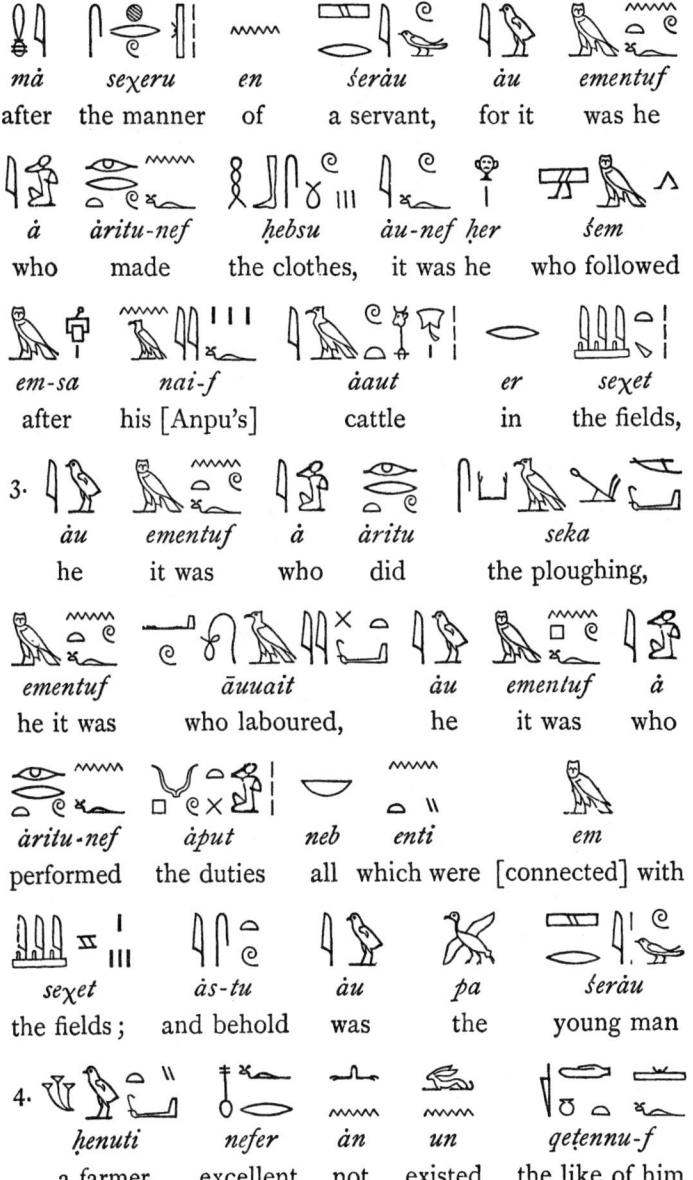

má	seχeru	en	śeràu	àu	ementuf
after	the manner	of	a servant,	for it	was he

à	àritu-nef	ḥebsu	àu-nef ḥer	śem
who	made	the clothes,	it was he	who followed

em-sa	nai-f	àaut	er	seχet
after	his [Anpu's]	cattle	in	the fields,

3. àu	ementuf	à	àritu	seka
he	it was	who	did	the ploughing,

ementuf	àuuait	àu	ementuf	à
he it was	who laboured,	he	it was	who

àritu-nef	àput	neb	enti	em
performed	the duties	all	which were	[connected] with

seχet	às-tu	àu	pa	śeràu
the fields;	and behold	was	the	young man

4. ḥenuti	nefer	àn	un	qeṭennu-f
a farmer	excellent,	not	existed	the like of him

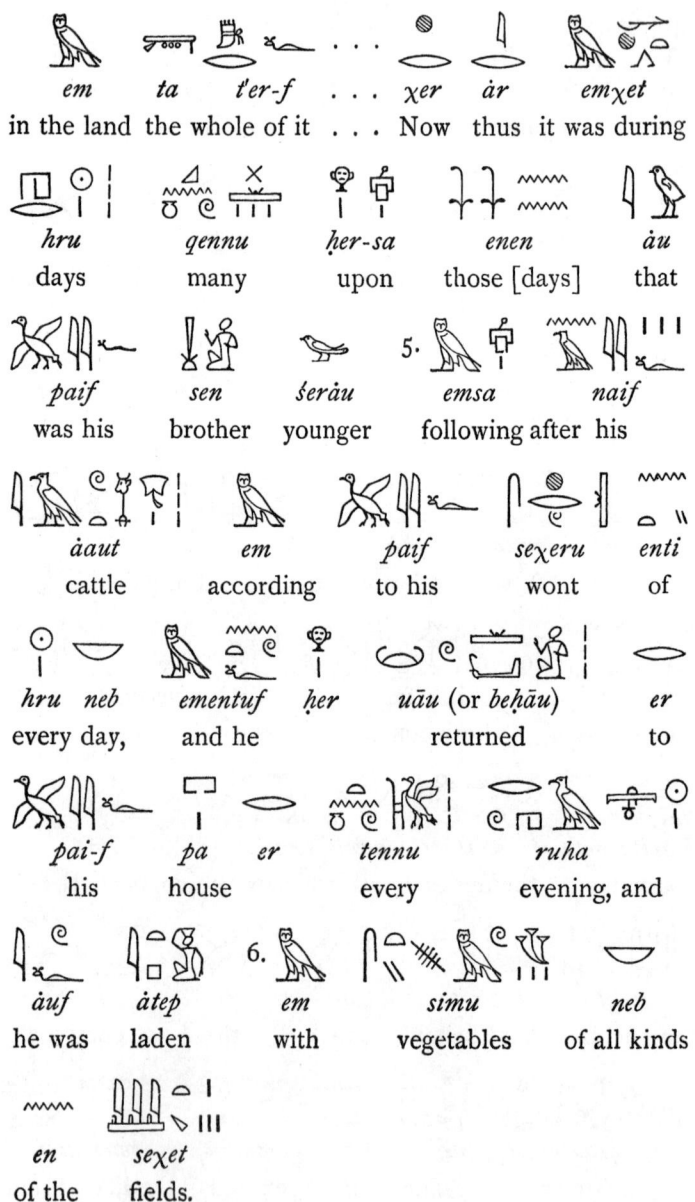

em	*ta*	*t'er-f*	... *χer*	*àr*	*emχet*
in the land	the whole of it	...	Now	thus	it was during

hru	*qennu*	*her-sa*	*enen*	*àu*
days	many	upon	those [days]	that

paif	*sen*	*seràu*	5. *emsa*	*naif*
was his	brother	younger	following after	his

àaut	*em*	*paif*	*seχeru*	*enti*
cattle	according	to his	wont	of

hru neb	*ementuf*	*her*	*uāu* (or *behāu*)	*er*
every day,	and he		returned	to

pai-f	*pa*	*er*	*tennu*	*ruha*
his	house		every	evening, and

àuf	*àtep*	6. *em*	*simu*	*neb*
he was	laden	with	vegetables	of all kinds

en	*seχet*
of the	fields.

A List of some of the Principal Hieroglyphic Signs and their Phonetic Values.

Men and Women.

àn	āχ	àm	śeps
ḥa	qa	àr	àmen
ur	qeṭ	sa	āb
ser	seḥer	fa	χer
àθi	tut	ḥeḥ	s
àau	à	ḥeḥ	māt
	beq		

Limbs, &c., of Men.

ṭep	ḥu	χu	sem
ḥrà	sept	ser	śem
ànem	ka	χen	àn
ut'a	χen	t	śes
àt	àn, àt	t'ebā	tet
àn	ā	ka, met	reṭ
àri	mā	sem	b
àr	neχt	ī	āā, āu
r	ṭā	seb	

ANIMALS.

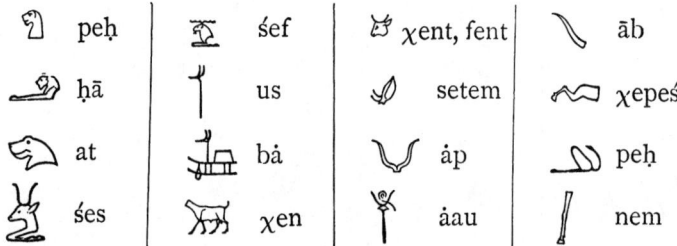

l, r	āb	nefer	áb
neb	sāb	ka	ba
ser	set	āā	máu

LIMBS, &c., OF ANIMALS.

peḥ	śef	χent, fent	āb
ḥā	us	setem	χepeś
at	bá	áp	peḥ
śes	χen	áau	nem

BIRDS.

Ḥeru, bak	ur	m	u
ba	ba	neḥ	pa
χu	mut	qem	ten
āq	se	ti	reχ
śerá	mer	a	t'a
			senṭ

PARTS OF BIRDS.

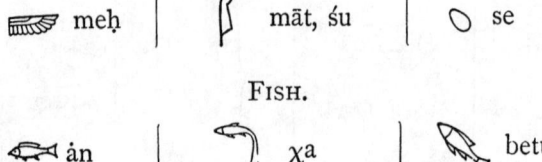

meḥ	māt, śu	se

FISH.

án	χa	betu

REPTILES.

sebek		t′			f
ḥefen		āf, net, χeb seχet			χeper
serq		kam			

TREES AND PLANTS.

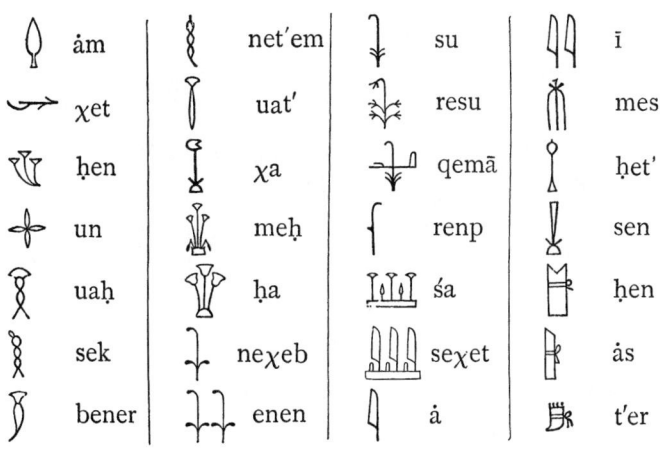

ȧm		net′em		su		ī
χet		uat′		resu		mes
ḥen		χa		qemā		ḥet′
un		meḥ		renp		sen
uaḥ		ha		śa		ḥen
sek		neχeb		seχet		ȧs
bener		enen		ȧ		t′er

CELESTIAL OBJECTS.

pet, ḥer		rā		χā		seb
θeḥen		χu		ȧbeṭ		

OBJECTS OF EARTH.

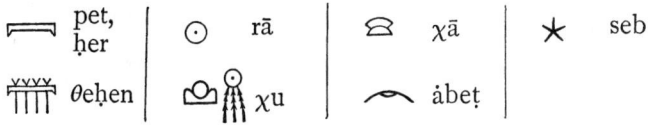

ta	ṭu	set	ȧner

WATER.

māu	n	ś	mer	āb

BUILDING.

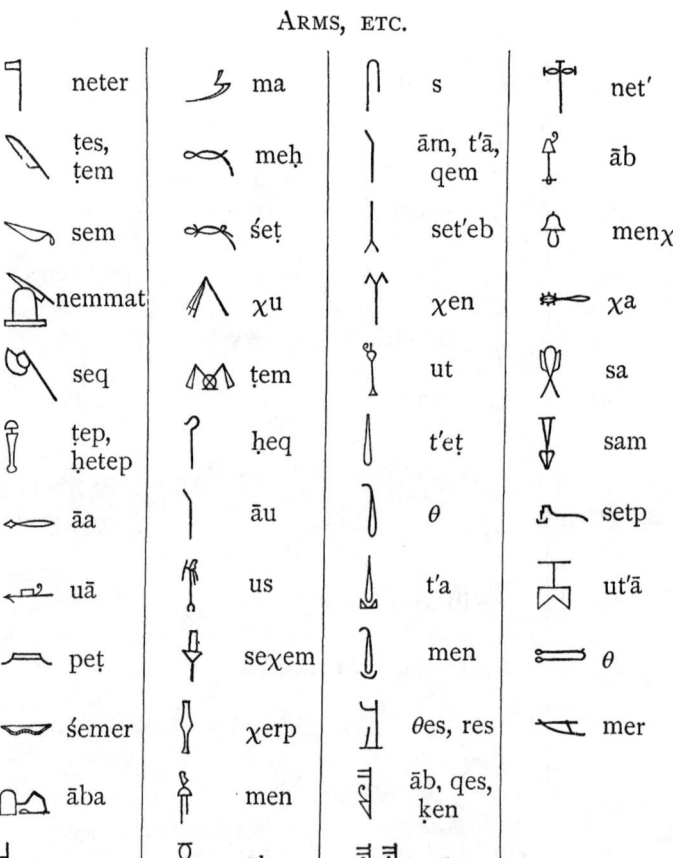

⊗	nu		seḥ		ā		ṭeṭ
	per		ḥeb		s		ȧuset
	ḥet		ȧneb		ȧn		

ARMS, ETC.

	neter		ma		s		net'
	ṭes, ṭem		meḥ		ām, t'ā, qem		āb
	sem		śeṭ		set'eb		menχ
	nemmat		χu		χen		χa
	seq		ṭem		ut		sa
	ṭep, ḥetep		ḥeq		t'eṭ		sam
	āa		āu		θ		setp
	uā		us		t'a		ut'ā
	peṭ		seχem		men		θ
	śemer		χerp		θes, res		mer
	āba		men		āb, qes, ḳen		
	qeṭ		āb		seḥ		

MUSICAL INSTRUMENTS.

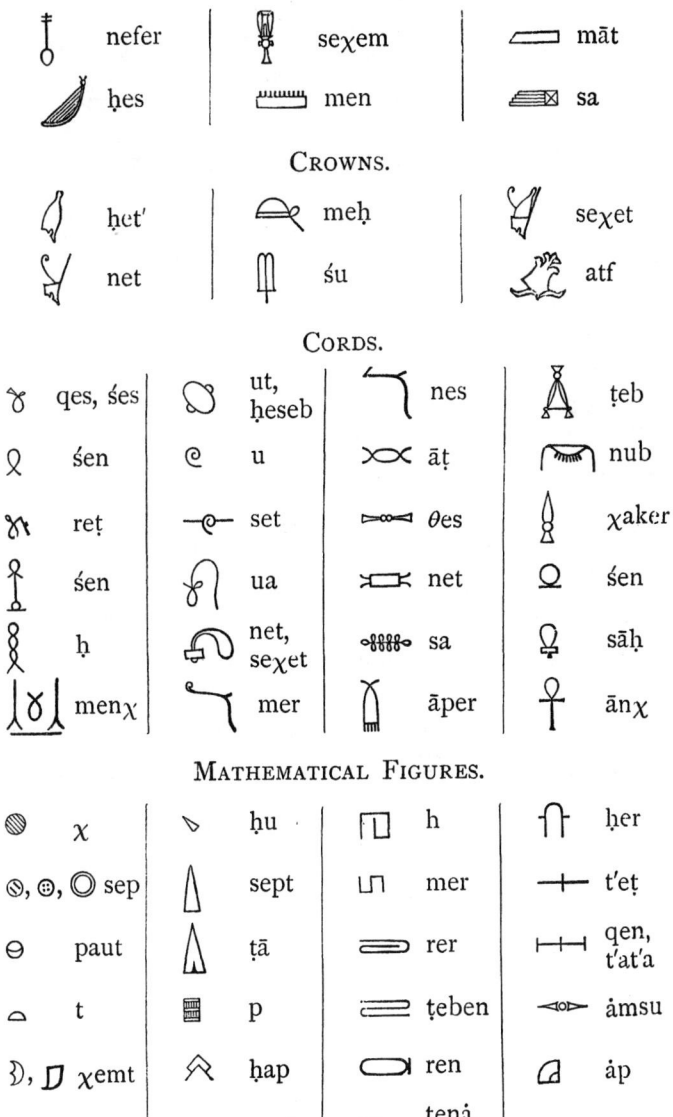

	nefer		seχem		māt
	ḥes		men		sa

CROWNS.

	ḥet′		meḥ		seχet
	net		śu		atf

CORDS.

	qes, śes		ut, ḥeseb		nes		ṭeb
	śen		u		āṭ		nub
	reṭ		set		θes		χaker
	śen		ua		net		śen
	ḥ		net, seχet		sa		sāḥ
	menχ		mer		āper		ānχ

MATHEMATICAL FIGURES.

	χ		ḥu		h		ḥer
	sep		sept		mer		t′eṭ
	paut		ṭā		rer		qen, t′at′a
	t		p		ṭeben		ȧmsu
	χemt		ḥap		ren		ȧp
	q		uu, ur, śes		tenȧ, peχ		

VASES, ETC.

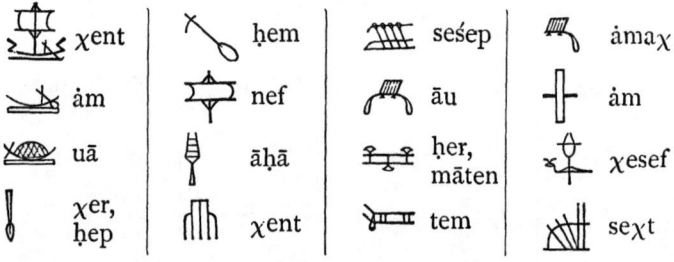

ʊ	nu		qebḥ		ta		χer
	χnem		ḥen		ta		k
	åb		må		ḥetep		neb
	ḥes		āu, āb		åa		ḥeb
	χent		ba		ḳ		nā, ån

SHIPS, ETC.

	χent		ḥem		seśep		åmaχ
	åm		nef		āu		åm
	uā		āḥā		her, māten		χesef
	χer, ḥep		χent		tem		seχt

DETERMINATIVES.

	to call		of women		of birds
	to pray		of birth		of goddesses
	to rejoice		to see		of trees
	to dance		of strength		of grain
	to plough		to give		of heaven
	foes		to walk, stand		of light
	of men		of flesh		of country
	of gods		to breathe, smell		of towns

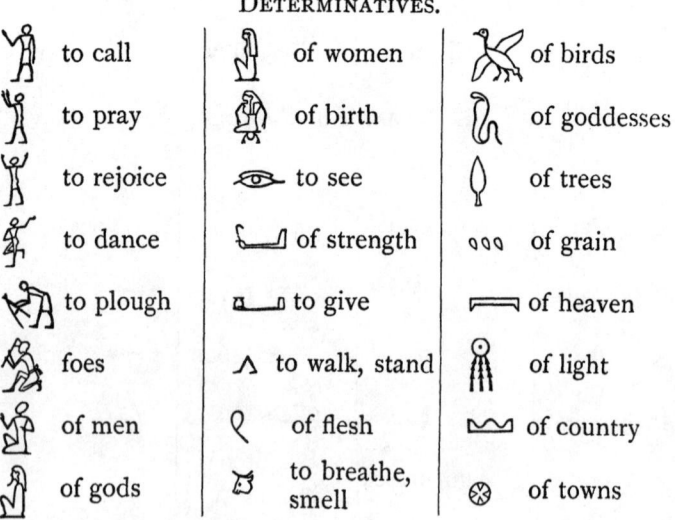

DETERMINATIVES—*continued.*

☽ of iron	○ ○ ○ of metals	▽ of festival
〰〰〰 of water	⎧ writing, ⎪ computation, ⎨ knowledge, ⎪ and abstract ⎩ ideas	⬡ of unguents
⊏⊐ of houses		⚏ of roads
⊂ of writing		⇘ of ships
ⵝ of ground	⋂ of fire	⟁ of winds

THE ARABIC ALPHABET.

Elif	ا	*a*	Zäd	ض	*ḍ* aspirated
Bâ	ب	*b*	Tâ	ط	*ṭ* palatal
Tâ	ت	*t*	Zâ	ظ	*z* palatal
Thâ	ث	*th* = θ	'Ain	ع †	
Gîm	ج	*g* (like *g* in *gin*)*	Ghain	غ	*g* guttural ‡
Hâ	ح	*ḥ* (a smooth guttural aspirate)	Fâ	ف	*f*
			Ḳâf	ق	*ḳ* guttural
Khâ	خ	*ch* (like *ch* in *loch*)	Kâf	ك	*k*
Dâl	د	*d*	Lâm	ل	*l*
Zâl	ذ	*th* (like *th* in *that*)	Mîm	م	*m*
Râ	ر	*r*	Nûn	ن	*n*
Zây	ز	*z*	Hâ	ه	*h*
Sîn	س	*s*	Wâw	و	*w*
Shîn	ش	*sh* (like *sh* in *shut*)	Yâ	ى	*y*
Ṣad	ص	*ṣ* (like *ss* in *hiss*)			

* Pronounced hard in Egypt.
† Usually unpronounceable by Europeans.
‡ Accompanied by a rattling sound.

THE COPTIC ALPHABET (31 letters).*

ⲁ	*a*	ⲙ	*m*	ⲯ	*ps*
ⲃ	*b*	ⲛ	*n*	ⲱ	*ô*
ⲅ	*g*	ⳉ	*x* or *ks*	ⳡ	*sh*
ⲇ	*d*	ⲟ	*o*	ϥ	*f*
ⲉ	*e*	ⲡ	*p*	ⳃ	*χ* or *ch*
ⲍ	*z*	ⲣ	*r*	ⳉ	*h*
ⲏ	*ê*	ⲥ	*s*	ⲝ	*ǧ*
ⲑ	*th*	ⲧ	*t*	ϭ	*č*
ⲓ	*i*	ⲩ	*y*	†ϯ	*ti*
ⲕ	*k*	ⲫ	*ph*		
ⲗ	*l*	ⲭ	*ch*		

* In the Boheiric dialect there are thirty-two.

† Six letters of the Coptic alphabet are modifications of the forms of Egyptian characters in demotic. *See* p. 40. The names of the letters in Coptic are ⲁⲗⲫⲁ, ⲃⲓⲇⲁ, ⲅⲁⲙⲙⲁ, ⲇⲁⲗⲇⲁ, ⲉⲓ, ⲍⲓⲧⲁ, ⲏⲧⲁ, ⲑⲓⲧⲁ, ⲓⲁⲩⲧⲁ, ⲕⲁⲡⲡⲁ, ⲗⲁⲩⲗⲁ, ⲙⲓ, ⲛⲓ, ⳉⲓ, ⲟ, ⲡⲓ, ⲣⲟ, ⲥⲓⲙⲁ, ⲧⲁⲩ, ⲩⲉ (ϩⲉ), ⲫⲓ, ⲭⲓ, ⲯⲓ, ⲁⲩ, ⳡⲉⲓ, ϥⲉⲓ, ⳃⲉⲓ, ϩⲟⲣⲓ, ⲝⲁⲛⳉⲓⲁ, ϭⲓⲙⲁ, ϯ.

EGYPTIAN.						ALEXANDRIAN MONTHS (COPTIC FORMS).		
⌒ 𝖨𝖨𝖨 ⊙	àbeṭ	uā	śat	Month one of sowing	ⲑⲱⲟⲩⲧ	August	29	*
⌒ 𝖨𝖨𝖨 ⊙	àbeṭ	sen	śat	Month two of sowing	ⲡⲁⲟⲡⲓ	September	28	
⌒ 𝖨𝖨𝖨 ⊙	àbeṭ	chemt	śat	Month three of sowing	ⲁⲑⲱⲣ	October	28	
⌒ 𝖨𝖨𝖨 ⊙	àbeṭ	fṭu	śat	Month four of sowing	ⲭⲟⲓⲁⲕ	November	27	
⌒ ▱ ⊙	àbeṭ	uā	pert	Month one of growing	ⲧⲱⲃⲓ	December	27	
⌒ ▱ ⊙	àbeṭ	sen	pert	Month two of growing	ⲙⲉⲭⲓⲣ	January	26	
⌒ ▱ ⊙	àbeṭ	chemt	pert	Month three of growing	ⲫⲁⲙⲉⲛⲱⲑ	February	25	
⌒ ▱ ⊙	àbeṭ	fṭu	pert	Month four of growing	ⲫⲁⲣⲙⲟⲩⲑⲓ	March	27	
⌒ ≈ ⊙	àbeṭ	uā	śet	Month one of inundation	ⲡⲁⲭⲟⲛ	April	26	
⌒ ≈ ⊙	àbeṭ	sen	śet	Month two of inundation	ⲡⲁⲱⲛⲓ	May	26	
⌒ ≈ ⊙	àbeṭ	chemt	śet	Month three of inundation	ⲉⲡⲏⲡ	June	25	
⌒ ≈ ⊙	àbeṭ	fṭu	śet	Month four of inundation	ⲙⲉⲥⲱⲣⲏ	July	25	

* The days for the beginnings of these months were first fixed at Alexandria about B.C. 30.

The ancient Egyptians had : I. the vague or civil year, which consisted of 365 days; it was divided into twelve months of thirty days each, and five intercalary days were added at the end; II. the Sothic year of $365\frac{1}{4}$ days. The first year of a Sothic period began with the rising of Sirius or the dog-star, on the 1st of the month Thoth, when it coincided with the beginning of the inundation; III. the Egyptian solar year,* which was a quarter of a day shorter than the Sothic year, an error which corrected itself in 1460 fixed years or 1461 vague years. The true year was estimated approximately by the conjunction of the sun with Sirius. Dr. Brugsch thinks (*Egypt under the Pharaohs*, Vol. II., p. 176) that as early as B.C. 2500 *four* different forms of the year were already in use, and that the "little year" corresponded with the lunar year, and the "great year" with a lunar year having intercalated days. Each month was dedicated to a god.† The Egyptians dated their stelæ and documents by the day of the month and the year of the king who was reigning at the time. The Copts first dated their documents according to the years of the INDICTION; the indictions were periods of fifteen years, and the first began A.D. 312. In later times the Copts made use of the era of the Martyrs, which was reckoned from the 29th of August, A.D. 284. About the ninth century after Christ they began to adopt the Muḥammedan era of the Hijrah or "flight," which was reckoned from A.D. 622.

* It was practically the same as the civil year.

† Some of the Coptic names of the months show that they have een derived from the ancient Egyptian : thus Thôth is from , *Teḥuti*, Pachôn from *Chensu*, Athôr from , *Ḥet-Ḥeru*, Mesôre from *mes-Ḥeru*, "the birth of Horus" festival, etc. The Copts have I. an agricultural year, and II. an ecclesiastical year; the latter consists of twelve months of thirty days, with a thirteenth month called Nissi of five or six intercalary days.

THE RELIGION AND GODS OF EGYPT.

The religion of the ancient Egyptians is one of the most difficult problems of Egyptology, and though a great deal has been written about it during the last few years, and many difficulties have been satisfactorily explained, there still remain unanswered a large number of questions connected with it. In all religious texts the reader is always assumed to have a knowledge of the subject treated of by the writer, and no definite statement is made on the subject concerning which very little, comparatively, is known by students to-day. For example, in the texts inscribed inside the pyramids of Unàs, Pepi, and Tetà (B.C. 3300–3233), we are brought face to face with religious compositions which mention the acts and relationships of the gods, and refer to beliefs, and give instructions for the performance of certain acts of ritual which are nowhere explained. It will be remembered that Ptolemy II. Philadelphus instructed Manetho to draw up a history of the religion of the ancient Egyptians. If such a work was needed by the cultured Greek who lived when the religion of ancient Egypt, though much modified, was still in existence, how much more is it needed now? The main beliefs of the Egyptian religion were always the same. The attributes of one god might be applied to another, or one god might be confused with another; the cult of one god might decline in favour of another, or new gods might arise and become popular, but the foundation of the religion of Egypt remained unchanged. Still, it is asserted by some that the religion of the dynasties of the Early Empire was simpler and more free from speculation than that of the Middle and New Empires, in which the nature and mutual relationships of the gods were discussed and theogonies formulated. Speaking generally the gods of Egypt were the everlasting and unalterable powers of nature, *i.e.*, 'day and night,' 'light and darkness,' etc. The great god of the Egyptians, Rā, or Åmen-Rā, as he was called in the Middle Empire, was said to be the maker of all things; the various gods Horus, Åtmu, etc., were merely forms of him. Rā was self-begotten, and hymns to him never tire in declaring his absolute and perfect unity in terms which resemble those of the Hebrew Scriptures. It will be seen from the translation of a hymn given in the following pages that he is made to possess every attribute, natural and spiritual, which Christian peoples ascribe to God Almighty. The one doctrine, however, which lived persistently and unchanged in the Egyptian mind for five thousand years, is that of a future life. During the earliest dynasties beautiful, and enduring tombs * were built in order that the bodies which were placed in them might be preserved until such time as the resurrection of the body should take place. It is clear from the papyri that man was supposed to possess a body, a soul, *ba*, a 'genius' *ka*, and an intelligence, *χu*. The body, freed from all its most corruptible portions, was preserved by being filled with bitumen, spices, and

---

* "Les belles tombes que l'on admire dans les plaines de Thèbes et de Saḳḳârah ne sont donc pas dues à l'orgueil de ceux qui les ont érigées. Une pensée plus large a présidé à leur construction. Plus les matériaux sont énormes, plus on est sûr que les promesses faites par la religion recevront leur exécution. En ces sens, les Pyramides ne sont pas des monuments 'de la vaine ostentation des rois'; elles sont des obstacles impossibles à renverser, et les preuves gigantesques d'un dogme consolant." (Mariette, *Notices des Principaux Monuments*, p. 44.)

aromatic drugs, and having been bandaged in many a fold of linen, lay in its tomb, ready to take part in the life which was inherited by those who were deemed worthy of it.

After the death of a man it was thought that he was taken into the hall of the god Osiris, judge of the dead, and that his conscience, symbolized by the heart, was weighed in the balance before him. Thoth, the scribe of the gods, stood there with his reed and palette to write down the result, while his associate, a cynocephalus ape 🐒, sat over the middle of the beam of the balance, and watched the index pointer. The man's soul, and destiny, and nurse, and cradle stood by, watching the weighing of the heart by Anubis against a feather, ∫, emblematic of Law. If the result were favourable, the dead man was led by Horus into the presence of Osiris, where stood the four children of Horus, Amset, Ḥāpi, Ṭuamāutef, and Ḳebḥsenuf (to each of whom certain intestines were dedicated), upon a lotus flower which sprung forth from under the throne of Osiris; and after making offerings to the god, the dead man passed into everlasting life. If the result were unfavourable, the Devourer, a beast part lion, part hippopotamus, and part horse, stepped forward and claimed the dead man as his. Annihilation was the result.

After death the soul of the dead man was supposed to have many enemies to combat, just as the sun was supposed to spend the time between his rising and setting in fighting the powers of mist, darkness, and night. These he vanquished by the knowledge and use of certain "words of power." The deceased was also supposed to be condemned to perform field labours in the nether-world, but to avoid this, stone, wooden, or Egyptian porcelain figures were placed in his tomb to do the work for him. After undergoing all these troubles and trials, the soul went into the abode of beatified spirits, and there it did everything wished by it, and remained in bliss until it rejoined its body in the tomb. The soul of the dead man entered successively into a phœnix (*bennu*), a heron, a swallow, a snake, a crocodile, etc.

In the hall of Osiris the soul was supposed to affirm before forty-two gods that it had not committed any of the forty-two sins which are detailed in good papyri at full length as follows :—

"I am not a doer of what is wrong, I am not a plunderer,
"I am not a robber, I am not a slayer of men, I do not
"stint the quantity of corn, I am not a niggard, I do not
"seize the property of the gods, I am not a teller of lies, I
"am not a monopolizer of food, I am no extortioner, I am
'not unchaste, I am not the cause of others' tears, I am
"not a dissembler, I am not a doer of violence, I am not
"a domineering character, I do not pillage cultivated land,
"I am not an eavesdropper, I am not a chatterer, I do not
"dismiss a case through self-interest, I am not unchaste
"with women or men, I am not obscene, I am not an
"exciter of alarms, I am not hot in speech, I do not turn a
"deaf ear to the words of righteousness, I am not foul-
"mouthed, I am not a striker, I am not a quarreller, I do
"not revoke my purpose, I do not multiply clamour in
"reply to words, I am not evil-minded or a doer of evil, I
"am not a reviler of the king, I put no obstruction upon
"the water, I am not a bawler, I am not a reviler of
"the god, I am not fraudulent, I am not sparing in
"offerings to the gods, I do not deprive the dead of the
"funereal cakes, I do not take away the cakes of the child
"or profane the god of my locality, I do not kill sacred
"animals." (Renouf, *Introduction to Papyrus of Ani*, p. 17, col. 2.)

It is tolerably evident then that grand tombs were not

built as mere objects of pride, but as "everlasting habitations" which would serve to preserve the body from decay, and be ready to be re-inhabited by the soul at the proper season.   Greek authors have written much about the beliefs of the Egyptians; but the greater number of their statements are to be received with caution.   They wrote down what they were told, but were frequently mis· informed.

The papyri which have come down to us show that the moral conceptions of the Egyptians were of a very high order : and works like the Maxims of Ptaḥ-ḥetep and the Maxims of Ani show clearly that a man's duty to his god and to his fellow-man was laid down in a distinct manner.   Such works will compare very favourably with the Proverbs of Solomon and the Wisdom of Jesus the son of Sirach.

The religious literature of the Egyptians includes a large number of works, of which the most important is the collection of chapters generally called the Book of the Dead ; in Egyptian its name is *per em hru*, "Coming forth by day."   Selections from this work were written in the hieratic character upon coffins as early as the XIIth dynasty (B.C. 2500), and this practice was continued down to the time of the Roman Empire.   The walls of tombs were covered with extracts from it, and scribes and people of rank had buried with them large rolls of papyrus inscribed with its principal chapters, and ornamented with vignettes explanatory of the text which ran beneath.   Some of the chapters in the work are of very great antiquity ; and so far back as B.C. 2500 the text was so old, and had been copied so often, that it was already not to be understood.   Many parts of it are obscure, and many utterly corrupt ; but the discovery from time to time of ancient papyri with accurate readings tends to clear up many doubtful points, and to bring out the right meaning of certain parts of the work.

The following is a list of the most important gods with their names in hieroglyphs; it will be readily seen how very many of them are merely forms of the sun-god Rā, and how many of them have the same attributes :—

CHNEMU,* the 'Moulder,' , is represented with the head of a ram, and is one of the oldest gods of the Egyptian religion. He was thought to possess some of the attributes of Āmen, Rā, and Ptaḥ, and shared with the last-named god the attribute of "maker of mankind." At Philæ he is represented making man out of clay on a potter's wheel. Chnemu put together the scattered limbs of the dead body of Osiris, and it was he who constructed the beautiful woman who became the wife of Bata in the Tale of the Two Brothers. Like Āmen-Rā he is said to be the father of the gods. His cult had great vogue in the regions round about the first cataract, where he was always associated with Aneq and Sati. In bas-reliefs he is usually coloured green, and wears the *atef* crown with uræi, etc.

CHNEMU.

* The authorities for the figures of the gods are given by Lanzone in his *Dizionario di Mitologia Egizia.*

† The following are the crowns most commonly met with on the monuments :—

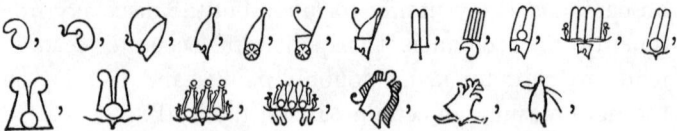

PTAḤ 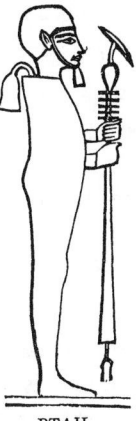, the 'Opener,' perhaps the oldest of all the gods of Egypt, was honoured with a temple and worshipped at Memphis from the time of the Ist dynasty. He is said to be the father of the gods, who came forth from his eye, and of men, who came forth from his mouth. He is represented in the form of a mummy, and he holds a sceptre composed of *usr*, 'strength,' *ānch*, 'life,' and *ṭeṭ*, 'stability.' With reference to his connection with the resurrection and the nether-world, he is called PTAḤ-SEKER-ÀUSAR, and is then represented as a little squat boy, at times wearing a beetle on his head. He is at times represented with Isis and Nephthys, and then appears to be a form of Osiris.

PTAḤ.

TMU , or ÀTMU , was the 'Closer' of the day or night.

ÀTMU.

MUT.

Mut ⟨𓄿⟩, the 'Mother,' was one of the divinities of the Theban triad; she was supposed to represent Nature, the mother of all things.

Cheperá ⟨𓆣⟩, the 'Creator,' was associated with Ptaḥ, and was supposed to be the god who caused himself to come into existence. He is represented with a beetle for his head. In later days he was supposed to be the father of the gods and creator of the universe, and the attributes which had been applied to Rā during the Middle Empire were transferred to him.

Bast ⟨𓎰⟩ was principally worshipped in Lower Egypt at Bubastis, where a magnificent temple was built in her honour (see p. 109); she is represented with the head of a cat, and was associated with Ptaḥ. The correct reading of her name appears to be Sechet, and she represents the flame of the Sun.

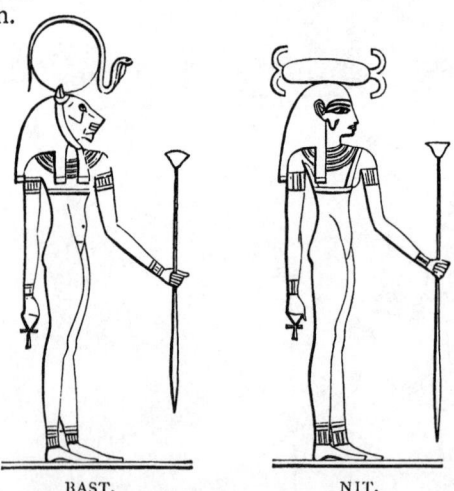

BAST.   NIT.

Nit, ⟨𓈖⟩, the 'Weaver,' was a counterpart of the goddess Mut; she is also identified with Hathor. She was the goddess of hunting, and is represented holding bows and arrows; she is usually coloured green.

RĀ, ⟨glyphs⟩, the Sun-god, was the creator of gods and men; his emblem was the sun's disk. His worship was very ancient, and he was said to be the offspring of Nut, or the sky. He assumed the forms of several other gods, and is at times represented by the lion, cat, and hawk. In papyri and on bas-reliefs he is represented with the head of a hawk and wears a disk, in front of which is a uræus ⟨glyph⟩. He was particularly adored at Thebes. When he rose in the morning he was called Ḥeru-chuti or Harmachis; and at night, when he set, he was called Ȧtmu, or 'the closer.' During the night he was supposed to be engaged in fighting Ȧpepi, the serpent, who, at the head of a large army of fiends, personifications of mist, darkness, and cloud, tried to overthrow him. The battle was fought daily, but Rā always conquered, and appeared day after day in the sky.

HORUS, ⟨glyphs⟩, Ḥeru, is the morning sun, and is also represented as having the head of a hawk; he was said to be son of Isis and Osiris, and is usually called the "avenger of his father," in reference to his defeat of Set.

RA.

HORUS.

ÁMEN-RĀ ⟨ ⟩, Mut, and Chonsu formed the great triad* of Thebes. Ámen-Rā was said to be the son of Ptaḥ, and he seems to have usurped the attributes of many of the gods. The word Ámen means 'hidden.' His chief titles were "lord of the thrones of the two lands," and "king of the gods." He is represented as wearing horns and feathers, and holding 'rule,' 'dominion,' 'power,' and 'stability.' The god ÁMSU was a form of Ámen-Rā. The exalted position which Ámen-Rā, originally a mere local deity, occupied at Thebes, will be best understood from the translation of a hymn to him written in hieratic during the XVIIIth or XIXth dynasty :—

ÁMEN-RĀ.

" Adoration of Ámen-Rā, the bull in Heliopolis, president of all the gods, beautiful god, beloved one, the giver of the life of all warmth to all beautiful cattle !

" Hail to thee, Ámen-Rā, lord of the thrones of the two lands, at the head of the Ápts.† The bull of his mother, at the head of his fields, the extender of footsteps, at the head of the "land of the South," ‡ lord of the Mat'au, § prince of Araby, lord of the sky, eldest son of earth, lord

---

* In the principal temple of each province the chief deity was associated with other gods ; . . . . . hence from an early period triads (consisting of the principal god, a female deity and their offspring) or enneads consisting of nine gods. (Renouf, *Hibbert Lectures*, p. 83.)

† The great temple at Karnak.

‡ Ethiopia and Asia.   § A country in Asia.

of things which exist, establisher of things, establisher of all things.

"One in his times, as among the gods. Beautiful bull of the cycle of the gods, president of all the gods, lord of Law, father of the gods, maker of men, creator of beasts, lord of things which exist, creator of the staff of life, maker of the green food which makes cattle to live. Form made by Ptaḥ, beautiful child, beloved one. The gods make adorations to him, the maker of things which are below, and of things which are above. He shines on the two lands sailing through the sky in peace. King of the South and North, the SUN (Rā), whose word is law, prince of the world! The mighty of valour, the lord of terror, the chief who makes the earth like unto himself. How very many more are his forms than those of any (other) god! The gods rejoice in his beauties, and they make praises to him in the two great horizons, at (his) risings in the double horizon of flame. The gods love the smell of him when he, the eldest born of the dew, comes from Araby, when he traverses the land of the Mat'au, the beautiful face coming from Neter-ta.† The gods cast themselves down before his feet when they recognize their lord in his majesty, the lord of fear, the mighty one of victory, the mighty of Will, the master of diadems, the verdifier of offerings (?), the maker of *t'efau* food.

"Adorations to thee, O thou maker of the gods, who hast stretched out the heavens and founded the earth! The untiring watcher, Âmsu-Âmen, lord of eternity, maker of everlasting, to whom adorations are made (literally, lord of adorations), at the head of the Âpts, established with two horns, beautiful of aspects; the lord of the uræus crown,

* Compare Psalm cx. 3.

† *I.e.*, "Divine land," a name frequently given on the monuments to indicate the lands which lie to the south of Egypt between the Nile and the Red Sea,

exalted of plumes, beautiful of tiara, exalted of the white crown; the serpent *mehen*, and the two uræi are the (ornaments) of his face; the double crown, helmet and cap are his decorations in (his) temple. Beautiful of face he receives the *atef* crown   ; beloved of the south and north is it, he is master of the *sechti* crown   . He receives the âmsu sceptre   , (and is) lord of the. . . . . . and of the whip. Beautiful prince, rising with the white crown   , lord of rays, creator of light! The gods give acclamations to him, and he stretches out his hands to him that loves him. The flame makes his enemies fall, his eye overthrows the rebels, it thrusts its copper lance into the sky and makes the serpent Nâk* vomit what it has swallowed.

* Nâk is one of the names of Āpepi, the demon of mist, cloud, and night, who was supposed to swallow up the sun daily; he was the enemy, *par excellence*, whom the Sun-god Rā was supposed to fight against and overcome. Āpepi was represented under the form of a serpent with knives stuck in his back   . Compare the following extract from the service for his destruction which was recited daily in the temple of Amen-Rā, at Thebes: "Fall down upon thy face, Āpepi, enemy of Rā! The flame coming forth from the eye of Horus comes against thee, a mighty flame which comes forth from the eye of Horus, comes against thee. Thou art thrust down into the flame of fire which rushes out against thee, a flame which is fatal to thy soul, thy intelligence, thy words of power, thy body and thy shade. The flame prevails over thee, it drives darts into thy soul, it makes an end of whatever thou hast, and sends goads into thy form. Thou hast fallen by the eye of Horus, which is mighty over its enemy, which devours thee, and which leads on the mighty flame against thee; the eye of Rā prevails over thee, the flame devours thee, and nothing of thee remains. Get thee back, thou art hacked in pieces, thy soul is parched, thy name is buried in oblivion, silence covers it, it is overthrown; thou art put an end to and buried under threefold oblivion. Get thee back, retreat thou, thou art cut in pieces and removed from him that is in his shrine. O, Āpepi, thou doubly crushed one, an end to thee, an end to thee! Mayest thou never rise up again! The eye of Horus prevails over thee

"Hail to thee, Rā, lord of Law, whose shrine is hidden, master of the gods, the god Cheperà in his boat; by the sending forth of (his) word the gods spring into existence. Hail god Àtmu, maker of mortals. However many are their forms he causes them to live, he makes different the colour of one man from another. He hears the prayer of him that is oppressed, he is kind of heart to him that calls unto him, he delivers him that is afraid from him that is strong of heart, he judges between the mighty and the weak.

"The lord of intelligence, knowledge (?) is the utterance of his mouth. The Nile cometh by his will, the greatly beloved lord of the palm tree comes to make mortals live. Making advance every work, acting in the sky, he makes to come into existence the sweet things of the daylight; the gods rejoice in his beauties, and their hearts live when they see him. O Rā, adored in the Àpts, mighty one of risings in the shrine; O Àni,* lord of the festival of the new moon, who makest the six days festival and the festival of the last quarter of the moon; O prince, life, health, and strength! lord of all the gods, whose appearances are in the horizon, president of the ancestors of Auker;† his name is hidden from his children in his name 'Àmen.'

"Hail to thee, O thou who art in peace, lord of dilation of heart (*i.e.*, joy), crowned form, lord of the *ureret* crown, exalted of the plumes, beautiful of tiara, exalted of the white crown, the gods love to look upon thee; the double crown of Upper and Lower Egypt is established upon thy brow. Beloved art thou in passing through the two lands.

and devours thee daily, according to that which Rā decreed should be done to thee. Thou art thrown down into the flame of fire which feeds upon thee; thou art condemned to the fire of the eye of Horus which devours thee, thy soul, thy body, thy intelligence and thy shade."— British Museum Papyrus, 10188, col. xxiv.

* ⿰ , a form of Rā.

† A common name for a necropolis.

Thou sendest forth rays in rising from thy two beautiful eyes. The *pāt* (ancestors, *i.e.*, the dead) are in raptures of delight when thou shinest, the cattle become languid when thou shinest in full strength; thou art loved when thou art in the sky of the south, thou art esteemed pleasant in the sky of the north. Thy beauties seize and carry away all hearts, the love of thee makes the arms drop; thy beautiful creation makes the hands tremble, and (all) hearts to melt at the sight of thee.

"O Form, ONE, creator of all things, O ONE, ONLY, maker of existences! Men came forth from his two eyes, the gods sprang into existence at the utterance of his mouth. He maketh the green herb to make cattle live, and the staff of life for the (use of) man. He maketh the fishes to live in the rivers, the winged fowl in the sky; he giveth the breath of life to (the germ) in the egg, he maketh birds of all kinds to live, and likewise the reptiles that creep and fly; he causeth the rats to live in their holes, and the birds that are on every green twig. Hail to thee, O maker of all these things, thou ONLY ONE.

"Is he of many forms in his might! He watches all people who sleep, he seeks the good for his brute creation. O Åmen, establisher of all things, Åtmu and Harmachis,* all people adore thee, saying, ' Praise to thee because of thy resting among us; homage to thee because thou hast created us.' All creatures say 'Hail to thee,' and all lands praise thee; from the height of the sky, to the breadth of the earth, and to the depths of the sea art thou praised. The gods bow down before thy majesty to exalt the Will of their creator; they rejoice when they meet their begetter, and say to thee, Come in peace, O father of the fathers of all the gods, who hast spread out the sky and hast founded the earth, maker of things which are,

---

* These three names are the names of the Sun-god at mid-day, evening, and morning respectively.

creator of things which exist, prince, life, health, strength ! president of the gods. We adore thy will, inasmuch as thou hast made us, thou hast made (us) and given us birth, and we give praises to thee by reason of thy resting with us.

"Hail to thee, maker of all things, lord of Law, father of the gods, maker of men, creator of animals, lord of grain, making to live the cattle of the hills ! Hail Åmen, bull, beautiful of face, beloved in the Åpts, mighty of risings in the shrine, doubly crowned in Heliopolis, thou judge of Horus and Set in the great hall.* President of the great cycle of the gods, ONLY ONE,† without his second, at the head of the Åpts, Åni at the head of the cycle of his gods, living in Law every day, the double horizoned Horus of the East ! He has created the mountain (or earth), the silver, the gold, and genuine lapis lazuli at his Will . . . . Incense and fresh *ānti* ‡ are prepared for thy nostrils, O beautiful face, coming from the land of the Mātʹau, Åmen-Rā, lord of the thrones of the two lands, at the head of the Åpts, Åni at the head of his shrine. King, ONE among the gods, myriad are his names, how many are they is not known ; shining in the eastern horizon and setting in the western horizon, overthrowing his enemies by his birth at dawn every day. Thoth exalts his two eyes, and makes him to set in his splendours ; the gods rejoice in his beauties which those who are in his . . . . . . exalt. Lord of the *sekti* § boat, and of the *āṭet* ‖ boat, which travel over the sky for thee in peace. Thy sailors rejoice when they see Nåk overthrown, his limbs stabbed with the knife, the fire devouring him, his foul soul beaten out of his foul body, and his feet carried away. The gods rejoice, Rā is satisfied,

* See page 92.
† Compare " The Lord our God is ONE," Deut. vi. 4.
‡ A perfume brought into Egypt from the East.
§ The boat in which Rā sailed to his place of setting in the West.
‖ The boat in which Rā sailed from his place of rising in the East.

Heliopolis is glad, the enemies of Âtmu are overthrown, and the heart of Nebt-ānch * is happy because the enemies of her lord are overthrown. The gods of Cher-āba are rejoicing, those who dwell in the shrines are making obeisance when they see him mighty in his strength (?) Form (?) of the gods of law, lord of the Âpts in thy name of 'maker of Law.' Lord of *t'efau* food, bull . . . . . . in thy name of 'Âmen bull of his mother.' Maker of mortals, making . . . . . become, maker of all things that are in thy name of Âtmu Cheperâ. Mighty Law making the body festal, beautiful of face, making festal the breast. Form of attributes (?), lofty of diadem, the two uræi fly by his forehead. The hearts of the *pātu* go forth to him, and unborn generations turn to him ; by his coming he maketh festal the two lands. Hail to thee, Âmen-Rā, lord of the thrones of the two lands ! his town loves his shining." †

Isis, ⌂, Âuset, the mother of Horus and wife of Osiris, ⌂ , Âusar was the daughter of Nut, or the sky ; she married her brother Osiris. Her sister Nephthys ⌂ and her brother Set likewise married one another. This last couple conspired against Isis and Osiris, and Set having induced his brother Osiris to enter a box, closed the lid down and threw it into the Nile ; the box was carried down by the river and finally cast up on the sea shore. Set having found the box once more, cut the body of Osiris into fourteen pieces, which he cast over the length and breadth of the land. As soon as

ISIS.

* *I.e.*, "the lady of life," a name of Isis.
† See *Records of the Past*, Vol. II., pp. 127–136, and Grébaut, *Hymne à Ammon Râ*.

Isis heard what had happened, she went about seeking for the pieces, and built a temple over each one; she found all save one. Osiris, however, had become king of the nether-world, and vengeance was taken by his son Horus upon his brother Set. Osiris is usually represented in the form of a mummy, holding in his hands ⌐ 'dominion,' ⌐ 'life,' ⌐ 'rule,' and ⌐ 'power.' He is called 'the lord of Abydos,' 'lord of the holy land, lord of eternity and prince of everlasting,' 'the president of the gods,' 'the head of the corridor of the tomb,' 'bull of the west,' 'judge of the dead,' etc., etc.

The writers of Egyptian mythological texts always assume their readers to possess a knowledge of the history of the murder of Osiris by Set, and of the wanderings and troubles of his disconsolate wife Isis. The following extracts from Plutarch's work on the subject will supply certain information not given in the Egyptian texts.

"Osiris, being now become king of Egypt, applied himself towards civilizing his countrymen by turning them from their former indigent and barbarous course of life; he moreover taught them how to cultivate and improve the fruits of the earth; he gave them a body of laws to regulate their conduct by, and instructed them in that reverence and worship which they were to pay to the gods; with the same good disposition he afterwards travelled over the rest of the world, inducing the people everywhere to submit to his discipline; not indeed compelling them by force of arms, but persuading them to yield to the strength of his reasons, which were conveyed to them in the most agreeable manner, in hymns and songs accompanied with instruments of music; from

OSIRIS.

which last circumstance the Greeks conclude him to have been the same person with their Dionysius or Bacchus. During the absence of Osiris from his kingdom, Typhon had no opportunity of making any innovations in the State, Isis being extremely vigilant in the government, and always upon her guard. After his return, however, having first persuaded seventy-two other persons to join with him in the conspiracy, together with a certain queen of Ethiopia named Aso, who chanced to be in Egypt at that time, he contrived a proper stratagem to execute his base designs. For having privily taken the measure of Osiris's body, he caused a chest to be made exactly of the same size with it, as beautiful as might be, and set off with all the ornaments of art. This chest he brought into his banqueting room ; where after it had been much admired by all who were present, Typhon, as it were in jest, promised to give it to any one of them whose body upon trial it might be found to fit. Upon this the whole company, one after another, go into it. But as it did not fit any of them, last of all Osiris lays himself down in it ; upon which the conspirators immediately ran together, clapped the cover upon it, then fastened it down on the outside with nails, pouring likewise melted lead over it. After this they carried it away to the river-side, and con- veyed it to the sea by the Tanaïtic mouth of the Nile ; which, for this reason, is still held in the utmost abomina- tion by the Egyptians, and never named by them but with proper marks of detestation. These things, say they, were thus executed upon the 17th day of the month Athôr, when the sun was in Scorpio, in the 28th year of Osiris's reign ; though there are others who tell us that he was no more than twenty-eight years old at this time.

"The first who knew of the accident which had befallen their king, were the Pans and Satyrs who inhabited the country round Chemmis (Panopolis or Aḥmîm); and they immediately acquainting the people with the news, gave the first occasion to the name of Panic Terrors, which has ever since been made use of to signify any sudden affright or amazement of a multitude. As to Isis, as soon as the report reached her, she immediately cut off one of the locks of her hair, and put on mourning apparel upon the very spot where she then happened to be, which accordingly from this accident has ever since been called Coptos, or the *City of Mourning*, though some are of opinion that this word rather signifies *Deprivation*. After this she wandered everywhere about the country full of disquietude and perplexity in search of the chest, enquiring of every person she met with, even of some children whom she chanced to see, whether they knew what was become of it. Now it so happened that these children had seen what Typhon's accomplices had done with the body, and accordingly acquainted her by what mouth of the Nile it had been conveyed into the sea . . . . .

"At length she received more particular news of the chest, that it had been carried by the waves of the sea to the coast of Byblos, and there gently lodged in the branches of a bush of Tamarisk, which in a short time had shot up into a large and beautiful tree, growing round the chest and enclosing it on every side, so that it was not to be seen ; and further, that the king of the country, amazed at its unusual size, had cut the tree down, and made that part of the trunk wherein the chest was concealed a pillar to support the roof of his house. These things, say they, being made known to Isis in an extraordinary manner, by the report of demons, she immediately went to Byblos ; * where, setting herself down by the side of a fountain, she refused to speak to any body excepting only to the queen's women who chanced to be there ; these she saluted and caressed in the kindest manner possible, plaiting their hair for them, and transmitting

* *I.e.*, the papyrus swamps.

into them part of that wonderfully grateful odour which issued from her own body . . . . . The queen therefore sent for her to court, and after a further acquaintance with her, made her nurse to one of her sons . . . . . The goddess, discovering herself, requested that the pillar which supported the roof of the king's house might be given to her; which she accordingly took down, and then easily cutting it open, after she had taken out what she wanted, she wrapt up the remainder of the trunk in fine linen, and pouring perfumed oil upon it, delivered it into the hands of the king and queen . . . . . . When this was done, she threw herself upon the chest, making at the same time such a loud and terrible lamentation over it as frighted the younger of the king's sons who heard her out of his life. But the elder of them she took with her, and set sail with the chest for Egypt . . . . .

"No sooner was she arrived in a desert place, where she imagined herself to be alone, but she presently opened the chest, and laying her face upon her dead husband's, embraced his corpse, and wept bitterly.

"Isis intending a visit to her son Horus, who was brought up at Butus, deposited the chest in the meanwhile in a remote and unfrequented place; Typhon, however, as he was one night hunting by the light of the moon accidentally met with it; and knowing the body which was enclosed in it, tore it into several pieces, fourteen in all, dispersing them up and down in different parts of the country. Upon being made acquainted with this event, Isis once more sets out in search of the scattered fragments of her husband's body, making use of a boat made of the reed papyrus in order the more easily to pass through the lower and fenny parts of the country. For which reason, say they, the crocodile never touches any persons who sail in this sort of vessel, as either fearing the anger of the goddess, or else respecting it on account of its having once carried her. To this occasion, therefore, it is to be imputed that there are so many different sepulchres of Osiris shewn in Egypt; for we are told that wherever Isis met with any of the scattered limbs of her husband, she there buried it. There are others, however, who contradict this relation, and tell us that this variety of sepulchres was owing rather to the policy of the queen, who, instead of the real body, as was pretended, presented these several cities with the image only of her husband; and that she did this not only to render the honours which would by this means be paid to his memory more extensive, but likewise that she might hereby elude the malicious search of Typhon; who, if he got the better of Horus in the war wherein they were going to be engaged, distracted by this multiplicity of sepulchres, might despair of being able to find the true one. . . . . . .

"After these things Osiris, returning from the other world, appeared to his son Horus, encouraged him to the battle, and at the same time instructed him in the exercise of arms. He then asked him, 'what he thought the most glorious action a man could perform?' to which Horus replied, 'to revenge the injuries offered to his father and mother.' This reply much rejoiced Osiris . . . . We are moreover told that amongst the great numbers who were continually deserting from Typhon's party was the goddess Thoueris, and that a serpent pursuing her as she was coming over to Horus, was slain by his soldiers. Afterwards it came to a battle between them, which lasted many days; but victory at length inclined to Horus, Typhon himself being taken prisoner. Isis, however, to whose custody he was committed, was so far from putting him to death, that she even loosed his bonds and set him at liberty. This action of his mother so extremely incensed Horus, that he laid hands upon her and pulled off the ensign of royalty which she wore on her head; and instead thereof Hermes clapt on an helmet made in the shape of an ox's head.

. . . . After this there were two other battles fought between them, in both of which Typhon had the worst. . . . . . .

"Such, then, are the principal circumstances of this famous story, the more harsh and shocking parts of it, such as the cutting in pieces of Horus and the beheading of Isis, being omitted." (Plutarch, *De Iside et Osiride*, xii–xx. Squire's translation.)

In the calendar of the lucky and unlucky days of the Egyptian year, the directions concerning the 26th day of the month of Thoth, which is marked ⌂⌂⌂⌂⌂, or "thrice unlucky," say, "Do nothing at all on this day, for it is the day on which Horus fought against Set. Standing on the soles of their feet they aimed blows at each other like men, and they became like two bears of hell, lords of Cher-āba. They passed three days and three nights in this manner, after which Isis made their weapons fall. Horus fell down, crying out, 'I am thy son Horus,' and Isis cried to the weapons, saying, 'Away, away, from my son Horus' . . . . Her brother Set fell down. and cried out, saying, 'Help, help!' Isis cried out to the weapons, 'Fall down.' Set cried out several times, 'Do I not wish to honour my mother's brother?' and Isis cried out to the weapons, 'Fall down—set my elder brother free'; then the weapons fell away from him. And Horus and Set stood up like two men, and each paid no attention to what they had said. And the majesty of Horus was enraged against his mother Isis like a panther of the south, and she fled before him. On that day a terrible struggle took place, and Horus cut off the head of Isis; and Thoth transformed this head by his incantations, and put it on her again in the form of a head of a cow." (Chabas, *Le Calendrier*, p. 29.)

NEPHTHYS, 𓊮, Nebt-ḥet, sister of Osiris and Isis, is generally represented standing at the bier of Osiris lamenting him. One myth relates that Osiris mistook her for Isis, and that ANUBIS, the god of the dead, was the result of the union.

SET, , the god of evil, appears to have been worshipped in the earliest times. He was the opponent of Horus in a three days' battle, at the end of which he was defeated. He was worshipped by the Hyksos, and also by the Cheta ; but in the later days of the Egyptian empire he was supposed to be the god of evil, and was considered to be the chief fiend and rebel against the sun-god Rā.

ANUBIS, , Ȧnpu, the god of the dead, is usually represented with the head of a jackal.

SEB, , was the husband of Nut, the sky, and father of Osiris, Isis, and the other gods of that cycle.

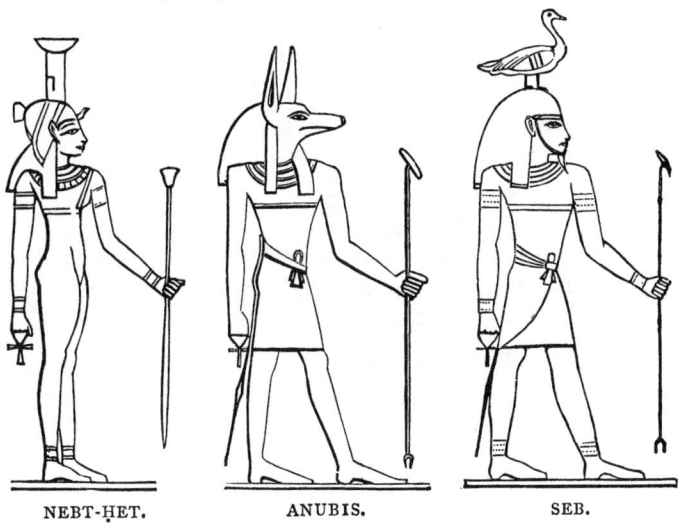

NEBT-ḤET.   ANUBIS.   SEB.

THOTH, , Teḥuti, 'the measurer,' was the scribe of the gods, and the measurer of time and inventor of numbers. In the judgment hall of Osiris he stands by the side of the balance holding a palette and reed ready to record the result of the weighing as announced by the dog-headed ape who sits on the middle of the beam of the scales. In one aspect he is the god of the moon, and is represented with the head of an ibis.

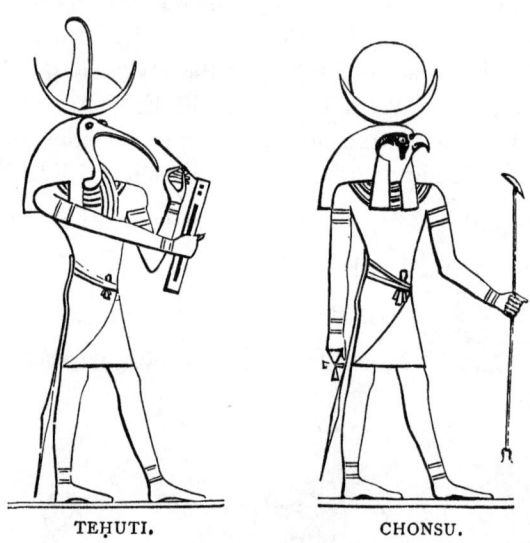

TEḤUTI. CHONSU.

CHONSU, [hieroglyphs], was associated with Åmen-Rā and Mut in the Theban triad. He was the god of the moon, and is represented as hawk-headed and wearing the lunar disk and crescent. His second name was Nefer-ḥetep, and he was worshipped with great honour at Thebes.

SEBEK, [hieroglyphs], the crocodile-headed god, was worshipped at Kom-Ombos and in the Fayûm.

Î-EM-ḤETEP (Imouthis), [hieroglyphs], was the son of Ptaḥ.

SHU, [hieroglyphs], and TEFNUT, [hieroglyphs], were the children of Seb and Nut, and represented sunlight and moisture respectively.

ATHOR, or HATHOR, [glyph], Het-Heru, 'the house of Horus,' is identified with Nut, the sky, or place in which she brought forth and suckled Horus. She was the wife of Átmu, a form of Rā. She is represented as a woman wearing a headdress in the shape of a vulture, and above it a disk and horns. She is called 'mistress of the gods,' 'lady of the sycamore,' 'lady of the west,' and 'Hathor of Thebes.' She is the female power of nature, and has some of the attributes of Isis, Nut, and Mut. She is often represented under the form of a cow coming out of the Theban hills.

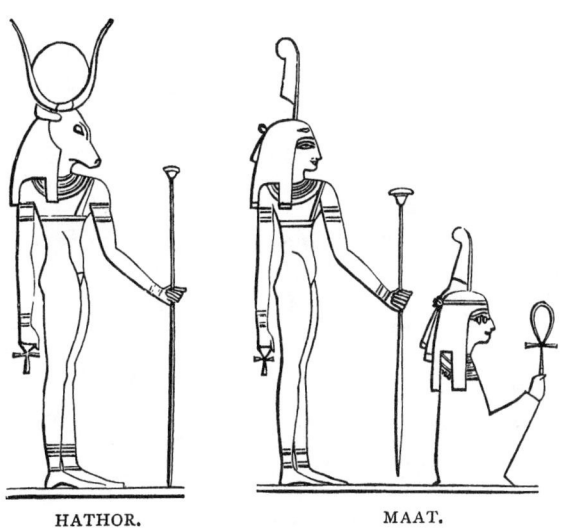

HATHOR.   MAAT.

MĀĀT, [glyphs], the goddess of 'Law,' was the daughter of the Sun-god Rā ; she is represented as wearing the feather [glyph], emblematic of law [glyph].

HĀPI, [glyphs], the god of the Nile, is represented wearing a cluster of flowers on his head [glyph] ; he is coloured red and green, probably to represent the colours of the water of the Nile immediately before and just after the beginning of the inundation.

SERAPIS, *i.e.*, Osiris-Apis, , was a god introduced into Egypt during the reign of the Ptolemies;* he is represented with the head of a bull wearing a disk and uræus. He is said to be the second son of Ptaḥ. The worship of Apis at Memphis goes back to the earliest times; the Serapeum, discovered there by M. Mariette, contained the tombs of Apis bulls from the time of Amenophis III. (about B.C. 1550) down to the time of the Roman Empire. See page 155.

* "..... the Lagids, as well as the Seleucids, were careful of disturbing the foundations of the old religion of the country ; ..... they introduced ..... the Greek god of the lower world, Pluto, into the native worship, under the hitherto little mentioned name of the Egyptian god Serapis, and then gradually transferred to this the old Osiris worship." Mommsen, *Provinces of the Roman Empire*, Vol. II., p. 265.

LOWER EGYPT.

ALEXANDRIA.

Alexandria was founded B.C. 332 by Alexander the Great who began to build his city on the little town of Rakoti, just opposite to the island of Pharos. King Ptolemy I. Soter made this city his capital : and having founded the famous library and museum, he tried to induce the most learned men of his day to live there. His son and successor Ptolemy II. Philadelphus, continued the wise policy of his father, and Alexandria became famous as a seat of learning. The keeper of the museum during the reign of Ptolemy III. Euergetes I. was Aristophanes of Byzantium. During the siege of the city by the Romans in the time of Cæsar, B.C. 48, the library of the museum was burnt ;* but Antony after-wards gave Cleopatra a large collection of manuscripts which formed the nucleus of a second library. In the early centuries of our era the people of Alexandria quarrelled perpetually among themselves,† the subjects of dispute

---

* This collection numbered 200,000 MSS., and formed the famous Pergamenian library founded by Eumenes II., king of Pergamus, B.C. 197.

† " . . . . . the Alexandrian rabble took on the slightest pretext to stones and to cudgels. In street uproar, says an authority, himself Alexandrian, the Egyptians are before all others ; the smallest spark suffices here to kindle a tumult. On account of neglected visits, on account of the confiscation of spoiled provisions, on account of ex-clusion from a bathing establishment, on account of a dispute between the slave of an Alexandrian of rank and a Roman foot-soldier as to the value or non-value of their respective slippers, the legions were under the necessity of charging among the citizens of Alexandria . . . . . In these riots the Greeks acted as instigators . . . . . but in the further course of the matter the spite and savageness of the Egyptian proper came into the conflict. The Syrians were cowardly, and as soldiers the Egyptians were so too ; but in a street tumult they were able to develope a courage worthy of a better cause." (Mommsen, *Provinces of the Roman Empire*, Vol. II., p. 265.)

being matters connected with Jews and religious questions. St. Mark is said to have preached the Gospel here. Meanwhile the prosperity of the town declined and the treasury became empty.

Alexandria was captured by Chosroes (A.D. 619), and by 'Amr ibn el-'Âṣi, a general of 'Omar, A.D. 641. The decline of Alexandria went on steadily, until it became in the middle ages little more, comparatively, than a moderate sized sea-port town, with a population of some thousands of people. In the present century a little of its prosperity was restored by Muḥammad 'Ali, who in 1819 built the Maḥmûdîyeh canal to bring fresh water to the town from the Rosetta arm of the Nile. Its population to-day is about 300,000, and includes large and wealthy colonies of Jews and Greeks.

The Christians were persecuted at Alexandria with great severity by Decius (A.D. 250), by Valerianus (A.D. 257), and by Diocletian (A.D. 304). For a large number of years the city was disturbed by the fierce discussions on religious dogmas between Arius and Athanasius, George of Cappadocia and Athanasius, the Anthropomorphists and their opponents, and Cyril and Nestorius. The Christian sects supported their views by violence, and the ordinary heathen population of the town rebelled whenever they could find a favourable opportunity.

The most important ancient buildings of Alexandria were :—

The **Lighthouse** or **Pharos,** one of the seven wonders of the world, was built by Sostratus of Cnidus, for Ptolemy Philadelphus, and is said to have been about 600 feet high. All traces of this wonderful building have now disappeared. The embankment or causeway called the HEPTASTADIUM * (from its length of seven stades), was made either by Ptolemy Philadelphus or his father Ptolemy Soter ; it divided the

---

* The Heptastadium joined the ancient town and the Island of Pharos ; a large part of the modern town is built upon it.

harbour into two parts. The eastern port is only used by native craft, on account of its sandy shoals ; the western port is the Eunostos Harbour, which at present is protected by a breakwater about one mile and three-quarters along. The MUSEUM and **Library of Alexandria** were founded by Ptolemy I., and greatly enlarged by his son Ptolemy Philadelphus. When this latter king died it was said to contain 100,000 manuscripts. These were classified, arranged, and labelled by Callimachus ; when it was burnt down in the time of Julius Cæsar, it is thought that more than 750,000 works were lost. Copies of works of importance were made at the expense of the State, and it is stated that every book which came into the city was seized and kept, and that a copy only of it was returned to the owner. Antony handed over to Cleopatra about 200,000 manuscripts (the Pergamenian Library), and these were made the foundation of a second library. Among the famous men who lived and studied in this library were Eratosthenes, Strabo, Hipparchus, Archimedes, and Euclid. The **Serapeum** was built by Ptolemy Soter, and was intended to hold the statue of a god from Sinope, which was called by the Egyptians ' Osiris-Apis,' or Serapis. It stood close by Rakoti to the east of Alexandria near ' Pompey's Pillar,' and is said to have been one of the most beautiful buildings in the world ; it was filled with remarkable statues and other works of art. It was destroyed by the Christian fanatic Theophilus,* Patriarch of Alexandria, during the reign of Theodosius II. The LIBRARY of the Serapeum is said to have contained about 300,000 manuscripts, which were burnt by 'Amr ibn el-'Âsi at the command of the Khalif 'Omar, A.D. 641 ; these were sufficiently numerous, it is said, to heat the public baths of Alexandria for six

---

* " . . . the perpetual enemy of peace and virtue ; a bold, bad man, whose hands were alternately polluted with gold and with blood." (Gibbon, *Decline*, Chap. xxvii.)

months.*   The Sôma formed a part of the Cæsareum, and contained the bodies of Alexander the Great and the Ptolemies, his successors.   The Theatre, which faced the island of Antirhodus, the Sôma, and the Museum and Library, all stood in the royal buildings in the Bruchium quarter of the town, between Lochias and the Heptastadium. The stone sarcophagus (now in the British Museum, No. 10), which was thought to have belonged to Alexander the Great, was made for Nectanebus I., the first king of the XXXth

---

* " The spirit of Amrou ('Amr ibn el-'Âṣi) was more curious and liberal than that of his brethren, and in his leisure hours the Arabian chief was pleased with the conversation of John, the last disciple of Ammonius, and who derived the surname of *Philoponus* from his laborious studies of grammar and philosophy.   Emboldened by this familiar intercourse, Philoponus presumed to solicit a gift, inestimable in *his* opinion, contemptible in that of the Barbarians : the royal library, which alone, among the spoils of Alexandria, had not been appropriated by the visit and the seal of the conqueror.   Amrou was inclined to gratify the wish of the grammarian, but his rigid integrity refused to alienate the minutest object without the consent of the caliph ; and the well-known answer of Omar was inspired by the ignorance of a fanatic. 'If these writings of the Greeks agree with the book of God, they are useless and need not be preserved: if they disagree, they are pernicious and ought to be destroyed.'   The sentence was executed with blind obedience : the volumes of paper or parchment were distributed to the 4,000 baths of the city ; and such was their incredible multitude that six months were barely sufficient for the consumption of this precious fuel." (Gibbon, *Decline and Fall*, chap. li.)   The chief authority for this statement is Bar-Hebraeus (born A.D. 1226, died at Marâghah in Âdhurbâigan, July 30th, 1286), and it has been repeated by several Arabic writers.   Both Gibbon and Renaudot thought the story incredible, but there is no reason why it should be.   Gibbon appears to have thought that the *second* Alexandrian library was pillaged or destroyed when Theophilus, Patriarch of Alexandria, destroyed the image of Serapis ; there is, however, no proof that it was, and it seems more probable that it remained comparatively unhurt until the arrival of 'Amr ibn el-'Âṣi.   See the additional notes in Gibbon, ed. Smith, Vol. III., p. 419, and Vol. VI., p. 338.

dynasty, B.C. 378. The PANEUM, or temple of Pan, is probably represented by the modern Kôm ed-Dîk. The JEWS' QUARTER lay between the sea and the street, to the east of Lochias. The NECROPOLIS was situated at the west of the city. The GYMNASIUM stood a little to the east of the Paneum, on the south side of the street which ends, on the east, in the Canopic Gate.

Pompey's Pillar was erected by Pompey, a Roman prefect, in honour of Diocletian, some little time after A.D. 302.* It is made of granite brought from Aswân; the shaft is about 70 feet, and the whole monument, including its pedestal, is rather more than 100 feet high. The fragments of the columns which lie around the base of this pillar are thought to have belonged to the Serapeum.

A few years ago there were to be seen in Alexandria the two famous granite obelisks called **Cleopatra's Needles.** They were brought from Heliopolis during the reign of the Roman Emperor Augustus, and set up before the Temple of Cæsar. Until quite lately one of them remained upright; the other had fallen. They are both made of Aswân granite; one measured 67 feet in height, the other 68½ feet; the diameter of each is about 7½ feet. The larger obelisk was given by Muḥammad 'Ali to the English early in this century, but it was not removed until 1877, when it was transported to England at the expense of Sir Erasmus Wilson, and it now stands on the Thames Embankment. The smaller obelisk was taken to New York a few years later. The inscriptions show that both were made during the reign of Thothmes III., about B.C. 1600, and that Rameses II., who lived about 250 years later, added lines of inscriptions recording his titles of honour and greatness.

---

* The Greek inscription recording this fact is published in Boeckh, *Corpus Inscriptionum Græcarum*, t. iii., p. 329, where it is also thus restored : Τὸν [ὁσ]ιώτατον Αὐτοκράτορα, τὸν πολιοῦχον 'Αλεξανδρείας, Διοκλητιανὸν τὸν ἀνίκητον πο[μπήϊ]ος ἔπαρχος Αἰγύπτου. . . . . .

The **Catacombs,** which were built early in the fourth century of our era, are on the coast near the harbour and on the coast near the new port.

The **Walls** of the city were built by Muḥammad ʻAli, and appear to have been laid upon the foundation of ancient walls.

On the south side of Alexandria lies Lake Mareotis, which in ancient days was fed by canals running from the Nile. During the middle ages the lake nearly dried up, and the land which became available for building purposes in consequence was speedily covered with villages. In the year 1801, the English dug a canal across the neck of land between the lake and the sea, and flooded the whole district thus occupied. During the last few years an attempt has been made to pump the water out; it would seem with considerable success.

Between Alexandria and Cairo are the following important towns:—

I. DAMANHÛR* (Eg.,  Ṭemȧi en-Ḥeru, 'Town of Horus,' the capital of the Mudîrîyeh of Beḥêreh. This was the Hermopolis Parva of the Romans.

II. KAFR EZ-ZAIYÂT, on the east side of the river, situated among beautiful and fertile fields.

III. ṬANṬA, the capital of Gharbîyeh, situated between the Rosetta and Damietta arms of the Nile. This town is celebrated for three *Fairs*, which are held here in January, April, and August, in honour of the Muḥammedan saint Seyyid el-Bedawi, who was born at Fez about A.D. 1200, and who lived and died at Ṭanṭa. Each fair lasts eight days, and the greatest day in each fair is the Friday; the most important fair is that held in August.

IV. BENHA el-ʻAsal, 'Benha of the Honey,' the capital of

* It is called ϯⲙⲁⲓⲛϩⲱⲣ by the Copts.

Ḳalyûb. It obtained this name because a Copt called Makawkas * sent, among other gifts, a jar of honey to Muḥammad the Prophet. Quite close to this town are the ruins of the ancient city of Athribis.

About forty miles to the east of Alexandria lies the town of Rosetta, not far from the ancient Bolbitane. It was founded towards the end of the ninth century, and was once a flourishing seaport; it has become famous in modern times on account of the trilingual inscription, called the **'Rosetta Stone,'** which was found here in 1799 by a French officer called Boussard. This inscription was inscribed on a block of basalt, and contained a decree by the Egyptian priests in honour of Ptolemy V., Epiphanes, dated in the eighth year of his reign (B.C. 196). The hieroglyphic, demotic, and Greek texts enabled Young and Champollion to work out the phonetic values of a number of the hieroglyphic characters employed to write the names of the Greek rulers. The stone is preserved in the British Museum.

---

* Makawkas was "Prince of the Copts," and "Governor of Alexandria and Egypt"; he was a Jacobite, and a strong hater of the Melchites or "Royalists." He was invited to become a follower of Muḥammad the Prophet, but he declined. When Egypt was captured by 'Amr ibn el-'Âṣi he betrayed the Copts, but by means of paying tribute he secured to himself the liberty of professing the Christian religion, and he asked that, after his death, his body might be buried in the church of St. John at Alexandria. He sent, as gifts to the Prophet, two Coptic young women, sisters, called Maryam and Shirîn; two girls, one eunuch, a horse, a mule, an ass, a jar of honey, an alabaster jar, a jar of oil, an ingot of gold, and some Egyptian linen. (Gagnier, *La vie de Mahomet*, pp. 38, 73.) The Arabic geographers state that the best honey in Egypt comes from Benha.

SUEZ AND THE SUEZ CANAL.

The town of Suez practically sprang into existence during the building of the Suez Canal, which was opened in 1869; before that time it was an insignificant village with a few hundred inhabitants. Ancient history is almost silent about it, even if it be identified with Clysma* Praesidium. It is situated at the north end of the Gulf of Suez, and is now important from its position at the south end of the Suez Canal. A fresh-water canal from Cairo to Suez was built in 1863, but before the cutting of this canal the inhabitants obtained their water either from the Wells of Moses (about eight miles from Suez) or Cairo. It was at one time considered to be near the spot where the Israelites crossed the 'Sea of Sedge'; there is little doubt, however, that the passage was made much nearer the Mediterranean.

The neck of land which joins Asia to Africa, or the Isthmus of Suez, is nearly one hundred miles wide; on the south side is the Gulf of Suez, on the north the Mediterranean. The Red Sea and the Mediterranean appear to have been united in ancient days. Modern investigations have proved that so far back as the time of Rameses II. or earlier a canal was cut between Pelusium and Lake Timsaḥ, and it is almost certain that it was well fortified. The Asiatics who wished to invade Egypt were compelled to cross the Isthmus of Suez, and a canal would not only serve as a water barrier against them, but be useful

---

* Clysma, in Arabic Ḳulzum, is said by the Arabic geographers to have been situated on the coast of the sea of Yemen, on the Egyptian side, at the far end, three days from Cairo and four days from Pelusium. (Juynboll, *Lex. Geog. Arab.*, t. ii., p. ٢٢٢.)

as a means of transport for troops from one point to another. The name of the place Ḳanṭara, 'a bridge,' a little to the north of Isma'ilîya, seems to point to the fact of a ford existing here from very early times. Nekau (B.C. 610) began to make a canal at Bubastis, between the Nile and the Red Sea, but never finished it; it was continued in later times by Darius, and Ptolemy Philadelphus made a lock for it; still later we know that the Mediterranean and Red Seas were joined by a canal. The emperor Trajan made a canal from Cairo to the Red Sea, which, having become impassable, was re-opened by 'Omar's general, 'Amr ibn el-'Âṣi, after his capture of Egypt.

In the Middle Ages various attempts were made in a half-hearted manner to cut a new canal across the Isthmus, but although several royal personages in and out of Egypt were anxious to see the proposed work begun, nothing was seriously attempted until 1798, when Napoleon Bonaparte directed M. Lepère to survey the route of a canal across the Isthmus. M. Lepère reported that the difference between the levels of the Red Sea and Mediterranean was thirty-three feet, and, that, therefore, the canal was impossible.* Although several scientific men doubted the accuracy of M. Lepère's conclusion, the fact that the level of the two seas is practically the same was not proved until M. Linant Bey, Stephenson, and others examined the matter in 1846. It was then at once evident that a canal *was* possible. M. de Lesseps laid the plans for a canal before Sa'îd Pasha in 1854; two years afterwards they were sanctioned, and two years later the works began. The original plan proposed to make a

---

* This was the opinion of some classical writers : compare Aristotle, *Meteorologica*, i. 14, 27 ; Diodorus, i. 23 ; and Strabo, xvii. 1, 25. The Arabic writer Mas'ûdi relates that a certain king tried to cut a canal across this isthmus, but that on finding that the waters of the Red Sea stood at a higher level than those of the Mediterranean, he abandoned his project. (*Les Prairies d'Or*, t. iv. p. 97.)

canal from Suez to Pelusium, but it was afterwards modified, and by bringing the northern end into the Mediterranean at Port Sa'îd, it was found possible to do away with the lock at each end, which would have been necessary had it embouched at Pelusium.   The **fresh-water canal** from Bûlâk to Suez, with an aqueduct to Port Sa'îd, included in the original plan, was completed in 1863.   The filling of the Bitter Lakes with sea-water from the Mediterranean was begun on the 18th March, 1869, and the whole canal was opened for traffic on November 16th of the same year. The cost of the canal was about £19,000,000.

The buoyed channel which leads into the canal at the Suez end is 300 yards across in the widest part.   The average width of the dredged channel is about 90 feet, and the average depth about 28 feet.   At Shalûf et-Terrâbeh the excavation was very difficult, for the ground rises about twenty feet above the sea-level, and the elevation is five or six miles long.   A thick layer of hard rock 'cropped' up in the line of the canal, and the work of removing it was of no slight nature.   On a mound not quite half-way between Suez and Shalûf are some granite blocks bearing traces of cuneiform and hieroglyphic inscriptions recording the name of Darius.   They appear to be the remains of one of a series of buildings erected along the line of the old canal which was restored and probably completed by Darius. At Shalûf the width of the canal is about 90 feet, and shortly after leaving this place the canal enters the Small Bitter Lake, which is about seven miles long.   Before reaching the end of it is, on the left, another mound on which were found the ruins of a building which was excavated by M. de Lesseps.   Granite slabs were found there inscribed with the name of Darius in Persian cuneiform characters and in hieroglyphics.   The canal next passes through the Great Bitter Lake (about fifteen miles long), and a few kilometres farther along it passes through the rock, upon which was built by Darius another monument to tell passers-by that he it was who made the canal. The track of the canal through the Bitter Lakes is marked by a double row of buoys ; the distance between each buoy is 330 yards, and the space between the two rows is about thirty yards. At a little distance to the north of the Bitter Lake is Ṭusân, which may be easily identified by means of the tomb of the Muḥammedan saint Ennedek. Shortly after Lake Timsaḥ, or the 'Crocodile Lake,' is reached, on the north side of which is the town of Isma'îlîya, formerly the head-quarters of the staff in charge of the various works connected with the construction of the canal. The canal channel through the lake is marked by buoys as in the Bitter Lakes. Soon after re-entering the canal the plain of El-Gisr, or the 'bridge,' is entered ; it is about fifty-five feet above the level of the sea. Through this a channel about eighty feet deep had to be cut. Passing through Lake Balâḥ, el-Ḳanṭara, 'the bridge,' a place situated on a height between the Balâḥ and Menzaleh Lakes, is reached. It is by this natural bridge that every invading army must have entered Egypt, and its appellation, the 'Bridge of Nations,' is most appropriate. On the east side of the canal, not far from el-Ḳanṭara, are some ruins of a building which appears to have been built by Rameses II., and a little beyond Ḳanṭara begins Lake Menzaleh. About twenty miles to the east are the ruins of Pelusium. The canal is carried through Lake Menzaleh in a perfectly straight line until it reaches Port Sa'îd.

The town of Port Sa'îd is the product of the Suez Canal, and has a population of about 12,000. It stands on the island which forms part of the narrow tract of land which separates Lake Menzaleh from the Mediterranean. The first body of workmen landed at the spot which afterwards became Port Sa'îd in 1859, and for many years the place was nothing but a factory and a living-place for workmen.

The harbour and the two breakwaters which protect it are remarkable pieces of work ; the breakwater on the east is about one mile, and that on the west is about one and five-eighths of a mile in length, and is being lengthened yearly to protect the harbour from the mud-carrying current which always flows from the west, and would block up the canal but for the breakwater. Near the western breakwater is the lighthouse, about 165 feet high ; the electric light is used in it, and can be seen for a distance of twenty miles. The port is called Sa'îd in honour of Sa'îd Pasha. The fresh water used is brought in iron pipes laid along the western side of the canal from Isma'îlîya. The choice fell upon this spot for the Mediterranean end of the canal because water sufficiently deep for ocean-going ships was found within two miles of the shore. The total length of the canal, including the buoyed channel at the Suez end, is about one hundred miles.

CAIRO TO SUEZ.

On the line between Cairo and Suez the following important places are passed :—

I. Shibîn el-Ḳanâṭir, the stopping place for those who wish to visit the ' Jewish Hill ' or Tell el-Yahûdîyyeh, where Onia, the high priest of the Jews, built a temple by the permission of Ptolemy Philometor, in which the Egyptian Jews might worship. The site of the town was occupied in very early times by a temple and other buildings which were set up by Rameses II. and Rameses III. ; a large number of the tiles which formed parts of the walls of these splendid works are preserved in the British Museum.

II. Zaḳâzîḳ, the capital of the Sherḳîyeh province, is a town of about 40,000 inhabitants ; the railway station stands about one mile from the mounds which mark the site of the famous old city of Bubastis,* or Tell Basṭa. The chief article of commerce here is cotton. Not far from Zakâzîk flows the Fresh-water Canal from Cairo to Suez, which in many places exactly follows the route of the old canal which was dug during the XIXth dynasty.

Bubastis, Bubastus, or Tell Basṭa (the Pibeseth = " House of Bast " of Ezekiel xxx. 17), was the capital of the Bubastites nome in the Delta, and was situated on the eastern side of the Pelusiac arm of the Nile. The city was dedicated to the goddess Bast, the animal sacred to whom was the cat, and was famous for having given a dynasty of kings (the XXIInd) to Egypt. To the south of the city were the lands which Psammetichus I. gave to his Ionian and Carian mercenaries, and on the north side was the canal which Nekau (Necho) dug between the Nile and the Red Sea. The city was captured by the Persians B.C. 352, and the walls, the entire circuit of which was three miles, were dismantled. Recent excavations have shown beyond doubt that the place was inhabited during the earliest dynasties, and that many great kings of Egypt delighted to build temples there. The following description of the town and the festival celebrated there will be found of interest : " Here is a temple of Bubastis deserving of mention. Other temples are larger and more magnificent, but none more beautiful than this. The goddess Bubastis is the same as the Greek Diana. Her temple stands in an island surrounded on all sides by water, except at the entrance passage. Two separate canals lead from the Nile to the entrance, which diverging to the right and left, surround the temple. They are about 100 feet broad, and planted with trees. The vestibule is 60 feet high, and ornamented with very fine figures six

---

* From the hieroglyphic ⌐ 𓊪𓏏𓂉 *Pa-Bast*, Coptic ⲡⲟⲩⲃⲁⲥⲧ; it was the metropolis of the 18th nome of Lower Egypt, "where the soul of Isis lived in [the form] of Bast."

cubits in height.   The temple stands in the centre of the
town, and in walking round the place you look down upon
it on every side, in consequence of the foundations of the
houses having been elevated, and the temple still continuing
on its original level.   The sacred enclosure is encompassed
by a wall, on which a great number of figures are sculptured ;
and within it is a grove, planted round the shrine of the
temple, with trees of a considerable height.   In the shrine is
the statue of the goddess.   The sacred enclosure is 600 feet
in length by the same in breadth.   The street which corre-
sponds with the entrance of the temple crosses the public
square, goes to the east, and leads to the temple of Mercury :
it is about 1,800 feet long and 400 feet wide, paved and
planted on each side with large trees." *   The goddess
Bast who was worshipped there is represented as having the
head of a lioness or cat.   She wore a disk, with a uræus,
and carried the sceptre ⌐ or ⌐.   She was the female counterpart of Ptaḥ, and was one of the triad of Memphis.   Properly
speaking her name is Sechet ⚱ ◉ 🜊.   She is called
'Lady of Heaven,' and 'The great lady, beloved of Ptaḥ.' †
The nature of the ceremony on the way to Bubastis, says
Herodotus, ‡ is this :—" They go by water, and numerous
boats are crowded with persons of both sexes.   During the
voyage several women strike cymbals and tambourines ;
some men play the flute ; the rest singing and clapping
their hands.   As they pass near a town, they bring the boat

* Herodotus, ii. 137, 138, translated by Wilkinson, "Ancient
Egyptians," iii. p. 35.

† She is a form of Hathor, and as wife of Ptaḥ, was the mother of
Nefer-Àtmu and I-em-ḥetep.   She was the personification of the
power of light and of the burning heat of the sun ; it was her duty to
destroy the demons of night, mist and cloud, who fought against the
sun.

‡ Book II. 60.

close to the bank. Some of the women continue to sing and strike cymbals; others cry out as long as they can, and utter reproaches against the people of the town, who begin to dance, while the former pull up their clothes before them in a scoffing manner. The same is repeated at every town they pass upon the river. Arrived at Bubastis, they celebrate the festival, sacrificing a great number of victims; and on that occasion a greater consumption of wine takes place than during the whole of the year; for according to the accounts of the people themselves, no less than 700,000 persons of both sexes are present, besides children."

The fertile country round about Zaḳâzîḳ is probably a part of the Goshen of the Bible.

III. Abu Ḥammâd, where the Arabian desert begins.

IV. Tell el-Kebîr, a wretched village, now made famous by the victory of Lord Wolseley over 'Arabi Pasha in 1882.

V. Maḥsamah, which stands on the site of a town built by Rameses II. Near this place is Tell el-Maskhûta, which some have identified with the Pithom which the Israelites built for the king of Egypt who oppressed them.

VI. Isma'îlîya (see p. 107).

VII. Nefîsheh. Here the fresh water canal divides into two parts, the one going on to Suez, and the other to Isma'îlîya.

CAIRO.

Cairo (from the Arabic Ḳâhira, 'the Victorious,' because the planet Ḳâhir or Mars was visible on the night of the foundation of the city) is situated on the right or eastern bank of the Nile, about ten miles south of the division of the Nile into the Rosetta and Damietta branches. It is called in Arabic Maṣr * : it is the largest city in Africa, and its population must be now about half a million souls. Josephus says that the fortress of the Babylon of Egypt, which stood on the spot occupied by old Cairo or Fosṭâṭ, was founded by the Babylonian mercenary soldiers of Cambyses, B.C. 525; Diodorus says that it was founded by Assyrian captives in the time of Rameses II., and Ctesias is inclined to think that it was built in the time of Semiramis. The opinions of the two last mentioned writers are valuable in one respect, for they show that it was believed in their time that Babylon of Egypt was a very ancient foundation. During the reign of Augustus it was the headquarters of one of the legions that garrisoned Egypt, and remains of the town and fortress which these legionaries occupied are still to be seen a little to the north of Fosṭâṭ. The word Fosṭâṭ † means a 'tent,' and the place is so called from the tent of 'Amr ibn el-'Aṣi, which was pitched there when he besieged Egypt, A.D. 638, and to which he returned after his capture of Alexandria. Around his tent lived a large number of his followers, and

---

* Maṣr is a form of the old name Mîṣrî (Hebrew *Misraim*), by which it is called in the cuneiform tablets, B.C. 1550.

† Arab. فسطاط, another form of فساط, = Byzantine Greek Φοσσάτον.

these being joined by new comers, the city of Fosṭâṭ at length arose. It was enlarged by Aḥmed ibn Ṭulûn, who built a mosque there; by Khamarûyeh, who built a palace there; but when the Fâṭimite Khalif Mu'izz conquered Egypt (A.D. 969), he removed the seat of his government from there, and founded Maṣr el-Ḳâhira, "Maṣr the Victorious," near Fosṭâṭ. Fosṭâṭ, which was also known by the name of Maṣr, was henceforth called Maṣr el-'Atîka. During the reign of Ṣalâḥeddîn the city was surrounded with walls and the citadel was built. Sulṭân after Sulṭân added handsome buildings to the town, and though it suffered from plagues and fires, it gained the reputation of being one of the most beautiful capitals in the Muhammedan empire. In 1517 it was captured by Selim I., and Egypt became a pashalik of the Turkish empire, and remained so until its conquest by Napoleon Bonaparte in 1798. Cairo was occupied by Muḥammad 'Ali in 1805, and the massacre of the Mamelukes took place March 1, 1811.

THE MUSEUM AT GÎZEH.

The Egyptian antiquities which are now exhibited at Gîzeh were, until the end of 1889, preserved at Bûlâḳ, where they occupied the site of the old post-office. The founding of the Bûlâḳ museum is due to the energy and perseverance of Auguste Ferdinand Mariette. This distinguished Frenchman was born at Boulogne-sur-Mer on February 11th, 1821. His ancestors were not unknown in the literary world. He was educated at Boulogne, and was made professor there when he was twenty years of age. He seems to have tried his hand at various professions, and to have studied archæological matters whenever he had a little leisure. His attention was first drawn to the study of Egyptian archæology by the examination of a collection of Egyptian antiquities which had been made by Vivant

Denon, one of the artists attached to the French Expedition in Egypt. Soon after this he wrote a paper on the list of kings which was found at Karnak and brought to Paris by Prisse, and sent it to Charles Lenormant. This gentleman, together with Maury, de Saulcy and Longpérier, advised him to come to Paris, where he soon obtained an appointment on the staff of the Louvre. As the salary paid to the young man was not sufficient to keep him, he resolved to ask the French Government to provide him with the necessary funds to go to Egypt, where he wished to try his fortune. The plea urged by him was that he wished to study the Coptic language and literature in the convents of Egypt, and with his application for funds he sent in a treatise which he had drawn up on Coptic matters. The petition was favourably received, and he set out for Egypt in the summer of 1850. Having arrived in Egypt, he found that it was not easy to obtain access to the libraries of the convents, for the Patriarch had insisted that they should be carefully guarded from strangers. While at Saḳḳârah, one day he discovered by accident a sphinx, which mentioned the names of Osiris-Ḥâpi or Serapis, similar to one that he had seen at Cairo. He remembered that the Serapeum at Memphis was described by ancient authors as standing on a sandy plain, and he believed that he had really found the spot where it stood and its ruins. He obtained labourers and set to work to dig, and discovered about one hundred and fifty sphinxes and two chapels; these objects and many other indications caused him to believe that he had actually found the Serapeum. The excavations were stopped for a short time, but were recommenced after a sum of money had been voted by the French Government. At the end of 1851 Mariette entered the Serapeum, and found there sixty-four Apis bulls, stelæ, etc., etc. As the dates when the bulls were placed in the Serapeum were stated, they afforded a valuable help in fixing the chronology of Egypt as far back as the XVIIIth dynasty. In 1853 he discovered a granite temple near Gîzeh ; and shortly afterwards he was appointed Assistant-Curator at the Louvre. In 1858 he was created Bey by Sa'îd Pasha, and the foundation of an Egyptian museum at Bûlâk was entrusted to him. About the same time he began a large series of excavations in several places at once, and the scene of his labours extended from one end of Egypt to the other. At Abydos he cleared out the temple of Seti I., two temples of Rameses II., and a large number of tombs; at Denderah, a temple of Hathor ; at Thebes he removed whole villages and mountains of earth from the temples at Karnak, Medînet-Habu and Dêr el-Baḥari ; and at Edfu he removed from the roof of the temple a village of huts and cleared out its interior. He was the author of several large works in which he gave accounts of his different labours, and published fac-similes of the texts on the monuments which he had discovered. He died at Cairo on January 17th, 1881, and was entombed in a sarcophagus which stood in the court-yard of Bûlâk Museum; his remains were removed to Gîzeh with the antiquities of the Museum. He was succeeded as Director by M. Maspero, who has in turn been succeeded by M. Grébaut.

The national Egyptian collection at Gîzeh surpasses every other collection in the world, by reason of the number of the monuments in it which were made during the first six dynasties, and by reason of the fact that the places from which the greater number of the antiquities come are well ascertained. Here may be seen stelæ of nobles who lived during the IIIrd dynasty; of Ptaḥ-ḥetep of the Vth dynasty; monuments which belong to the little-known period during which the kings of the VIIth to the XIth dynasty reigned ; a stele of the Theban king Ântefâa (XIth dynasty); and a number of sphinxes and other objects which Mariette thought were executed under the rule of the Hyksos kings. The statue of Chephren, the "Shêkh el-Beled," the jewellery of Queen Âāh-Ḥetep, the mother of Âḥmes, the first king of the XVIIIth dynasty; the Dêr el-Baḥari mummies, the list of kings from Saḳḳârah, the Ethiopian monuments from Gebel Barkal, the stele of Canopus, and other such unique objects, have given the collection a world-wide reputation. The stele inscribed with the decree of Canopus contains a hieroglyphic inscription with translations of it into demotic and Greek. The subject-matter is a decree of a body of priests who met together at Canopus B.C. 238, in which they express their determination to establish a new order of priesthood in the name of the reigning king Ptolemy III. Euergetes I., in recognition of the many benefits which he had conferred upon the country of Egypt; they also decide to erect statues of the dead princess Berenice, and to put up copies of this trilingual inscription inscribed on bronze slabs in every temple of the first and second rank. This stone is as valuable as remarkable, for the inscriptions prove beyond all doubt that the method of decipherment employed by Champollion was correct.

In former days the collection of scarabs at Bûlâḳ was valuable and nearly complete.

Among the papyri is one, of great value, which is inscribed with a work written by a scribe called Ani; containing advice to his son Chonsu-ḥetep as to judicious behaviour in all the various scenes of life. In it he exhorts him to avoid every vice and excess in anything, to love and cherish his mother, not to cause her pain by any unwise action, and to act as she would wish; to be submissive to his superiors and kind to his inferiors; to behave with modesty and due regard to the feelings of others; and to remember that death will come. The

work has much in common with the Maxims of Ptaḥ-ḥetep*
and the Book of Proverbs. Another papyrus of great value
is the fragment which treats of the geography of the Fayûm
and Lake Moeris. With the arrival of the Dêr el-Baḥari mummies there came some important copies of the Book of the
Dead belonging to the best period of the Theban recension
of that interesting work. It is much to be wished that the
Administration of the Museum would publish from time to
time fac-similes of the most important inscriptions which are
found, and if they could be accompanied with translations
or summaries of their contents the science of Egyptology
would be much advanced. It is understood that a scientific
classification of all the objects in the Museum according to
the period to which they belong is in contemplation ; if this
is ever carried out the Museum will become a valuable
school for students of Egyptian archæology.

It had long been felt by scholars and others that the
old buildings at Bûlâḳ, where such valuable antiquities
were stored, were quite inadequate to the wants of the
Egyptian collection. There was no room whatever for
expansion, and each year the danger caused by the inundation grew more serious ; in the year 1878 the Nile
waters actually entered the Museum. As the whole neighbourhood round about was filled with granaries and ware-
houses packed with inflammable matter, the need for
removing the collection to a larger and a safer place became
very pressing. At the end of 1888 it was definitely decided
by the authorities to remove the antiquities from Bûlâk to
the palace at Gîzeh. The work was begun in 1889, and
was continued throughout the summer and autumn of that
year; the opening of the new Museum to visitors took place
on January 12, 1890.

---

* The maxims of Ptaḥ-ḥetep are inscribed upon the Prisse papyrus,
which was written about B.C. 2500 ; they were composed during the
reign of Àssa, the eighth king of the Vth dynasty, about B.C. 3366.

Briefly, the new arrangement is as follows—

In the FIRST ROOM are to be found all the monuments which belong to a period anterior to the pyramids of Gîzeh, that is to say, anterior to the IVth dynasty. Here too are several objects which were discovered by Mariette at Saḳḳârah and Mêdûm, and a few which were excavated at Mît Rahineh in 1888. The statue of the priest is perhaps the oldest known.

In the SECOND ROOM is a selection from the most beautiful and important of the monuments of the IVth, Vth and VIth dynasties, including the large statues of Ptaḥ-ḥetep and the Shêkh el-Beled.

In the THIRD ROOM are the statues of Chephren, Mycerinus, Usr-en-Rā and Men-kau-Ḥeru.

The FOURTH, FIFTH, and SIXTH ROOMS contain stelæ and other objects inscribed with texts of the Ancient Empire.

The SEVENTH, EIGHTH, and NINTH ROOMS contain statues and bas-reliefs.

In the TENTH and ELEVENTH ROOMS are, among other objects, a tomb from Saḳḳârah and the mummy of Mentu-em-saf, the fourth king of the VIth dynasty.

The TWELFTH ROOM is occupied with monuments of the Ancient Empire brought from Upper Egypt.

Following on here, too, are the antiquities which belong to the unknown period between the VIth and the XIth dynasties; and after these come the monuments of the XIIth dynasty, and those which are thought to be the product of the time when the Hyksos or Shepherd kings ruled over Egypt.

The galleries, which are close by, contain the stelæ, bas-reliefs, and statues of the New Empire, and the monuments of the Ethiopian kings from Gebel Barkal. It is intended to gather together in their proper order all the antiquities which represent the Greek, Roman, and Arabic domination of Egypt.

On the first floor are rooms for the exhibition of flowers from the tombs, coins, figures of gods in bronze, and Egyptian porcelain, scarabs, furniture, household goods, arms, tools, papyri, wooden objects, etc., etc. In a large room near at hand are the famous Dêr el-Baḥari mummies, among them being Âḥmes (Amāsis), Seti I., Rameses II., and Rameses III.

COPTIC CHURCHES IN CAIRO.*

The Church of MÂR MÎNÂ lies between Fosṭâṭ and Cairo; it was built in honour of St. Menas, an early martyr, who is said to have been born at Mareotis, and martyred during the persecution of Galerius Maximinus at Alexandria. The name Mînâ, or Menâ, probably represents the Coptic form of Menâ, ⌷ ⌶ , the name of the first historical king of Egypt. The church was probably founded during the fourth century, and it seems to have been restored in the eighth century; the first church built to Mâr Mînâ was near Alexandria. The church measures 60 feet × 50 feet; it contains some interesting pictures, and a very ancient bronze candelabrum in the shape of two winged dragons, with seventeen sockets for lighted tapers. On the roof of the church is a small bell in a cupola.

About half-a-mile beyond the Dêr† containing the church of St. Menas, lies the Dêr of Abu's Sêfên, in which are situated the churches al-'Aḍra (the Virgin), Anba Shenûti, and Abu's Sêfên. The last-named church was built in the tenth century, and is dedicated to St. Mercurius, who is

---

* The authorities for the following facts relating to Coptic Churches are Butler's *Coptic Churches of Egypt*, 2 vols., 1884 ; and Curzon, *Visits to Monasteries in the Levant.*

† Arabic ﺩﻳﺮ "convent, monastery."

called "Father of two swords," or Abu's Sêfên.   The church measures 90 feet × 50 feet, and is built chiefly of brick; there are no pillars in it.   It contains a fine ebony partition dating from A.D. 927, some interesting pictures, an altar casket dating from A.D. 1280, and a marble pulpit.   In this church are chapels dedicated to Saints Gabriel, John the Baptist, James, Mâr Buktor, Antony, Abba Nûb, Michael, and George.   Within the Dêr of Abu's Sêfên is the "Convent of the Maidens;" the account of Mr. Butler's discovery of this place is told by him in his *Coptic Churches of Egypt*, Vol. I, p. 128.   The church of the Virgin was founded probably in the eighth century.

The church of Abu Sargah, or Abu Sergius, stands well towards the middle of the Roman fortress of Babylon in Egypt.   Though nothing is known of the saint after whom it was named, it is certain that in A.D. 859 Shenûti was elected patriarch of Abu Sargah; the church was most probably built much earlier, and some go so far as to state that the crypt (20 feet × 15 feet) was occupied by the Virgin and her Son when they fled to Egypt to avoid the wrath of Herod.   "The general shape of the church is, or was, a nearly regular oblong, and its general structure is basilican.   It consists of narthex, nave, north and south aisle, choir, and three altars eastward each in its own chapel: of these the central and southern chapels are apsidal, the northern is square ended . . . . . .   Over the aisles and narthex runs a continuous gallery or triforium, which originally served as the place for women at the service.   On the north side it stops short at the choir, forming a kind of transept, which, however, does not project beyond the north aisle . . . . . .   On the south side of the church the triforium is prolonged over the choir and over the south side-chapel.   The gallery is flat-roofed while the nave is covered with a pointed roof with framed principals like that at Abu's Sêfên . . . . . .   Outside, the roof of Abu Sargah is plastered over with cement showing the king-posts projecting above the ridge-piece. Over the central part of the choir and over the haikal the roof changes to a wagon-vaulting; it is flat over the north transept, and a lofty dome overshadows the north aisle chapel...... The twelve monolithic columns round the nave are all, with one exception, of white marble streaked with dusky lines...... The exceptional column is of red Assuân granite, 22 inches in diameter...... The wooden pulpit...... is of rosewood inlaid with designs in ebony set with ivory edgings...... The haikal-screen projects forward into the choir as at Al 'Adra.. ... is of very ancient and beautiful workman- ship; pentagons and other shapes of solid ivory, carved in relief with arabesques, being inlaid and set round with rich mouldings...... The upper part of the screen contains square panels of ebony set with large crosses of solid ivory, most exquisitely chiselled with scrollwork, and panels of ebony carved through in work of the most delicate and skilful finish." (Butler, *Coptic Churches*, Vol. I., pp. 183– 190, ff.) The early carvings representing St. Demetrius, Mâr George, Abu's Sêfên, the Nativity, and the Last Supper, are worthy of careful examination.

The Jewish synagogue near Abu Sargah was originally a Coptic church dedicated to St. Michael, which was sold to the Jews by a patriarch called Michael towards the end of the ninth century; it measures 65 feet × 35 feet, and is said to contain a copy of the Law written by Ezra.

A little to the south-east of Abu Sargah is the church dedicated to the Virgin, more commonly called El- Mu'allakah, or the 'hanging,' from the fact that it is sus- pended between two bastions, and must be entered by a staircase. The church is triapsal, and is of the basilican order. It originally contained some very beautiful screens, which have been removed from their original positions and made into a sort of wall, and, unfortunately, modern stained glass has been made to replace the old. The cedar doors, sculptured in panels, are now in the British Museum. The cedar and ivory screens are thought to belong to the eleventh century. The church is remarkable in having no choir, and Mr. Butler says it is "a double-aisled church, and as such is remarkable in having no transepts." The pulpit is one of the most valuable things left in the church, and probably dates from the twelfth century; in the wooden coffer near it are the bones of four saints. Authorities differ as to the date to be assigned to the founding of this church, but all the available evidence now known would seem to point to the sixth century as the most probable period; at any rate, it must have been before the betrayal of the fortress of Babylon to 'Amr by the Monophysite Copts in the seventh century.

A little to the north-east of Abu Sargah is the church of St. Barbara, the daughter of a man of position in the East, who was martyred during the persecution of Maximinus; it was built probably during the eighth century. In the church is a picture of the saint, and a chapel in honour of St. George. At the west end of the triforium are some mural paintings of great interest.

Within the walls of the fortress of Babylon, lying due north of Abu Sargah, are the two churches of Mâr Girgis and the Virgin.

To the south of the fortress of Babylon, beyond the Muḥammedan village on the rising ground, lie the Dêr of Bablûn and the Dêr of Tadrus. In Dêr el-Bablûn is a church to the Virgin, which is very difficult to see. It contains some fine mural paintings, and an unusual candlestick and lectern; in it also are chapels dedicated to Saints Michael and George. This little building is about fifty-three feet square. Dêr el-Tadrus contains two churches dedicated to Saints Cyrus and John of Damanhûr in the

Delta ; there are some fine specimens of vestments to be seen there.

A short distance from the Mûski is a Dêr containing the churches of the Virgin, St. George, and the chapel of Abu's Sêfên. The church of the Virgin occupies the lower half of the building, and is the oldest in Cairo. The chapel of Abu's Sêfên is reached through a door in the north-west corner of the building, and contains a wooden pulpit inlaid with ivory. The church of St. George occupies the upper part of the building, and is over the church of the Virgin.

In the Greek (Byzantine) quarter of Cairo is the Dêr el-Tadrus, which contains the churches of St. George and the Virgin.

The Coptic churches of Cairo contain a great deal that is interesting, and are well worth many visits. Though the fabrics of many of them are not older than the sixth, seventh, or eighth century of our era, it may well be assumed that the sites were occupied by Coptic churches long before this period.

The Mosques of Cairo.

Speaking generally there are three types of mosque * in Cairo : 1, the court-yard surrounded by colonnades, as the Mosques of 'Amr and Tulûn ; 2, the court yard surrounded by four gigantic arches, as in the Mosque of Sultân Hasan, etc. ; and 3, the covered yard beneath a dome, as in the Mosque of Muhammad 'Ali.

The Mosque of 'AMR in Fostât, or Old Cairo, is the oldest mosque in Egypt, its foundation having been laid A.H. 21 = A.D. 643. The land upon which it was built was given by 'Amr ibn el-'Asi and his friends after they had become masters of the fortress of Babylon. Of 'Amr's edifice very

---

* The word "mosque" is derived from the Arabic مسجد a "place of prayer."

little remains, for nearly all the building was burnt down at the end of the ninth century. Towards the end of the third quarter of the tenth century the mosque was enlarged and rebuilt, and it was subsequently decorated with paintings, etc.; the splendour of the mosque is much dwelt upon by Makrîzî. The court measures 350 feet × 400 feet. The building contains 366 pillars—one row on the west side, three rows on the north and south sides, and six rows on the east side; one of the pillars bears the name of Muḥammad. In the north-east corner is the tomb of 'Abdallah, the son of 'Amr.

The Mosque of AḤMED IBN ṬULÛN (died A.D. 884) is the oldest in Maṣr el-Ḳâhira, or New Cairo, having been built A.D. 879, under the rule of Khalif Mu'tamid (A.D. 870–892). It is said to be a copy of the Ka'ba at Mecca, and to have taken two or three years to build. The open court is square, and measures about 300 feet from side to side ; in the centre is the Ḥanafîyyeh (حنفية) or fountain for the Turks. On the north, west, and south side is an arcade with walls pierced with arches ; on the east side are five arcades divided by walls pierced with arches. The wooden pulpit is a famous specimen of wood carving, and dates from the thirteenth century. Around the outside of the minaret of this mosque is a spiral staircase, which is said to have been suggested by its founder. The mosque is called the " Fortress of the Goat," because it is said to mark the spot where Abraham offered up the ram ; others say that the ark rested here.

The Mosque of ḤÂKIM (A.D. 996–1020), the third Fâṭimite Khalif, was built on the plan of mosque of ibn Ṭulûn (see above) ; the date over one of the gates is A.H. 393 = A.D. 1003. The Museum of Arab art is located here.

The Mosque EL-AZHAR is said to have been founded

by Jôhar, the general of Mu'izz, about A.D. 980. The plan
of the principal part was the same as that of the mosque of
'Amr, but very little of the original building remains. It
was made a university by the Khalif 'Aziz (A.D. 975–996),
and great alterations were made in the building by different
Sultâns in the twelfth, thirteenth, fifteenth, sixteenth, and
eighteenth centuries; Sa'îd Pasha made the last in A.D. 1848.
The minarets belong to different periods; the mosque has six
gates, and at the principal of these, the "Gate of the Barbers,"
is the entrance. On three of the sides of the open court are
compartments, each of which is reserved for the worshippers
who belong to a certain country. The Lîwân of the mosque
is huge, and its ceiling is supported upon 380 pillars of
various kinds of stone; it is here that the greater part of
the students of the university carry on their studies. The
number of students varies from 10,000 to 13,000, and the
education, from the Muḥammedan point of view, is perhaps
the most thorough in the whole world.

In the Citadel are:—1. The Mosque of Ṣalâheddîn
Yûsuf, built A.D. 1171–1198; 2. The Mosque of Sulêmân
Pasha or Sulṭân Selîm, built A.H. 391 = A.D 1001.

The Muristân Kalaûn, originally a hospital, contains the
tomb of El-Manṣûr Kalaûn (A.D. 1279–1290), which is
decorated with marble mosaics.

The Mosque-tomb of Muḥammad en-Nâṣir (A.D. 1293–
1341), son of Kalaûn, stands near that of Kalaûn.

The Mosque of SULṬÂN ḤASAN, built of stone taken
from the pyramids of Gîzeh, is close to the citadel, and is
generally considered to be the grandest in Cairo. It was
built by Ḥasan, one of the younger sons of Sultân Nâṣir, and
its construction occupied three years, A.D. 1356–1358. It
is said that when the building was finished the architect's
hands were cut off to prevent his executing a similar work
again. This story, though probably false, shows that the
mosque was considered of great beauty, and the judgment

of competent critics of to-day endorses the opinion of it which was prevalent in Ḥasan's time. Ḥasan's tomb is situated on the east side of the building. The remaining minaret* is about 280 feet high, the greatest length of the mosque is about 320 feet, and the width about 200 feet. In the open court are two fountains which were formerly used, one by the Egyptians, and one by the Turks. On the eastern side are still to be seen a few of the balls which were fired at the mosque by the army of Napoleon.

The Mosque of Barḳûḳ (A.D. 1382–1399) contains the tomb of the daughter of Barḳûḳ.

The Mosque of MUAIYAD, one of the Circassian Mamelukes, was founded between the years 1412–1420; it is also known as the "Red Mosque," from the colour of the walls outside. "Externally it measures about 300 feet by 250, and possesses an internal court, surrounded by double colonnades on three sides, and a triple range of arches on the side looking towards Mecca, where also are situated—as in that of Barḳûḳ—the tombs of the founder and his family. A considerable number of ancient columns have been used in the erection of the building, but the superstructure is so light and elegant, that the effect is agreeable." † The bronze gate in front belonged originally to the mosque of Sulṭân Ḥasan.

The Mosque of ḲAIT Bey (A.D. 1468–1496), one of the last independent Mameluke sulṭâns of Egypt, is about eighty feet long and seventy feet wide; it has some fine mosaics, and is usually considered the finest piece of architecture in Cairo.

The Mosque el-Ghûri was built by the Sulṭân Kanṣuweh el-Ghûri early in the sixteenth century; it is one of the most beautiful mosques in Cairo.

---

* From the Arabic مَنَارَة "place of light."

† Fergusson, *Hist. of Architecture*, Vol. II., p. 516.

The Mosque of Sittah Zênab was begun late in the last century; it contains the tomb of Zênab, the granddaughter of the Prophet.

The Mosque begun by Muḥammad 'Ali in the Citadel, was finished in 1857 by Sa'îd Pasha, after the death (in 1849) of that ruler; it is built of alabaster from the quarries of Beni Suêf. As with nearly all mosques built by the Turks, the church of the Hagia Sophia at Constantinople served as the model, but the building is not considered of remarkable beauty. The mosque is also a square covered by a large dome and four small ones. In the south-east corner is the tomb of Muḥammad 'Ali, and close by is the mimbar (منبر) or pulpit; in the recess on the east side is the Ḳibla (قبلة), or spot to which the Muḥammedan turns his face during his prayers. The court is square, with one row of pillars on each of its four sides, and in the centre is the fountain for the Turks; the clock in the tower on the western side was presented to Muḥammad 'Ali by Louis Philippe.

The Mosque of el-Ḥasanên, *i.e.*, the mosque of Ḥasan and Ḥusên, the sons of 'Ali the son-in-law of the Prophet, is said to contain the head of Ḥusên who was slain at Kerbela A.D. 680; the head was first sent to Damascus and afterwards brought to Cairo.

In the Mosque of el-Akbar the dancing dervishes perform.

THE TOMBS OF THE KHALIFS.*

These beautiful buildings are situated on the eastern side of the city, and contain the tombs of the members of the

---

* The word "Khalif," Arabic خليفة, *Khalîfah*, means "successsor" (of Muḥammad) or "vicar" (of God upon earth), and was a title applied to the head of the Muslim world. The last Khalîfah died in Egypt *about* A.D. 1517.

families of the Circassian Mameluke Sulṭâns who reigned from A.D. 1382–1517.   The tomb-mosques of Yûsuf, el Ashraf, and the tomb of el-Ghûri (A.D. 1501–1516) are to the north-east of the Bâb en-Naṣr; the tomb-mosques of Yûsuf and el-Ashraf are only to be seen by special permission.   In the tomb-mosque of Barḳûḳ are buried that sulṭân, his son the Sulṭân Farag (A.D. 1399–1412), and various other members of the family.   The limestone pulpit and the two minarets are very beautiful specimens of stone work.   To the west of this tomb-mosque is the tomb of Sulṭân Sulêmân, and near that are the tombs of the Seven Women, the tomb-mosque of Bursbey (A.D. 1422–1438), the Maʿbed er-Rifâʿi, and the tomb of the mother of Bursbey. The most beautiful of all these tombs is the tomb-mosque of Ḳait Bey (A.D. 1468–1496), which is well worthy of more than one visit.

THE TOMBS OF THE MAMELUKES.*

Of the builders of these tombs no history has been preserved; the ruins, however, show that they must have been very beautiful objects.   Some of the minarets are still very fine.

THE CITADEL.

The Citadel was built by Ṣalâḥeddîn, A.D. 1166, and the stones used were taken from the pyramids of Gîzeh; it formed a part of the large system of the fortifications of Cairo which this Sulṭân carried out so thoroughly.   Though admirably situated for commanding the whole city, and as a fortress in the days before long range cannon were invented, the site was shown in 1805 to be ill chosen for the purposes

---

* The word "Mameluke" means a "slave," Arabic مَمْلُوك, plur. مَمَالِيك.

of defence in modern times, by Muḥammad 'Ali, who, by means of a battery placed on the Moḳaṭṭam heights, compelled Khurshîd Pasha to surrender the citadel. In the narrow way, with a high wall, through the Bâb el-Azab, which was formerly the most direct and most used means of access to it, the massacre of the Mamelukes took place by the orders of Muḥammad 'Ali, A.D. 1811. The single Mameluke who escaped is said to have made his horse leap down from one of the walls of the Citadel; he refused to enter the narrow way.

Joseph's Well.

This well is not called after Joseph the Patriarch, as is usually supposed, but after the famous Ṣalâḥeddîn (Saladin), whose second name was Yûsuf or Joseph. The shaft of this well, in two parts, is about 280 feet deep, and was found to be choked up with sand when the Citadel was built; Saladin caused it to be cleared out, and from his time until 1865 its water was regularly drawn up and used. This well was probably sunk by the ancient Egyptians.

The Library.

This valuable institution was founded by Isma'îl in 1870, and contains the library of Muṣṭafa Pasha; the number of works in the whole collection is said to be about 24,000. Some of the copies of the Ḳorân preserved there are among the oldest known.

Ezbekîyeh Garden.

This garden or "place," named after the Amîr Ezbeki, the general of Ḳait Bey (A.D. 1468—1496), was made in 1870 by M. Barillet, and has an area of about twenty acres.

The Nilometer in the Island of Rôḍa.

The Nilometer here is a pillar, which is divided into seventeen parts, each representing a cubit, *i.e.*, $21\frac{1}{3}$ inches, and each cubit is divided into twenty-four parts. This pillar is placed in the centre of a well about sixteen feet square; the lower end is embedded in the foundations, and the upper end is held in position by a beam built into the side walls. The well is connected with the Nile by a channel. The first Nilometer at Rôḍa is said to have been built by the Khalif Sulêmân (A.D. 715—717), and about one hundred years later the building was restored by Mâmûn (A.D. 813—833). At the end of the eleventh century a dome resting upon columns was built over it. When the Nile is at its lowest level it stands at the height of seven cubits in the Nilometer well, and when it reaches the height of $15\frac{2}{3}$ cubits, the shêkh of the Nile proclaims that sufficient water has come into the river to admit of the cutting of the dam which prevents the water from flowing over the country. The difference between the highest rise and the lowest fall of the Nile at Cairo is about twenty-five feet. The cutting of the dam takes place some time during the second or third week in August, at which time there are general rejoicings. When there happens to be an exceptionally high Nile, the whole island of Rôḍa is submerged, and the waters flow over the Nilometer to a depth of two cubits, a fact which proves that the bed of the Nile is steadily rising, and one which shows how difficult it is to harmonize all the statements made by Egyptian, Greek, and Arabic writers on the subject. As the amount of taxation to be borne by the people has always depended upon the height of the inundation, attempts were formerly made by the governments of Egypt to prove to the people that there never was a low Nile.

HELIOPOLIS.*

About five miles to the north-east of Cairo stands the
little village of Maṭariyyeh †, built upon part of the site of
Heliopolis, where may be seen the sycamore tree, usually
called the "Virgin's Tree," under which tradition says that
the Virgin Mary sat and rested during her flight to Egypt;
it was planted some time towards the end of the XVIIth
century, and was given to the Empress Eugénie by Ismaʿîl
on the occasion of the opening of the Suez Canal. Beyond
the "Virgin's Tree" is the fine Aswân granite obelisk which
marks the site of the ancient town of Heliopolis, called
"On" in Gen. xli. 45, "House of the Sun" in Jeremiah

* Called in Egyptian ⸺⸺, *Ȧnnu meḫt*, "Annu of the
North," to distinguish it from ⸺⸺, *Ȧnnu Qenȧu*, "Annu
of the South," *i.e.*, Hermonthis.

† مَطَرِيّة, Juynboll, *op. cit.*, t. iii., p. 110. At this place the balsam
trees, about which so many traditions are extant, were said to grow.
The balsam tree was about a cubit high, and had two barks; the
outer red and fine, and the inner green and thick. When the
latter was macerated in the mouth, it left an oily taste and an
aromatic odour. Incisions were made in the barks, and the liquid
which flowed from them was carefully collected and treated; the
amount of balsam oil obtained formed a tenth part of all the liquid
collected. The last balsam tree cultivated in Egypt died in 1615, but
two were seen alive in 1612; it is said that they would grow nowhere
out of Egypt. They were watered with the water from the well at
Maṭariyyeh in which the Virgin Mary washed the clothes of our Lord
when she was in Egypt. The oil was much sought after by the
Christians of Abyssinia and other places, who thought it absolutely
necessary that one drop of this oil should be poured into the water in
which they were baptized. See Wansleben, *L'Histoire de l'Eglise
d'Alexandrie*, pp. 88–93; *Abd-allatif* (ed. de Sacy), p. 88.

xliii. 13, and "Eye or Fountain of the Sun" by the Arabs. Heliopolis was about twelve miles from the fortress of Babylon, and stood on the eastern side of the Pelusiac arm of the Nile, near the right bank of the great canal which passed through the Bitter Lakes and connected the Nile with the sea. Its ruins cover an area three miles square. The greatest and oldest Egyptian College or University for the education of the priesthood and the laity stood here, and it was here that Ptolemy II. Philadelphus, sent for Egyptian manuscripts when he wished to augment the library which his father had founded.

The **obelisk** is sixty-six feet high, and was set up by Usertsen I. ⟨ ☉ 𓎟 𐩒 ⟩ about B.C. 2433 ; a companion obelisk remained standing in its place until the seventh century of our era, and both were covered with caps of *smu* (probably copper) metal. During the XXth dynasty the temple of Heliopolis was one of the largest and wealthiest in all Egypt, and its staff was numbered by thousands. When Cambyses visited Egypt the glory of Heliopolis was well on the wane, and after the removal of the priesthood and sages of the temple to Alexandria by Ptolemy II. its downfall was well assured. When Strabo visited it (B.C. 24), the greater part of it was in ruins ; but we know from Arab writers that many of the statues remained *in situ* at the end of the twelfth century. Heliopolis had a large population of Jews, and it will be remembered that Joseph married the daughter of Pa-ṭâ-pa-Rā (Potiphar) a priest of On (Ȧnnu) or Heliopolis. It lay either in or very near the Goshen of the Bible. The Mnevis bull, sacred to Rā, was worshipped at Heliopolis, and it was here that the phœnix or palm-bird brought its ashes after having raised itself to life at the end of each period of five hundred years. Alexander the Great halted here on his way from Pelusium to Memphis. Macrobius says that the Heliopolis of Syria, or Baalbek, was founded by a body of priests who left the ancient city of Heliopolis of Egypt.

THE PYRAMIDS OF GIZEH.

On the western bank of the Nile, from Abu Roâsh on the north to Mêdûm on the south, is a slightly elevated tract of land, about twenty-five miles long, on the edge of the Libyan desert, on which stand the pyramids of Abu Roâsh, Gîzeh, Zâwyet el-'Aryân, Abusîr, Saḳḳârah, and Dahshûr. Other places in Egypt where pyramids are found are El-lâhûn in the Fayûm, and Kullah near Esneh. The pyramids built by the Ethiopians at Meroë and Gebel Barkal are of a very late date (B.C. 600–100), and are mere copies, in respect of form only, of the pyramids in Egypt. It is well to state at once that the pyramids were tombs and nothing else. There is no evidence whatever to show that they were built for purposes of astronomical observations, and the theory that the Great Pyramid was built to serve as a standard of measurement is ingenious but worthless. The significant fact, so ably pointed out by Mariette, that pyramids are only found in cemeteries, is an answer to all such theories. Tomb-pyramids were built by kings and others until the XIIth dynasty. The ancient writers who have described and treated of the pyramids are given by Pliny (Nat. Hist., xxxvi. 12, 17). If we may believe some of the writers on them during the Middle Ages, their outsides must have been covered with inscriptions; these were probably of a religious nature.* In modern times they have been examined by Shaw (1721),

---

* " .... their surfaces exhibit all kinds of inscriptions written in the characters of ancient nations which no longer exist. No one knows what this writing is or what it signifies." Mas'ûdi (ed. Barbier de Meynard), t. ii., p. 404.

Pococke (1743), Niebuhr (1761), Davison (1763), Bruce (1768), Denon and Jumard (1799), Hamilton (1801), Caviglia (1817), Belzoni (1817), Wilkinson (1831), Howard Vyse and Perring (1837–38), Lepsius (1842–45), and Petrie (1881).

It appears that before the actual building of a pyramid was begun a suitable rocky site was chosen and cleared, a mass of rock if possible being left in the middle of the area to form the core of the building. The chambers and the galleries leading to them were next planned and excavated. Around the core a truncated pyramid building was made, the angles of which were filled up with blocks of stone. Layer after layer of stone was then built around the work, which grew larger and larger until it was finished. Dr. Lepsius thought that when a king ascended the throne, he built for himself a small but complete tomb-pyramid, and that a fresh coating of stone was built around it every year that he reigned; and that when he died the sides of the pyramids were like long flights of steps, which his successor filled up with right-angled triangular blocks of stone. The door of the pyramid was walled up after the body of its builder had been laid in it, and thus remained a finished tomb. The explanation of Dr. Lepsius may not be correct, but at least it answers satisfactorily more objections than do the views of other theorists on this matter. It has been pointed out that near the core of the pyramid the work is more carefully executed than near the exterior, that is to say, as the time for the king's death approached the work was more hurriedly performed.

During the investigations made by Lepsius in and about the pyramid area, he found the remains of about seventy-five pyramids, and noticed that they were always built in groups.

The pyramids of Gîzeh were opened by the Persians during the fifth and fourth centuries before Christ; it is probable that they were also entered by the Romans. Khalif Mâmûn (A.D. 813–833) entered the Great Pyramid, and found that others had been there before him. The treasure which is said to have been discovered there by him is probably fictitious. Once opened, it must have been evident to every one what splendid quarries the pyramids formed, and very few hundred years after the conquest of Egypt by the Arabs they were laid under contribution for stone to build mosques, etc., in Cairo. Early in the thirteenth century Melik el-Kâmil made a mad attempt to destroy the third pyramid built by Mycerinus; but after months of toil he only succeeded in stripping off the covering from one of the sides. It is said that Muḥammad 'Ali was advised to undertake the senseless task of destroying them all.

THE GREAT PYRAMID.

This, the largest of the three pyramids at Gîzeh, was built by Chufu  or Cheops, the second king of the IVth dynasty, B.C. 3733, who called it  *Chut.* His name was found written in red ink upon the blocks of stone inside it. All four sides measure in greatest length about 755 feet each, but the length of each was originally about 20 feet more; its height now is 451 feet, but it is said to have been originally about 481 feet. The stone used in the construction of this pyramid was brought from Ṭurra and Moḳaṭṭam, and the contents amount to 85,000,000 cubic feet. The flat space at the top of the pyramid is about thirty feet square, and the view from it is very fine.

The entrance (A) to this pyramid is, as with all pyramids, on the north side, and is about 45 feet above the ground. The passage A B C is 320 feet long, 3¼ feet high, and 4 feet

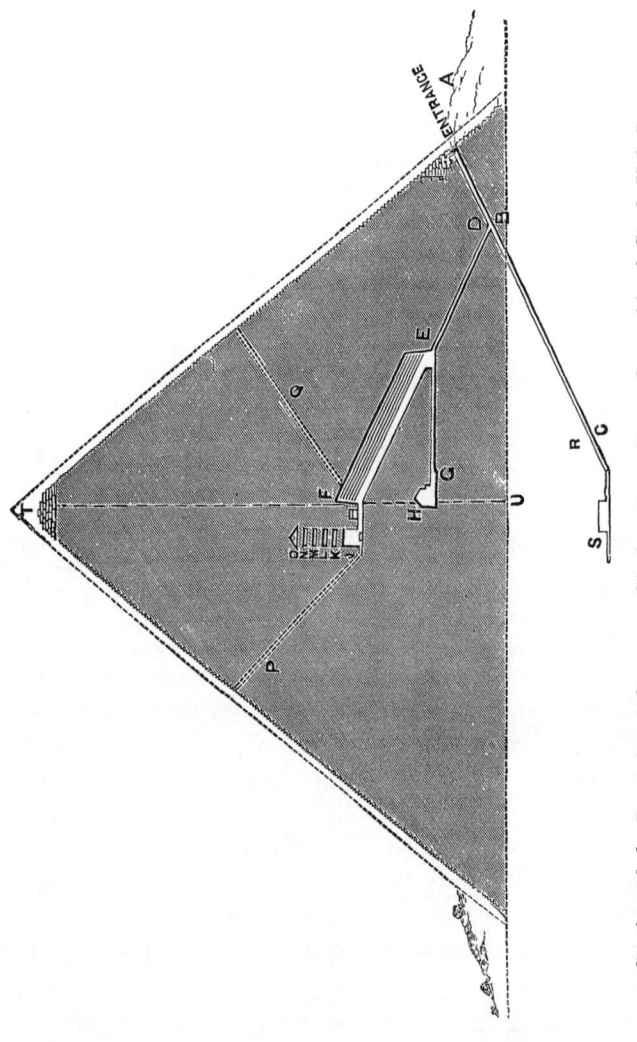

Section of the Pyramid of Cheops at Gizeh.   From Vyse, *Pyramids of Gizeh*, Vol. I., p. 2.

wide; at B is a granite door, round which the path at D has been made. The passage at D E is 125 feet long, and the large hall E F is 155 feet long and 28 feet high; the passage E G leads to the pointed-roofed Queen's Chamber H, which measures about 17 × 19 × 20 feet. The roofing in of this chamber is a beautiful piece of mason's work. From the large hall E F there leads a passage 22 feet long, the ante-chamber in which was originally closed by four granite doors, remains of which are still visible, into the King's Chamber, J, which is lined with granite, and measures about 35 × 17 × 19 feet. The five hollow chambers K, L, M, N, O were built above the King's Chamber to lighten the pressure of the superincumbent mass. In chamber O the name Chufu was found written. The air shafts P and Q measure 234 feet × 8 inches × 6 inches, and 174 feet × 8 inches × 6 inches respectively. A shaft from E to R leads down to the subterranean chamber S, which measures 46 × 27 × 10½ feet. The floor of the King's Chamber, J, is about 140 ft. from the level of the base of the pyramid, and the chamber is a little to the south-east of the line drawn from T to U. Inside the chamber lies the empty, coverless, broken red granite sarcophagus of Cheops, measuring 7½ × 3¼ × 3⅓ feet. The account of the building of this pyramid is told by Herodotus* as follows : "Now, they told me, that to the reign of Rhampsinitus there was a perfect distribution of justice, and that all Egypt was in a high state of prosperity; but that after him Cheops, coming to reign over them, plunged into every kind of wickedness. For that, having shut up all the temples, he first of all forbade them to offer sacrifice, and afterwards he ordered all the Egyptians to work for himself; some, accordingly, were appointed to draw stones from the quarries in the Arabian mountain down to the Nile, others he ordered to receive the stones when transported in vessels across the river, and to drag

* Bk. ii. 124–126.

them to the mountain called the Libyan. And they worked to the number of 100,000 men at a time, each party during three months. The time during which the people were thus harassed by toil, lasted ten years on the road which they constructed, along which they drew the stones, a work in my opinion, not much less than the pyramid; for its length is five stades (3,051 feet), and its width ten orgyæ (60 feet), and its height, where it is the highest, eight orgyæ (48 feet); and it is of polished stone, with figures carved on it: on this road these ten years were expended, and in forming the subterraneous apartments on the hill, on which the pyramids stand, which he had made as a burial vault for himself, in an island, formed by draining a canal from the Nile. Twenty years were spent in erecting the pyramid itself: of this, which is square, each face is eight plethra (820 feet), and the height is the same; it is composed of polished stones, and jointed with the greatest exactness; none of the stones are less than thirty feet. This pyramid was built thus; in the form of steps, which some call crossæ, others bomides. When they had first built it in this manner, they raised the remaining stones by machines made of short pieces of wood: having lifted them from the ground to the first range of steps, when the stone arrived there, it was put on another machine that stood ready on the first range; and from this it was drawn to the second range on another machine; for the machines were equal in number to the ranges of steps; or they removed the machine, which was only one, and portable, to each range in succession, whenever they wished to raise the stone higher; for I should relate it in both ways, as it is related. The highest parts of it, therefore, were first finished, and afterwards they completed the parts next following; but last of all they finished the parts on the ground and that were lowest. On the pyramid is shown an inscription, in Egyptian characters, how much was expended in radishes, onions, and garlic, for the workmen; which the interpreter,* as I well remember, reading the inscription, told me amounted to 1,600 talents of silver. And if this be really the case, how much more was probably expended in iron tools, in bread, and in clothes for the labourers, since they occupied in building the works the time which I mentioned, and no short time besides, as I think, in cutting and drawing the stones, and in forming the subterraneous excavation. [It is related] that Cheops reached such a degree of infamy, that being in want of money, he prostituted his own daughter in a brothel, and ordered her to extort, they did not say how much; but she exacted a certain sum of money, privately, as much as her father ordered her; and contrived to leave a monument of herself, and asked every one that came in to her to give her a stone towards the edifice she designed: of these stones they said the pyramid was built that stands in the middle of the three, before the great pyramid, each side of which is a plethron and a half in length." (Cary's translation.)

THE SECOND PYRAMID.

The second pyramid at Gîzeh was built by Chā-f-Rā, (𓏏𓎡𓇳), or Chephren, the third king of the IVth dynasty, B.C. 3666, who called it 𓊃△, *ur*. His name has not been found inscribed upon any part of it, but the fragment of a marble sphere inscribed with the name of Chā-f-Rā,

---

* Herodotus was deceived by his interpreter, who clearly made up a translation of an inscription which he did not understand. William of Baldensel, who lived in the fourteenth century, tells us that the outer coating of the two largest pyramids was covered with a great number of inscriptions arranged in lines. (Wiedemann, *Aeg. Geschichte*, p. 179.) If the outsides were actually inscribed, the text must have been purely religious, like those inscribed inside the pyramids of Pepi, Teta, and Unas.

which was found near the temple, close by this pyramid, confirms the statements of Herodotus and Diodorus Siculus, that Chephren built it. A statue of this king, now in the Gîzeh Museum, was found in the granite temple close by. This pyramid appears to be larger than the Great Pyramid because it stands upon a higher level of stone foundation; it was cased with stone originally and polished, but the greater part of the outer casing has disappeared. An ascent of this pyramid can only be made with difficulty. It was first explored in 1816 by Belzoni (born 1778, died 1823), the discoverer of the tomb of Seti I. and of the temple of Rameses II. at Abu Simbel. In the north side of the pyramid are two openings, one at the base and one about 50 feet above it. The upper opening led into a corridor 105 feet long, which descends into a chamber $46\frac{1}{2} \times 16\frac{1}{3} \times 22\frac{1}{2}$ feet, which held the granite sarcophagus in which Chephren was buried. The lower opening leads into a corridor about 100 feet long, which, first descending and then ascending, ends in the chamber mentioned above, which is usually called Belzoni's Chamber. The actual height is about 450 feet, and the length of each side at the base about 700 feet. The rock upon which the pyramid stands has been scarped on the north and west sides to make the foundation level. The history of the building of the pyramid is thus stated by Herodotus * : " The Egyptians say that this Cheops reigned fifty years; and when he died, his brother Chephren suc ceeded to the kingdom ; and he followed the same practices as the other, both in other respects, and in building a pyramid; which does not come up to the dimensions of his brother's, for I myself measured them; nor has it subterraneous chambers ; nor does a channel from the Nile flow to it, as to the other ; but this flows through an artificial aqueduct round an island within, in which they say the body of

* Bk. ii. 127.

Cheops is laid. Having laid the first course of variegated Ethiopian stones, less in height than the other by forty feet, he built it near the large pyramid. They both stand on the same hill, which is about 100 feet high. Chephren, they said, reigned fifty-six years. Thus 106 years are reckoned, during which the Egyptians suffered all kinds of calamities, and for this length of time the temples were closed and never opened. From the hatred they bear them, the Egyptians are not very willing to mention their names ; but call the pyramids after Philition, a shepherd, who at that time kept his cattle in those parts." (Cary's translation.)

THE THIRD PYRAMID.

The third pyramid at Gîzeh was built by Men-kau-Rā, ⟨○ ⬚ ⬚⟩, the fourth king of the IVth dynasty, about B.C. 3633, who called it ⬚ △, *Ḥer*. Herodotus and other ancient authors tell us that Men-kau-Rā, or Mycerinus, was buried in this pyramid, but Manetho states that Nitocris, a queen of the VIth dynasty, was the builder. There can be, however, but little doubt that it was built by Mycerinus, for the sarcophagus and the remains of the inscribed coffin of this king were found in one of its chambers by Howard Vyse in 1837. The sarcophagus, which measured $8 \times 3 \times 2\frac{1}{2}$ feet, was lost through the wreck of the ship in which it was sent to England, but the venerable fragments of the coffin are preserved in the British Museum, and form one of the most valuable objects in the famous collection of that institution. The inscription reads : " Osiris, king of the North and South, Men-kau-Rā, living for ever ! The heavens have produced thee, thou wast engendered by Nut (the sky), thou art the offspring of Seb (the earth). Thy mother Nut spreads herself over thee in her form as a divine mystery. She has granted thee to be a god, thou shalt nevermore have enemies, O king of the North and South, Men-kau-Rā, living for ever." This formula is one which is found upon coffins down to the latest period, but as the date of Mycerinus is known, it is possible to draw some interesting and valuable conclusions from the fact that it is found upon his coffin. It proves that as far back as 3,600 years before Christ the Egyptian religion was established on a firm base, that the doctrine of immortality was already deeply rooted in the human mind. The art of preserving the human body by embalming was also well understood and generally practised at that early date.

The pyramid of Men-kau-Rā, like that of Chephren, is built upon a rock with a sloping surface; the inequality of the surface in this case has been made level by building up courses of large blocks of stones. Around the lower part the remains of the old granite covering are visible to a depth of from 30 to 40 feet. It is unfortunate that this pyramid has been so much damaged; its injuries, however, enable the visitor to see exactly how it was built, and it may be concluded that the pyramids of Cheops and Chephren were built in the same manner. The length of each side at the base is about 350 feet, and its height is variously given as 210 and 215 feet. The entrance is on the north side, about thirteen feet above the ground, and a descending corridor about 104 feet long, passing through an ante-chamber, having a series of three granite doors, leads into one chamber about 40 feet long, and a second chamber about 44 long. In this last chamber is a shaft which leads down to the granite-lined chamber about twenty feet below, in which was found the sarcophagus and wooden coffin of Mycerinus, and the remains of a human body. It is thought that, in spite of the body of Mycerinus being buried in this pyramid, it was left unfinished at the death of this king, and that a succeeding ruler of

Egypt finished the pyramid and made a second chamber to hold his or her body. At a short distance to the east of this pyramid are the ruins of a temple which was probably used in connexion with the rites performed in honour of the dead king. In A.D. 1196 a deliberate and systematic attempt was made to destroy this pyramid by the command of the Muḥammedan ruler of Egypt. The account of the character of Mycerinus and of his pyramid as given by Herodotus is as follows: "They said that after him, Mycerinus,* son of Cheops, reigned over Egypt; that the conduct of his father was displeasing to him; and that he opened the temples, and permitted the people, who were worn down to the last extremity, to return to their employments, and to sacrifices; and that he made the most just decisions of all their kings. On this account, of all the kings that ever reigned in Egypt, they praise him most, for he both judged well in other respects, and moreover, when any man complained of his decision, he used to make him some present out of his own treasury and pacify his anger. . . . . . . This king also left a pyramid much less than that of his father, being on each side twenty feet short of three plethra; it is quadrangular, and built half way up of Ethiopian stone. Some of the Grecians erroneously say that this pyramid is the work of the courtesan Rhodopis; but they evidently appear to me ignorant who Rhodopis was; for they would not else have attributed to her the building such a pyramid, on which, so to speak, numberless thousands of talents were expended; besides, Rhodopis flourished in the reign of Amasis, and not at this time; for she was very many years later than those kings who left these pyramids." (Cary's translation.)

In one of the three small pyramids near that of Mycerinus the name of this king is painted on the ceiling.

* Book ii., 129, 134.

THE SPHINX.

The age of the **Sphinx** is unknown, and few of the facts connected with its history have come down to these days. Some years ago it was generally believed to have been made during the rule of the kings of the Middle Empire over Egypt, but when the stele which recorded the repairs made in the temple of the sphinx by Thothmes IV., B.C. 1533, came to light, it became certain that it was the work of one of the kings of the Ancient Empire. The stele records that one day during an after-dinner sleep, Harmachis appeared to Thothmes IV., and promised to bestow upon him the crown of Egypt if he would dig his image, *i.e.*, the Sphinx, out of the sand. At the end of the inscription part of the name of Chā-f-Rā or Chephren appears, and hence some have thought that this king was the maker of the Sphinx; as the statue of Chephren was subsequently found in the temple close by, this theory was generally adopted. An inscription found by Mariette near one of the pyramids to the east of the pyramid of Cheops shows that the Sphinx existed in the time of Chufu or Cheops. The Egyptians called the Sphinx *hu* 𓏤 𓅨 𓃭, and he represented the god Harmachis, *i.e.*, *Ḥeru-em-chut* 𓅃 𓈌 𓇳, "Horus in the horizon," or the rising sun, the conqueror of darkness, the god of the morning. On the tablet erected by Thothmes IV., Harmachis says that he gave life and dominion to Thothmes III., and he promises to give the same good gifts to his successor Thothmes IV. The discovery of the steps which led up to the Sphinx, a smaller Sphinx, and an open temple, etc., was made by Caviglia, who first excavated this monument; within the last few years very extensive excavations have been made round it by the Egyptian Government, and several hitherto unseen parts of it have been brought to view. The Sphinx is hewn out of the living rock, but pieces of stone have been added where necessary; the body is about 150 feet long, the paws are 50 feet long, the head is 30 feet long, the face is 14 feet wide, and from the top of the head to the base of the monument the distance is about 70 feet. Originally there probably were ornaments on the head, the whole of which was covered with a limestone covering, and the face was coloured red; of these decorations scarcely any traces now remain, though they were visible towards the end of the last century. The condition in which the monument now appears is due to the savage destruction of its features by the Muḥammedan rulers of Egypt, some of whom caused it to be used for a target. Around this imposing relic of antiquity, whose origin is wrapped in mystery, a number of legends and superstitions have clustered in all ages; but Egyptology has shown I. that it was a colossal image of Rā Harmachis, and therefore of his human representative upon earth, the king of Egypt who had it hewn, and II. that it was in existence in the time of, and was probably repaired by, Cheops and Chephren, who lived about three thousand seven hundred years before Christ.

THE TEMPLE OF THE SPHINX.

A little to the south-east of the Sphinx lies the large granite and limestone temple excavated by M. Mariette in 1853; statues of Chephren (now at Gîzeh) were found in it, and hence it has been generally supposed that he was the builder of it. It is a good specimen of the solid simple buildings which the Egyptians built during the Ancient Empire. In one chamber, and at the end of the passage leading from it, are hewn in the wall niches which were probably intended to hold mummies.

THE TOMB OF NUMBERS.

This tomb was made for Chā-f-Rā-ānch, a "royal relative" and priest of Chephren (Chā-f-Rā), the builder of the second pyramid. It is called the " tomb of numbers" because the numbers of the cattle possessed by Chāf-Rā-ānch are written upon its walls.

CAMPBELL'S TOMB.

This tomb, named after the British Consul-General of Egypt at that time, was excavated by Howard Vyse in 1837; it is not older than the XXVIth dynasty. The shaft is about 55 feet deep; at the bottom of it is a small chamber in which were found three sarcophagi in niches.

The pyramids of Gîzeh are surrounded by a large number of tombs of high officials and others connected with the services carried on in honour of the kings who built the pyramids. Some few of them are of considerable interest, and as they are perishing little by little, it is advisable to see as many of the best specimens as possible.

THE PYRAMIDS OF ABU ROÂSH.

These pyramids lie about six miles north of the Pyramids of Gîzeh, and are thought to be older than they. Nothing remains of one except five or six courses of stone, which show that the length of each side at the base was about 350 feet ; a passage about 160 feet long leading down to a subterranean chamber about 43 feet long. A pile of stones close by marks the site of another pyramid ; the others have disappeared. Of the age of these pyramids nothing certain is known. The remains of a causeway about a mile long leading to them are still visible.

THE PYRAMIDS OF ABUṢIR.

These pyramids, originally fourteen in number, were built by kings of the Vth dynasty, but only four of them are now standing, probably because of the poorness of the workmanship and the careless way in which they were put together. The most northerly pyramid was built by

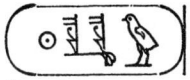 Saḥu-Rā, the second king of the Vth dynasty, B.C. 3533; its actual height is about 120 feet, and the length of each side at the base about 220 feet. The blocks of stone in the sepulchral chamber are exceptionally large. Saḥu-Rā made war in the peninsula of Sinai, he founded a town near Esneh, and he built a temple to Sechet at Memphis.

The pyramid to the south of that of Saḥu-Rā was built by  " *Usr-en-Rā, son of the Sun, An.*" This king, like Saḥu-Rā, also made war in Sinai. The largest of these three pyramids is now about 165 feet high and 330 feet square; the name of its builder is unknown. Abuṣir is the Busiris of Pliny.

BEDRASHÊN, MEMPHIS, AND SAKKÂRAH.

The ruins of **Memphis** and the antiquities at Sakkârah are usually reached by steamers or train from Cairo to Bedrashên. Leaving the river or station the village of Bedrashên is soon reached, and a short ride next brings the traveller to the village of Mît-Rahîneh. On the ground lying for some distance round about these two villages once stood the city of Memphis, though there is comparatively little left to show its limits. According to Herodotus (ii., 99), " Menes, who first ruled over Egypt, in the first place protected Memphis by a mound; for the whole river formerly ran close to the sandy mountain on the side of Libya; but Menes, beginning about a hundred stades above Memphis, filled in the elbow towards the south, dried up the old channel, and conducted the river into a canal, so as to make it flow between the mountains : this bend of the Nile, which flows excluded from *its ancient course,* is still carefully upheld by the Persians, being made secure every year; for if the river should break through and overflow in this part, there would be danger lest all Memphis should be flooded. When the part cut off had been made firm land by this Menes, who was first king, he in the first place built on it the city that is now called Memphis; for Memphis is situate in the narrow part of Egypt ; and outside of it he excavated a lake from the river towards the north and the west ; for the Nile itself bounds it towards the east. In the next place, *they relate* that he built in it the temple of Vulcan, which is vast and well worthy of mention." (Cary's translation.)

Whether Menes built the town or not, it is quite certain that the city of Memphis was of most ancient foundation.

The reason why the kings of Egypt established their capital there is obvious. From the peoples that lived on the western bank of the river they had little to fear, but on the eastern side they were always subject to invasions of the peoples who lived in Mesopotamia, Syria, and Arabia; with their capital on the western bank, and the broad Nile as a barrier on the east of it, they were comparatively safe. Added to this, its situation at the beginning of the Delta enabled it to participate easily of the good things of that rich country. The tract of land upon which Memphis stood was also fertile and well wooded. Diodorus speaks of its green meadows, intersected with canals, and of their pavement of lotus flowers; Pliny talks of trees there of such girth that three men with extended arms could not span them; Martial praises the roses brought from thence to Rome; and its wine was celebrated in lands remote from it. The site chosen was excellent, for in addition to its natural advantages it was not far from the sea-coast of the Delta, and holding as it were a middle position in Egypt, its kings were able to hold and rule the country from Philæ on the south to the Mediterranean on the north. In the inscriptions it is called 𓏠𓈖𓆴𓈉 *Men-nefer*,* "the beautiful dwelling," 𓉴𓏤𓊨𓂓 *Ḥet-Ptaḥ-ka*, "the temple of the double of Ptah," and 𓋹𓈖𓃀 Âneb-ḥet', "the white-walled city." The last name calls to mind the "White Castle" spoken of by classical writers. Tetâ, son of Menes, built his palace there, and Ka-Kau (𓍹𓂋𓆙𓆙𓍺), the second king of the IInd dynasty, B.C. 4100, established the worship of Apis there. During the rule of the IIIrd,

---

IVth, and VIth dynasties, the kings of which sprang from Memphis, that city reached a height of splendour which was probably never excelled. The most celebrated building there was the temple of Ptaḥ, which was beautified and adorned by a number of kings, the last of whom reigned during the XXVIth dynasty. The Hyksos ravaged, but did not destroy, the city; under the rule of the Theban kings, who expelled the Hyksos, the city flourished for a time, although Thebes became the new capital. When Rameses II. returned from his wars in the east, he set up a statue of himself in front of the temple of Ptaḥ there; Piānchi the Ethiopian besieged it; the Assyrian kings Esarhaddon and Assurbanipal captured it; Cambyses the Persian, having wrought great damage there, killed the magistrates of the city and the priests of the temple of Apis, and smote the Apis bull so that he died;* he established a Persian garrison there. After the founding of Alexandria, Memphis lost

---

* "When Cambyses arrived at Memphis, Apis, whom the Greeks call Epaphus, appeared to the Egyptians; and when this manifestation took place, the Egyptians immediately put on their richest apparel, and kept festive holiday. Cambyses seeing them thus occupied, and concluding that they made their rejoicings on account of his ill success, summoned the magistrates to Memphis; and when they came into his presence, he asked, 'why the Egyptians had done nothing of the kind when he was at Memphis before, but did so now, when he had returned with the loss of a great part of his army.' They answered, that their god appeared to them, who was accustomed to manifest himself at distant intervals, and that when he did appear, then all the Egyptians were used to rejoice and keep a feast. Cambyses, having heard this, said they lied, and as liars he put them to death. Having slain them, he next summoned the priests into his presence; and when the priests gave the same account, he said, that he would find out whether a god so tractable had come among the Egyptians; and having said this, he commanded the priests to bring Apis to him; they therefore went away to fetch him. This Apis, or Epaphus, is the calf of a cow incapable of conceiving another offspring; and the Egyptians say, that lightning descends upon the cow from heaven, and that from thence it brings

whatever glory it then possessed, and became merely the chief provincial city of Egypt. During the reign of Theodosius, a savage attack, the result of his edict, was made upon its temples and buildings by the Christians, and a few hundred years later the Muḥammedans carried the stones, which once formed them, across the river to serve as building materials for their houses and mosques. The circuit of the ancient city, according to Diodorus, was 150 stadia, or about thirteen miles.

The Colossal Statue of Rameses II.

This magnificent statue was discovered by Messrs. Caviglia and Sloane in 1820, and was presented by them to the British Museum. On account of its weight and the lack of public interest in such matters, it lay near the road leading from Bedrashên to Mît-Rahîneh, and little by little became nearly covered with the annual deposit of Nile mud; during the inundation the greater part of it was covered by the waters of the Nile. During the winter of 1886–87 Sir Frederick Stephenson collected a sum of money in Cairo for the purpose of lifting it out of the hollow in which it

forth Apis. This calf, which is called Apis, has the following marks : it is black, and has a square spot of white on the forehead ; and on the back the figure of an eagle ; and in the tail double hairs ; and on the tongue a beetle. When the priests brought Apis, Cambyses, like one almost out of his senses, drew his dagger, meaning to strike the belly of Apis, but hit the thigh ; then falling into a fit of laughter, he said to the priests, ' Ye blockheads, are there such gods as these, consisting of blood and flesh, and sensible to steel ? This, truly, is a god worthy of the Egyptians. But you shall not mock me with impunity.' Having spoken thus, he commanded those whose business it was, to scourge the priests, and to kill all the Egyptians whom they should find feasting. . . . But Apis, being wounded in the thigh, lay and languished in the temple ; and at length, when he had died of the wound, the priests buried him without the knowledge of Cambyses."—Herodotus, II. 27–29. (Cary's translation.)

lay, and the difficult engineering part of the task was ably accomplished by Major Arthur Bagnold, R.E.   This statue is made of a fine hard limestone, and measures about forty-two feet in height; it is probably one of the statues which stood in front of the temple of Ptaḥ, mentioned by Herodotus and Diodorus.   The prenomen of Rameses II.

Rā-usr-māt-setep-en-Rā, is inscribed on the belt of the statue, and on the end of the roll which the king carries in his hand are the words " Rameses, beloved of Åmen."   By the side of the king are figures of a daughter and son of Rameses.   The famous temple of Ptaḥ founded by Menes was situated to the south of the statue.

SAḲḲÂRAH.

The name Saḳḳârah is probably derived from the name of the Egyptian god Seker , who was connected with the resurrection of the dead.   The tract of land at Saḳḳârah which formed the great burial ground of the ancient Egyptians of all periods, is about four and a half miles long and one mile wide; the most important antiquities there are : I. the Step Pyramid ; II. the Pyramids of Unás, Tetá, and Pepi, kings of the Vth and VIth dynasties ; III. the Serapeum ; and IV. the Tomb of Thi.   Admirers of M. Mariette will be interested to see the house in which this distinguished *savant* lived.

I. The STEP PYRAMID is generally thought to have been built by the fourth king of the Ist dynasty (called Uenephes by Manetho, and Áta in the tablet of Abydos), who is said to have built a pyramid at Kochome (*i.e.*, Ka-Kam) near Saḳḳârah.   Though the date of this pyramid is not known accurately, it is probably right to assume that it is older than the pyramids of Gîzeh.   The door which led into the pyramid was inscribed with the name of a king called Rā-nub, and M. Mariette found the same name on one of the stelæ in the Serapeum. The steps of the pyramid are six in number, and are about 38, 36, 34½, 32, 31 and 29½ feet in height; the width of each step is from six to seven feet. The lengths of the sides at the base are: north and south 352 feet, east and west 396 feet, and the actual height is 197 feet. In shape this pyramid is oblong, and its sides do not exactly face the cardinal points. The arrangement of the chambers inside this pyramid is quite peculiar to itself.

II. The PYRAMID OF UNÁS ⟨ 𓆓𓏏𓏤 ⟩, called in Egyptian Nefer-âs-u, lies to the south-east of the Step Pyramid, and was reopened and cleared out in 1881 by M. Maspero, at the expense of Messrs. Thomas Cook and Son. Its original height was about 62 feet, and the length of its sides at the base 220 feet. Owing to the broken blocks of sand which lie round about it, Vyse was unable to give exact measurements. Several attempts had been made to break into it, and one of the Arabs who took part in one of these attempts, "Aḥmed the Carpenter," seems to have left his name inside one of the chambers in red ink. It is probable that he is the same man who opened the Great Pyramid at Gîzeh, A.D. 820. A black basalt sarcophagus, from which the cover had been dragged off, and an arm, a shin bone, some ribs and fragments of the skull from the mummy of Unâs, were found in the sarcophagus chamber. The walls of the two largest chambers and two of the corridors are inscribed with ritual texts and prayers of a very interesting character. Unâs, the last king of the Vth dynasty, reigned about thirty years. The Maṣṭabat el-Far‘ûn was thought by Mariette to be the tomb of Unâs, but some scholars thought that the 'blunted pyramid' at Dahshûr was his tomb, because his name was written upon the top of it.

The PYRAMID OF TETÀ ⟨ 𓏏𓎢 ⟩, called in Egyptian

Ṭeṭ-àsu, lies to the north-east of the Step Pyramid, and was opened in 1881. The Arabs call it the " Prison Pyramid," because local tradition says that it is built near the ruins of the prison where Joseph the patriarch was confined. Its actual height is about 59 feet; the length of its sides at the base is 210 feet, and the platform at the top is about 50 feet. The arrangement of the chambers and passages and the plan of construction followed is almost identical with that of the pyramid of Unàs. This pyramid was broken into in ancient days, and two of the walls of the sarcophagus chamber have literally been smashed to pieces by the hammer blows of those who expected to find treasure inside them. The inscriptions, painted in green upon the walls have the same subject matter as those inscribed upon the walls of the chambers of the pyramid of Unàs. According to Manetho, Tetà, the first king of the VIth dynasty, reigned about fifty years, and was murdered by one of his guards.

The PYRAMID OF PEPI I. or ⌈ 𓄿 𓅓 𓅬 𓇳 𓉴𓏥 ⌉ 'Rà-meri, son of the Sun, Pepi,' lies to the south-east of the Step Pyramid, and forms one of the central group of pyramids at Saḳḳârah, where it is called the Pyramid of Shêkh Abu Manṣûr; it was opened in 1880. Its actual height is about 40 feet, and the length of the sides at the base is about 250 feet; the arrangement of the chambers, etc., inside is the same as in the pyramids of Unàs and Tetà, but the ornamentation is slightly different. It is the worst preserved of these pyramids, and has suffered most at the lands of the spoilers, probably because having been constructed with stones which were taken from tombs ancient already in those days, instead of stones fresh from the quarry, it was more easily injured. The granite sarcophagus was broken to take out the mummy, fragments of which were found lying about on the ground; the cover too, smashed in pieces, lay on the ground close by. A small rose granite box, containing alabaster jars, was also found in the sarcophagus chamber. The inscriptions are, like those inscribed on the walls of the pyramids of Unàs and Tetà, of a religious nature; some scholars see in them evidence that the pyramid was usurped by another Pepi, who lived at a much later period than the VIth dynasty. The pyramid of Pepi I., the second king of the VIth dynasty, who reigned, according to Manetho, fifty-three years, was called in Egyptian by the same name as Memphis, *i.e.*, Men-nefer, and numerous priests were attached to its service. Pepi's kingdom embraced all Egypt, and he waged war against the inhabitants of the peninsula of Sinai. He is said to have set up an obelisk at Heliopolis, and to have laid the foundation of the temple at Denderah. His success as a conqueror was due in a great measure to the splendid abilities of one of his chief officers called Unà, who warred successfully against the various hereditary foes of Egypt on its southern and eastern borders.

III. The SERAPEUM or APIS MAUSOLEUM contained the vaults in which all the Apis bulls that lived at Memphis were buried. According to Herodotus, Apis "is the calf of a cow incapable of conceiving another offspring; and the Egyptians say that lightning descends upon the cow from heaven, and that from thence it brings forth Apis. This calf, which is called Apis, has the following marks: it is black, and has a square spot of white on the forehead, and on the back the figure of an eagle; and in the tail double hairs; and on the tongue a beetle." Above each tomb of an Apis bull was built a chapel, and it was the series of chapels which formed the Serapeum properly so called ; it was surrounded by walls like the other Egyptian temples, and it had pylons to which an avenue of sphinxes led. This remarkable place was excavated in 1850 by M. Mariette, who having seen in various parts of Egypt sphinxes upon which were written the names of Osiris–Apis, or Serapis, concluded that they must have come from the Serapeum or temple of Serapis spoken of by Strabo. Happening, by chance, to discover one day at Saḳḳârah a sphinx having the same characteristics, he made up his mind that he had lighted upon the remains of the long sought for building. The excavations which he immediately undertook, brought to light the Avenue of Sphinxes, eleven statues of Greek philosophers, and the vaults in which the Apis bulls were buried. These vaults are of three kinds, and show that the Apis bulls were buried in different ways at different periods: the oldest Apis sarcophagus laid here belongs to the reign of Amenophis III., about B.C. 1500. The parts of the Apis Mausoleum in which the Apis bulls were buried from the XVIIIth to the XXVIth dynasty are not visible ; but the new gallery, which contains sixty-four vaults, the oldest of which dates from the reign of Psammetichus I., and the most modern from the time of the Ptolemies, can be seen on application to the guardian of the tombs. The vaults are excavated on each side of the gallery, and each was intended to receive a granite sarcophagus. The names of Amāsis II., Cambyses, and Chabbesha are found upon three of the sarcophagi, but most of them are uninscribed. Twenty-four granite sarcophagi still remain in position, and they each measure about $13 \times 8 \times 11$ feet. The discovery of these tombs was of the greatest importance historically, for on the walls were found thousands of dated stelæ which gave accurate chronological data for the history of Egypt. These votive tablets mention the years, months, and days of the reign of the king in which the Apis bulls, in whose honour the tablets were set up, were born and buried. The Apis tombs had been rifled in ancient times, and only two of them contained any relics when M. Mariette opened them out.

IV. The TOMB OF THI lies to the north-east of the Apis

Mausoleum, and was built during the Vth dynasty, about B.C. 3500. Thi 〰〰 ⏑⏑, was a man who held the dignities of *smer*, royal councillor, superintendent of works, scribe of the court, confidant of the king, etc. ; he held also priestly rank as prophet, and was attached to the service of the pyramids of Abusîr. He had sprung from a family of humble origin, but his abilities were so esteemed by one of the kings, whose faithful servant he was, that a princess called Nefer-ḥetep-s was given him to wife, and his children Thi and Tamut ranked as princes. Thi held several high offices under Kakaȧ (⌷⌷⌷) and User-en-Rā (☉〰〰) kings of the Vth dynasty. The tomb or masṭaba of Thi is now nearly covered with sand, but in ancient days the whole building was above the level of the ground. The chambers of the tomb having been carefully cleared, it is possible to enter them and examine the most beautiful sculptures and paintings with which the walls are decorated. To describe these wonderful works of art adequately would require more space than can be given here ; it must be sufficient to say that the scenes represent Thi superintending all the various operations connected with the management of his large agricultural estates and farmyard, together with illustrations of his hunting and fishing expeditions.

The necropolis of Saḳḳârah contains chiefly tombs of the Ancient Empire, that is to say, tombs that were built during the first eleven dynasties ; many tombs of a later period are found there, but they are of less interest and importance, and in many cases small, but fine, ancient tombs have been destroyed to make them. As our knowledge of Egyptian architecture is derived principally from tombs and temples, a brief description of the most ancient tombs now known will not be out of place here ; the following observations on them are based upon the excellent articles of M. Mariette in the *Revue Archéologique*, S. 2ième, t. xix. p. 8 ff. The tombs

of the Ancient Empire found at Saḳḳârah belong to two
classes, in the commoner of which the naked body was
buried about three feet deep in the sand.   When the
yellowish-white skeletons of such bodies are found to-day,
neither fragments of linen nor pieces of coffins are visible ;
occasionally one is found laid within four walls roughly
built of yellow bricks made of sand, lime, and small stones.
A vaulted brick roof covers the space between the walls ; it
is hardly necessary to say that such tombs represent the last
resting places of the poor, and that nothing of any value is
ever found inside them.   The tombs of the better sort are
carefully built, and were made for the wealthy and the great;
such a tomb is usually called by the Arabs *maṣṭaba** (the
Arabic word for ' bench '), because its length in proportion
to its height is great, and reminded them of the long, low
seat common in Oriental houses, and familiar to them.
The maṣṭaba is a heavy, massive building, of rectangular
shape, the four sides of which are four walls symmetrically
inclined towards their common centre.   Each course of
stones, formed by blocks laid upon each other, is carried
a little behind the other.   The largest maṣṭaba measures
about 170 feet long by 86 feet wide, and the smallest about
26 feet by 20 feet : they vary in height from 13 to 30 feet.
The ground on which the maṣṭabas at Saḳḳârah are built
is composed of rock covered with sand to the depth of a
few feet ; their foundations are always on the rock.   Near
the pyramids of Gîzeh they are arranged in a symmetrical
manner ; they are oriented astronomically to the true north,
and their larger axes are always towards the north.   Though
they have, at first sight, the appearance of unfinished
pyramids, still they have nothing in common with pyramids
except their orientation towards the true north.   Maṣṭabas
are built of two kinds of stone and of bricks, and they are

---

* Pronounced *mastăba* (Arabic مَصْطَبَة).

usually entered on the eastern side ; their tops are quite flat. The interior of a mastaba may be divided into three parts : the chamber, the *sirdâb*,* or place of retreat, and the pit. The entrance is made through a door in the middle of the eastern or northern side, and though the interior may be divided into many chambers, it is usual only to find one. The walls of the interior are sometimes sculptured, and in the lower part of the chamber, usually facing the east, is a stele ; the stele alone may be inscribed and the walls unsculptured, but no case is known where the walls are sculptured and the stele blank. A table of offerings is often found on the ground at the foot of the stele. A little distance from the chamber, built into the thickness of the walls, more often to the south than the north, is a high, narrow place of retreat or habitation, called by the Arabs a *sirdâb*. This place was walled up, and the only communication between it and the chamber was by means of a narrow hole sufficiently large to admit of the entrance of the hand. One or more statues of the dead man buried in the mastaba were shut in here, and the small passage is said to have been made for the escape of the fumes of incense which was burnt in the chamber. The pit was a square shaft varying in depth from 40 to 80 feet, sunk usually in the middle of the larger axis of the mastaba, rather nearer the north than the south. There was neither ladder nor staircase, either outside or inside, leading to the funereal chamber at the bottom of the pit, hence the coffin and the mummy when once there were inaccessible. This pit was sunk through the mastaba into the rock beneath. At the bottom of the pit, on the south side, is an opening into a passage, about four feet high, which leads obliquely to the south-east ; soon after the passage increases in size in all directions, and becomes the sarcophagus chamber, which

---

* A *sirdâb*, strictly speakly, is a lofty, vaulted, subterranean chamber, with a large opening in the north side to admit air in the hot season.

is thus exactly under the upper chamber. The sarcophagus, rectangular in shape, is usually made of limestone, and rests in a corner of the chamber; at Saḳḳârah they are found uninscribed. When the mummy had been laid in the sarcophagus, and the other arrangements completed, the end of the passage near the shaft leading to the sarcophagus chamber was walled up, the shaft was filled with stones, earth, and sand, and the friends of the deceased might reasonably hope that he would rest there for ever. When M. Mariette found a maṣṭaba without inscriptions he rarely excavated it entirely. He found three belonging to one of the first three dynasties; forty-three of the IVth dynasty; sixty-one of the Vth dynasty; twenty-three of the VIth dynasty; and nine of doubtful date. The Egyptians called the tomb "the house of eternity," 𓉐𓏤 𓏏𓏤, *pa t'etta*.

MARIETTE'S HOUSE.

This house was the headquarters of M. Mariette and his staff when employed in making excavations in the Necropolis of Saḳḳârah. It is not easy to properly estimate the value to science of the work of this distinguished man. It is true that fortune gave him the opportunity of excavating some of the most magnificent of the buildings of the Pharaohs of all periods, and of hundreds of ancient towns; nevertheless it is equally true that his energy and marvellous power of work enabled him to use to the fullest extent the means for advancing the science of Egyptology which had been put in his hands. It is to be hoped that his house will be preserved on its present site as a remembrance of a great man who did a great work.

The TOMB OF PTAḤ-ḤETEP, a priest who lived during the Vth century, is a short distance from Mariette's house, and well worthy of more than one visit.

The Pyramids of Dahshûr.

These pyramids, four of stone and two of brick, lie about three and a half miles to the south of Maṣṭabat el-Far'ûn. The largest stone pyramid is about 326 feet high, and the length of each side at the base is about 700 feet; beneath it are three subterranean chambers. The second stone pyramid is about 321 feet high, and the length of its sides at the base is 620 feet; it is usually called the "Blunted Pyramid," because the lowest parts of its sides are built at one angle, and the completing parts at another. The larger of the two brick pyramids is about 90 feet high, and the length of the sides at the base is about 350 feet; the smaller is about 156 feet high, and the length of its sides at the base is about 343 feet.

The Quarries of Ma'ṣara and Ṭurra.

These quarries have supplied excellent stone for building purposes for six thousand years at least. During the Ancient Empire the architects of the pyramids made their quarrymen tunnel into the mountains for hundreds of yards until they found a bed of stone suitable for their work, and traces of their excavations are plainly visible to-day. The Egyptians called the Ṭurra quarry Re-āu, or Ta-re-āu, from which the Arabic name Ṭurra is probably derived. An inscription in one of the chambers tells us that during the reign of Amenophis III. a new part of the quarry was opened. Unà, an officer who lived in the reign of Pepi I., was sent to Ṭurra by this king to bring back a white limestone sarcophagus with its cover, libation stone, etc., etc.

The Pyramid of Mêdûm.

This pyramid, called by the Arabs *El Haram el-Kaddab*, or "the False Pyramid," is probably so named because it is unlike any of the other pyramids known to them ; it is said to have been built by Seneferu (⎡𝕝𝕝 ⟋ ⟍⎤), the first king of the IVth dynasty, but there is no evidence proving that he did.   The pyramid is about 115 feet high, and consists of three stages : the first is 70, the second 20, and the third about 25 feet high.   The stone for this building was brought from the Moḳaṭṭam hills, but it was never finished ; as in all other pyramids, the entrance is on the north side.   When opened in modern times the sarcophagus chamber was found empty, and it would seem that this pyramid had been entered and rifled in ancient days.   On the north of this pyramid are a number of maṣṭabas in which 'royal relatives' of Seneferu are buried ; the most interesting of these are those of Nefermat, one of his feudal chiefs (⎡▭ ⟋⎤ erpā ḫā), and Atet his widow.   The sculptures and general style of the work are similar to those found in the maṣṭabas of Saḳḳârah.

Wasṭa.

At **Wasṭa**, a town 55 miles from Cairo, is the railway junction for the Fayûm.   The line from Wasṭa runs west-wards, and its terminus is at Medînet el-Fayûm, a large Egyptian town situated a little distance from the site of Arsinoë in the Heptanomis,* called Crocodilopolis† by the Greeks, because the crocodile was here worshipped.   The Egyptians called the Fayûm Ta-she 𓎛𓏤 𓐩 "the lake district," and the name Fayûm is the Arabic form of the

---

* Heptanomis, or Middle Egypt, was the district which separated the Thebaïd from the Delta ; the names of the seven nomes were : Memphites, Heracleopolites, Crocodilopolites or Arsinoites, Aphroditopolites, Oxyrhynchites, Cynopolites, and Hermopolites. The greater and lesser Oases were always reckoned parts of the Heptanomis.

† In Egyptian 𓏰𓉐 𓐩 , *Neter ḥet Sebek.*

Coptic ⲪⲒⲞⲘ,* "the water." The Fayûm district has an area of about 850 square miles, and is watered by a branch of the Nile called the Baḥr-Yûsuf, which flows into it through the Libyan mountains. On the west of it lies the Birket el-Ḳurûn. This now fertile land is thought to have been reclaimed from the desert by Amenemḥāt III., a king of the XIIth dynasty. The Birket el-Ḳurûn was formerly thought to have been a part of Lake Moeris,† but more modern travellers place both it and the Labyrinth to the east of the Fayûm district. The Baḥr-Yûsuf is said by some to have been excavated under the direction of the patriarch Joseph, but there is no satisfactory evidence for this theory; strictly speaking it is an arm of the Nile, which has always needed cleaning out from time to time, and the Yûsuf, or Joseph, after whom it is named, was probably one of the Muḥammedan rulers of Egypt. Herodotus says‡ of Lake Moeris, "The water in this lake does not spring from the soil, for these parts are excessively dry, but it is conveyed through a channel from the Nile, and for six months it flows into the lake, and six months out again into the Nile. And during the six months that it flows out it yields a talent of silver (£240) every day to the king's treasury from the fish; but when the water is flowing into it, twenty minæ (£80)." The Labyrinth§ stood on the bank of Lake Moeris, and a number of its ruined chambers are still visible.

* From the Egyptian ⟨hieroglyphs⟩ , *Pa-iumā.*

† From the Egyptian *Ma-ur*, "great water."

‡ Bk. II., 149.

§ "Yet the labyrinth surpasses even the pyramids. For it has twelve courts enclosed with walls, with doors opposite each other, six facing the north, and six the south, contiguous to one another; and the same exterior wall encloses them. It contains two kinds of rooms, some under ground and some above ground over them, to the number of three thousand, fifteen hundred of each. The rooms above ground I myself went through, and saw, and relate from personal inspection.

Beni Suêf, 73 miles from Cairo, is the capital of the province bearing the same name, and is governed by a Mudîr. In ancient days it was famous for its textile fabrics, and supplied Aḥmîm and other weaving cities of Upper Egypt with flax. A main road led from this town to the Fayûm.

UPPER EGYPT.

Maghâghah, 106 miles from Cairo, is now celebrated for its large sugar manufactory, which is lighted by gas, and is well worth a visit ; the manufacturing of sugar begins here early in January.

About twenty-four miles farther south, lying inland, on the western side of the Nile, between the river and the Baḥr Yûsuf, is the site of the town of Oxyrhyncus, so called by the Greeks on account of the fish which they believed was worshipped there. The Egyptian name of the town was ⌐⌐ 𓅓𓏌 𓏏, Pa-māt′et, from which came the Coptic Pemge, ⲡⲉⲙ̅ϫⲉ, and the corrupt Arabic form Behnesa.

A little above Abu Girgeh, on the west bank of the Nile,

But the underground rooms I only know from report ; for the Egyptians who have charge of the building would on no account show me them, saying, that they were the sepulchres of the kings who originally built this labyrinth, and of the sacred crocodiles. I can therefore only relate what I have learnt by hearsay concerning the lower rooms ; but the upper ones, which surpass all human works, I myself saw ; for the passage through the corridors, and the windings through the courts, from their great variety, presented a thousand occasions of wonder as I passed from a court to the rooms, and from the rooms to the hall, and to the other corridors from the halls, and to other courts from the rooms. The roofs of all these are of stone, as also are the walls ; but the walls are full of sculptured figures. Each court is surrounded with a colonnade of white stone, closely fitted. And adjoining the extremity of the labyrinth is a pyramid, forty orgyæ (about 240 feet) in height, on which large figures are carved, and a way to it has been made under ground." Herodotus, Bk. II., 148 (Cary's translation).

is the town of El-Kais, which marks the site of the ancient Cynopolis or "Dog-city;" it was the seat of a Coptic bishop, and is called Kais, ⲔⲀⲓⲤ, in Coptic.

Thirteen miles from Abu Girgeh, also on the west bank of the Nile, is the town of Ḳlûṣanah, 134 miles from Cairo, and a few miles south, lying inland, is Samallût.

Farther south, on the east bank of the Nile, is Gebel eṭ-Têr, or the "Bird mountain," so called because tradition says that all the birds of Egypt assemble here once a year, and that they leave behind them when departing one solitary bird, that remains there until they return the following year to relieve him of his watch, and to set another in his place. As there are mountains called Gebel eṭ-Têr in all parts of Arabic-speaking countries, because of the number of birds which frequent them, the story is only one which springs from the fertile Arabic imagination. Gebel eṭ-Têr rises above the river to a height of six or seven hundred feet, and upon its summit stands a Coptic convent dedicated to Mary the Virgin, but called sometimes the "Convent of the Pulley," because the ascent to the convent is generally made by a rope and pulley. Leaving the river and entering a fissure in the rocks, the traveller finds himself at the bottom of a natural shaft about 120 feet long. When Robert Curzon visited this convent, he had to climb up much in the same way as boys used to climb up inside chimneys. The convent stands about 400 feet from the top of the shaft, and is built of small square stones of Roman workmanship; the necessary repairs have, however, been made with mud or sundried brick. The outer walls of the enclosure form a square which measures about 200 feet each way; they are 20 feet high, and are perfectly unadorned. Tradition says that it was founded by the Empress Helena,[*] and there is in this case no reason to doubt it. The church "is partly subterranean, being built in the recesses of an ancient stone

---

[*] Died about A.D. 328, aged 80. (Sozomen, *Eccles. Hist.*, II., 2.)

quarry; the other parts of it are of stone plastered over.
The roof is flat and is formed of horizontal beams of palm
trees, upon which a terrace of reeds and earth is laid.   The
height of the interior is about 25 feet.   On entering the
door we had to descend a flight of narrow steps, which led
into a side aisle about ten feet wide, which is divided from
the nave by octagon columns of great thickness supporting
the walls of a sort of clerestory.   The columns were surmounted by heavy square plinths almost in the Egyptian
style.   I consider this church to be interesting from its
being half a catacomb, or cave, and one of the earliest
Christian buildings which has preserved its originality . . . . .
it will be seen that it is constructed on the principle of a
Latin basilica, as the buildings of the Empress Helena
usually were." (Curzon, *Monasteries of the Levant*, p. 109.)
In Curzon's time the convent possessed fifteen Coptic books
with Arabic translations, and eight Arabic MSS.   As the
monks were, and are, dreadfully poor, they used to descend
the rock and swim out to any passing boat to beg for
charity; the Patriarch has forbidden this practice, but it is
not entirely discontinued.   Two or three miles from the
convent are some ancient quarries having rock bas-reliefs
representing Rameses III. making an offering to the crocodile god Sebek 𓆎 before Åmen-Rā.

MINYEH.

Minyeh, 156½ miles from Cairo, on the west bank of the
Nile, is the capital of the province of the same name; its
Arabic name is derived from the Coptic Mone, ⲘⲞⲚⲈ,
which in turn represents the Egyptian 𓏠 *Ment* in its old
name Chufu-menāt.   There is a large sugar factory here in
which about 2,000 men are employed.   A few miles south,
on the eastern side of the river, are some tombs, which
appear to have been hewn during the IIIrd or IVth dynasty.

BENI HASÂN.

Beni Hasân, 171 miles from Cairo, on the east bank of the Nile, is remarkable for the valuable historical tombs which are situated at a short distance from the site of the villages grouped under that name. The villages of the "Children of Hasân" were destroyed by order of Muḥammad 'Ali on account of the thievish propensities of their inhabitants. The **Speos Artemidos** is the first rock excavation visited here. The king who first caused this cavern to be hewn out was Thothmes III.; about 250 years later Seti I. made additions to it, but it seems never to have been finished. The cavern was dedicated to the lion-goddess Sechet, who was called Artemis by the Greeks; hence the name "cavern of Artemis." The portico had originally two rows of columns, four in each; the cavern is about 21 feet square, and the niche in the wall at the end was probably intended to hold a statue of Sechet.

There are about fifteen rock-tombs at Beni Hasân, but only two of them, those of Âmeni and Chnemu-ḥetep, are of interest generally speaking. They were all hewn during the XIIth dynasty, but have preserved the chief characteristics of the maṣṭabas of Saḳḳârah, that is to say, they consist of a chamber and a shaft leading down to a corridor, which ends in the chamber containing the sarcophagus and the mummy. As in the tombs at Aswân, a suitable layer of stone was sought for in the hill, and when found the tombs were hewn out. The walls were partly smoothed, and then covered with a thin layer of plaster upon which the scenes in the lives of the people buried there might be painted. The columns and the lower parts of some of the tombs are coloured red to resemble granite. The northern tomb is remarkable for columns somewhat resembling those subsequently termed **Doric.** Each of the four columns in the tomb is about 17 feet high, and has sixteen sides; the ceiling between each connecting beam, which runs from column to column, is vaulted. The columns in the southern tombs have lotus capitals, and are exceedingly graceful.

The **Tomb of Åmeni** belongs to the northern group of tombs; he is not the head of the family which was buried at Beni Hasân, as has been sometimes asserted, for he had no children. (*Recueil de Travaux*, I., p. 175.) Åmeni-Åmenemḫāt lived during the reign of Usertsen I., the second king of the XIIth dynasty; he was one of the feudal lords of Egypt, and chief of the nome of Meḥ or Antinoë, and chief president of the prophets. When quite a young man he was sent in the place of his father, who was too old for such work, to Ethiopia at the head of an army; he settled the frontiers of the country there, and came back to the king laden with spoil and tribute. In many other expeditions he was also perfectly successful. In the inscription on the tomb he says, " I have done all that I have said. I am a gracious and a compassionate man, and a ruler who loves his town. I have passed the course of years as the ruler of Meḥ, and all the labours of the palace have been carried out by my hands. I have given to the overseers of the temples of the gods of Meḥ 3,000 bulls with their cows, and I was in favour in the palace on account of it, for I carried all the products of the milk-bearing cows to the palace, and no contributions to the king's storehouses have been more than mine. I have never made a child grieve, I have never robbed the widow, I have never repulsed the labourer, I have never shut up a herdsman, I have never impressed, for forced labour, the labourers of a man who only employed five men; there was never a person miserable in my time, no one went hungry during my rule, for if there were years of scarcity I ploughed up all the arable land in the nome of Meḥ, up to its very frontiers on the north and south. By this means I made its people live and procured for them provisions, so that there was not a hungry person among them. I gave to the widow the same amount as I gave to the married woman, and I made no distinction between the great and the little in all that I gave. And, behold, when the inundation was great, and the owners of the land became rich thereby, I laid no additional tax upon the fields." The pictures on the walls represent scenes on the farm, the battle-field, the hunting ground and the river ; the various domestic pursuits of women are portrayed with wonderful skill. Ámeni-Ámenemḥāt, 𓏭𓈖𓏜𓏜, was the son of the lady Ḥennu ; the name of his father is not given.

The **Tomb of Chnemu-Ḥetep** also belongs to the northern group of tombs. Chnemu-ḥetep 𓊹𓃟𓊵𓏏𓊪 was one of the feudal lords of Egypt, a " royal relative," and the commandant of the land on the east side of the nome of Meḥ as far as the Arabian mountains ; he lived during the reign of (𓇓𓈖𓈖𓈖) 𓅐𓇳 (𓇋𓈖𓏜𓏏) " Nub-kau-Rā, son of the sun, Ámenemḥāt," the third king of the XIIth dynasty. Of the history of this Egyptian gentleman the following facts are known. During one of the expeditions which Ámenemḥāt I. made through Egypt, he raised to the rank of a feudal lord and "governor of the hilly land on the east of the nome of Meḥ," or Antinoë, the maternal grand-father of Chnemu-Ḥetep. In the reign of Usertsen I., the son of Ámenemḥāt I., the title of nobility conferred upon this man in the preceding reign was confirmed, and a large tract of land, lying between the Nile and the Libyan mountains, was added to his estates ; higher titles were also bestowed upon him in addition to those which he already possessed. The lands on the east side of the river, together with all his titles, passed into the hands of his eldest son Necht. Necht had a sister called Beqt, who likewise had a right to inherit all titles and property. She married a man called Neḥerá, the son of Sebek-ānch, and bore to him an only son called Chnemuḥetep; it was for him that this tomb was built. After a time, for some reason not stated, the inheritance of Menāt-Chufu,* which had been held by his uncle Necht, became vacant, and Amenemḥāt II. handed it over to the young man Chnemu-ḥetep, together with all the titles and honours which his grandfather had enjoyed by the command of Amenemḥāt I. and Usertsen I. Chnemu-ḥetep married a lady called Chati, by whom he had seven children; one of whom, by the favour of Amenemḥāt II., became the ruler of Menāt-Chufu. It has been said that Chnemu-ḥetep's grandfather was the Ameni-Amenemḥāt whose tomb lies close by; it is, however, distinctly said in the inscription on Chnemu-ḥetep's tomb that he was called Sebek-ānch. This tomb is famous for a remarkable scene painted on the north wall, which represents the arrival in Egypt of a family of thirty-seven persons belonging to the Āāmu, a Semitic race, who appear to have come thither to settle. The first person in the scene is the Egyptian "royal scribe, Nefer-ḥetep," who holds in his hands a piece of writing which states that in the sixth year of Usertsen II. thirty-seven people of the Āāmu brought to Chnemu-ḥetep, the son of a feudal lord, paint for the eyes called  *mest'emet.* Behind the scribe stands an Egyptian superintendent, and behind him the Āāmu chief Abesha, "the prince of the foreign country," together with his fellow-countrymen and women, who have come with him; in addition to the eye-paint, they bring a goat as a present for Chnemu-ḥetep. The men of the Āāmu wear beards, and carry bows and arrows; both men and women are dressed in garments of many colours. The home of the Āāmu lay to the east of Palestine. In this picture some have seen a representation of the arrival of Jacob's sons in Egypt to buy corn; there is no evidence for the support of this theory. That the Āāmu were shepherds or Hyksos is another theory that has been put forth. The paintings in Chnemu-ḥetep's tomb are if anything more beautiful than those in that of Āmeni, and they represent with wonderful fidelity the spearing of fish, the netting of birds, the hunting of wild animals, etc., etc.

In the other tombs are most interesting scenes connected with the daily occupations and amusements of the ancient Egyptians. It is much to be wished that copies of all these could be taken, for year by year they are slowly but surely disappearing.

RÔDA.

Rôda, 182 miles from Cairo, and the seat of a large sugar manufactory, lies on the west bank of the river, just opposite Shêkh 'Abâdeh, or Antinoë, a town built by Hadrian, and named by him after Antinous,* who was drowned here in the Nile. To the south of Antinoë lies the convent of Abu Honnês (Father John), and in the districts in the immediate neighbourhood are the remains of several Coptic buildings which date back to the fifth century of our era. A little to the south-west of Rôda, lying inland, are the remains of the city of Hermopolis Magna, called in Egyptian ☐☐, or ☐☐, Chemennu, in Coptic Shmûn, ϢⲘⲞⲨⲚ, and in Arabic Eshmûnên; the tradition which attributes the building of this city to Eshmûn, son of Miṣr, is worthless. The Greeks called it Hermopolis, because the Egyptians there worshipped Thoth, ☐, the scribe of the gods, who was named by the Greeks Hermes. A little distance from the town is the spot where large numbers of the ibis, a bird sacred to Thoth, were buried.

* A Bathynian youth, a favourite of the Emperor Hadrian.

MELÂWÎ.

Melâwî, 188 miles from Cairo, is situated on the west bank of the river.

HAGGI KANDÎL.

Haggi Kandîl, 195 miles from Cairo, lies on the east bank of the river, about five miles from the ruins of the city built by Chut-en-áten, ⟨ 𓄿𓏏𓈖𓇳 ⟩, or Amenophis IV., the famous "heretic" king of the XVIIIth dynasty, whose prenomen was ⟨ 𓇳𓄤𓆣𓏲𓂝 ⟩, Nefer-cheperu-Rā uā-en-Rā. Amenophis IV. was the son of Amenophis III., by a Mesopotamian princess called Thi, who came from the land of Mitanni. When the young prince Amenophis IV. grew up, it was found that he had conceived a rooted dislike to the worship of Ámen-Rā, the king of the gods and great lord of Thebes, and that he preferred the worship of the disk of the sun to that of Ámen-Rā; as a sign of his opinions he called himself "beloved of the sun's disk," instead of the usual and time-honoured "beloved of Ámen." The native Egyptian priesthood disliked the foreign queen, and the sight of her son with his protruding chin, thick lips, and other characteristic features of the negro race, found no favour in their sight; that such a man should openly despise the worship of Ámen-Rā was a thing intolerable to the priesthood, and angry words and acts were, on their part, the result. In answer to their objections the king ordered the name of Ámen-Rā to be chiselled out of all the monuments, even from his father's names. Rebellion then broke out, and Chut-en-áten thought it best to leave Thebes, and to found a new city for himself at a place between Memphis and Thebes, now called Tell el-Amarna. The famous architect Bek, whose father, Men, served under Amenophis III., designed the temple buildings, and in a very short time a splendid town with beautiful granite sculptures sprang out of the desert.

As an insult to the priests and people of Thebes, he built a sandstone and granite temple at Thebes in honour of the god Harmachis. When Chut-en-âten's new town, Chut-âten, "the splendour of the sun's disk," was finished, his mother Thi came to live there; and here the king passed his life quietly with his mother, wife, and seven daughters. He died leaving no male issue, and each of the husbands of his daughters became king. In 1887 a number of important cuneiform tablets, which confirmed in a remarkable manner many facts connected with this period of Egyptian history, were found at Tell el-Amarna (see page 13). The tombs in the rocks near Tell el-Amarna are of considerable interest.

GEBEL ABU FAḌAH.

Seventeen miles south of Haggi Ḳandîl, 212 miles from Cairo, on the east side of the river, is the range of low mountains about twelve miles long known by this name. Towards the southern end of this range there are some crocodile mummy pits.

MANFALÛṬ.

Manfalûṭ, $223\frac{1}{2}$ miles from Cairo, on the west bank of the Nile, occupies the site of an ancient Egyptian town; Leo Africanus says that the town was destroyed by the Romans, and adds that it was rebuilt under Muḥammedan rule. In his time he says that huge columns and buildings inscribed with hieroglyphs were still visible. The Coptic name Manbalot, "place of the sack,"* is the original of its Arabic name to-day.

ASYÛṬ.

Asyûṭ, $249\frac{1}{2}$ miles from Cairo, is the capital of the province of the same name, and the seat of the Inspector-General of Upper Egypt; it stands on the site of the

* ⲙⲁ ⲛ ⲃⲁⲗⲟⲧ.

ancient Egyptian city called —⋅— 𓄿 𓃭 𓊖 *Seut*, whence the
Arabic name Siût or Asyût, and the Coptic ⲥⲓⲱⲟⲩⲧ.
The Greeks called the city Lycopolis, or "wolf city,"
probably because the jackal-headed Anubis was worshipped
there. Asyût is a large city, with spacious bazaars and fine
mosques; it is famous for its red pottery and for its market,
held every Sunday, to which wares from Arabia and Upper
Egypt are brought. The American Missionaries have a
large establishment, and the practical, useful education of
the natives by these devoted men is carried on here, as well
as at Cairo, on a large scale. The Arabic geographers
described it as a town of considerable size, beauty, and
importance, and before the abandonment of the Sûdân by
the Khedive, all caravans from that region stopped there.
In the hills to the west of the town are a number of ancient
Egyptian tombs, which date back as far as the XIIIth
dynasty. A large number have been destroyed during the
present century for the sake of the limestone which forms
the walls. When M. Denon stayed here he said that the
number of hieroglyphic inscriptions which cover the tombs
was so great that many months would be required to read,
and many years to copy them. The disfigurement of the
tombs dates from the time when the Christians took up
their abode in them.

Fifteen miles farther south is the Coptic town of **Abu
Tîg**, the name of which appears to be derived from
ΑΠΟΘΗΚΗ, a "granary;" and 14½ miles beyond, 279 miles
from Cairo, is Kâu el-Kebîr (the ⲕⲱⲟⲩ of the Copts), which
marks the site of Antaeopolis, the capital of the Antaeopolite
nome in Upper Egypt. The temple which formerly existed
here was dedicated to Antaeus, the Libyan wrestler, who
fought with Hercules. In the plain close by it was thought
that the battle between Horus, the son of Osiris and Isis,
and Set or Typhon, the murderer of Osiris, took place;

Typhon was overcome, and fled away in the form of a crocodile. In Christian times Antaeopolis was the seat of a bishop.

Ṭaḥṭah, 291½ miles from Cairo, contains some interesting mosques, and is the home of a large number of Copts, in consequence of which, probably, the town is kept clean.

Sûhâk (Sohag), and the White and Red Monasteries.

Sûhâk, 317½ miles from Cairo, is the capital of the province of Girgeh; near it are the White and Red Monasteries.

The Dêr el-Abyaḍ or "**White Monastery,**" so-called because of the colour of the stone of which it is built, but better known by the name of Amba Shenûdah, is situated on the west bank of the river near Sûhâk, 317½ miles from Cairo. "The peculiarity of this monastery is that the interior was once a magnificent basilica, while the exterior was built by the Empress Helena, in the ancient Egyptian style. The walls slope inwards towards the summit, where they are crowned with a deep overhanging cornice. The building is of an oblong shape, about 200 feet in length by 90 wide, very well built of fine blocks of stone; it has no windows outside larger than loopholes, and these are at a great height from the ground. Of these there are twenty on the south side and nine at the east end. The monastery stands at the foot of the hill, on the edge of the Libyan desert, where the sand encroaches on the plain. . . . . . . The ancient doorway of red granite has been partially closed up." (Curzon, *Monasteries of the Levant*, p. 131.) There were formerly six gates; the single entrance now remaining is called the "mule gate," because when a certain heathen princess came riding on a mule to desecrate the church, the earth opened and swallowed her up. The walls enclose a space measuring about 240 feet by 133 feet. The convent was dedicated to Shenûti, a celebrated Coptic saint who lived in the fourth century of our era.*   Curzon says (*op. cit.*, p. 132) . . . . . . "The tall granite columns of the ancient church reared themselves like an avenue on either side of the desecrated nave, which is now open to the sky, and is used as a promenade for a host of chickens. . . . . The principal entrance was formerly at the west end, where there is a small vestibule, immediately within the door of which, on the left hand, is a small chapel, perhaps the baptistery, about twenty-five feet long, and still in tolerable preservation. It is a splendid specimen of the richest Roman architecture of the latter empire, and is truly an imperial little room. The arched ceiling is of stone; and there are three beautifully ornamented niches on each side. The upper end is semi-circular, and has been entirely covered with a profusion of sculpture in panels, cornices, and every kind of archi-tectural enrichment. When it was entire, and covered with gilding, painting, or mosaic, it must have been most gorgeous. The altar on such a chapel as this was probably of gold, set full of gems; or if it was the bapistery, as I suppose, it most likely contained a bath of the most precious jasper, or of some of the more rare kinds of marble, for the immersion of the converted heathen, whose entrance into the church was not permitted until they had been purified with the waters of baptism in a building without the door of the house of God" (p. 135). The library once contained over a hundred parchment books, but these were destroyed by the Mamelukes when they last sacked the convent.

The Dêr el-Aḥmar or **"Red Monastery,"** so-called be-cause of the red colour of the bricks of which it is built, was also built by the Empress Helena; it is smaller and

---

* Shenûdah, Coptic ⲱⲉⲛⲟⲩϯ Shenûti, was born A.D. 333; he died at midday on July 2, A.D. 451.

better preserved than the White Monastery, and was dedicated to the Abba Bêsa, the disciple and friend of Shenûti. The pillars of both churches were taken from Athribis, which lay close by; the orientation of neither church is exact, for their axes point between N.E. and N.E. by E. The ruined church of Armant near Thebes is built on the same model..

AḤMÎM.

A few miles south of Sûhâk, on the east bank of the river, lies the town of **Aḥmîm,** called Shmin or Chmim, ϣⲙⲓⲛ, Ⲭⲙⲓⲙ, by the Copts, and Panopolis by the Greeks; Strabo and Leo Africanus say that it was one of the most ancient cities of Egypt. The ithyphallic god Ȧmsu, identified by the Greeks with Pan, was worshipped here, and the town was famous for its linen weavers and stone cutters. Its Egyptian name was 𓏤 𓎢 𓆇 Ȧpu. In ancient days it had a large population of Copts, and large Coptic monasteries stood close by.

Menshiah, on the west bank of the river, 328½ miles from Cairo, stands on the site of a city which is said to have been the capital of the Panopolite nome; its Coptic name was Psôi, ⲯⲱⲓ. In the time of Shenûti the Blemmyes, a nomad warlike Ethiopian tribe, invaded Upper Egypt, and having acquired much booty, they returned to Psôi or Menshiah, and settled down there.

Girgeh, on the east bank of the river, 341½ miles from Cairo, has a large Christian population, and is said to occupy the site of the ancient This, whence sprang the first dynasty of historical Egyptian kings.

ABYDOS.*

Abydos,† in Egyptian ✶ⳃⳤ Åbṭu, Coptic ⲉⲃⲱⲧ, Arabic Harabat el-Madfûnah, on the west bank of the Nile, was one of the most renowned cities of ancient Egypt ; it was famous as the chief seat of the worship of Osiris in Upper Egypt, because the head of this god was supposed to be buried here. The town itself was dedicated to Osiris, and the temple in it, wherein the most solemn ceremonies connected with the worship of this god were celebrated, was more revered than any other in the land. The town and its necropolis were built side by side, and the custom usually followed by the Egyptians in burying their dead away from the town in the mountains was not followed in this case. Though the hills of fine white stone were there ready, the people of Abydos did not make use of them for funereal purposes ; the sandy plain interspersed every here and there with rocks was the place chosen for burial. The town of Abydos, a small town even in its best time, was built upon a narrow tongue of land situated between the canal, which lies inland some few miles, and the desert. It owed its importance solely to the position it held as a religious centre, and from this point of view it was the second city in Egypt. Thebes, Abydos, and Heliopolis practically represented the homes of religious thought and learning in Egypt. The necropolis of Abydos is not much older than the VIth dynasty, and the tombs found there

---

* The Temples at Abydos are visited by Messrs. Cook's travellers on the return journey to Cairo.

† Greek Ἄβυδος ; see Pape, *Wörterbuch*, p. 4. That the name was pronounced Abȳdos, and not Abўdos, is clear from :—

καὶ Σηστὸν καὶ Ἄβυδον ἔχον καὶ δῖαν Ἀρίσβην.

Iliad, ii., 836.

belonging to this period are of the mastaba class. During the XIth and XIIth dynasties the tombs took the form of small pyramids, which were generally built of brick, and the ancient rectangular form of tomb was revived during the XVIIIth dynasty. Abydos attained its greatest splendour under the monarchs of the XIth and XIIth dynasties, and though its plain was used as a burial ground as late as Roman times, it became of little or no account as early as the time of Psammetichus I. It has often been assumed that the town of Abydos is to be identified with This, the home of Menes, the first historical king of Egypt; the evidence derived from the exhaustive excavations made by M. Mariette does not support this assumption. No trace of the shrine of Osiris, which was as famous in Upper Egypt as was the shrine of the same god at Busiris in Lower Egypt, has been found in the temple; neither can any trace be discovered of the royal tombs which Rameses II. declares he restored. Plutarch says that wealthy inhabitants of Egypt were often brought to Abydos to be buried near the mummy of Osiris, and curiously enough, the tombs close to certain parts of the temple of Osiris are more carefully executed than those elsewhere. Of Abydos Strabo says (Bk. XVII., cap. i., sec. 42), "Above this city (Ptolemaïs) is Abydos, where is the palace of Memnon, constructed in a singular manner, entirely of stone, and after the plan of the Labyrinth, which we have described, but not composed of many parts. It has a fountain situated at a great depth. There is a descent to it through an arched passage built with single stones of remarkable size and workmanship. There is a canal which leads to this place from the great river. About the canal is a grove of Egyptian acanthus, dedicated to Apollo. Abydos seems once to have been a large city, second to Thebes. At present it is a small town. But if, as they say, Memnon is called Ismandes by the Egyptians, the Labyrinth might be a Memnonium, and the

work of the same person who constructed those at Abydos
and at Thebes; for in those places, it is said, are some
Memnonia. At Abydos Osiris is worshipped; but in the
temple of Osiris no singer, nor player on the pipe, nor on
the cithara, is permitted to perform at the commencement
of the ceremonies celebrated in honour of the god, as ¦s
usual in rites celebrated in honour of the gods." (Bk. XVII.
1, 44, Falconer's translation.) The principal monuments
which have been brought to light by the excavations of
M. Mariette at Abydos are:—

I. The **Temple of Seti I.,*** and the **Temple of
Rameses II.**

The 'Temple of Seti I., better known as the **Memnonium**, is built of fine white calcareous stone upon an
artificial foundation made of stone, earth and sand, which has
been laid upon a sloping piece of land; it was called Men-
māt-Rā,† after the prenomen of its builder. The Phœnician
graffiti show that the temple must have ceased to be used
at a comparatively early period. It would seem that it was
nearly finished when Seti I. died, and that his son Rameses
II. only added the pillars in front and the decoration.
Its exterior consists of two courts, A and B, the wall which
divides them, and the façade; all these parts were built by
Rameses II. The pillars are inscribed with religious scenes
and figures of the king and the god Osiris. On the large
wall to the south of the central door. is an inscription in
which Rameses II. relates all that he has done for the
honour of his father's memory, how he erected statues of

---

* The plans of the principal temples of Egypt printed in this book
are copied from those which accompany the *Rapport sur les Temples
Égyptiens adressé à S.E. Le Ministre des Travaux Publics* par Grand
Bey. This gentleman's plans were made as recently as 1888, and are
more complete than the more elaborate drawings given by Lepsius
in his *Denkmäler*, and by other *savants*.

† ☉ 𓏤 𓎛

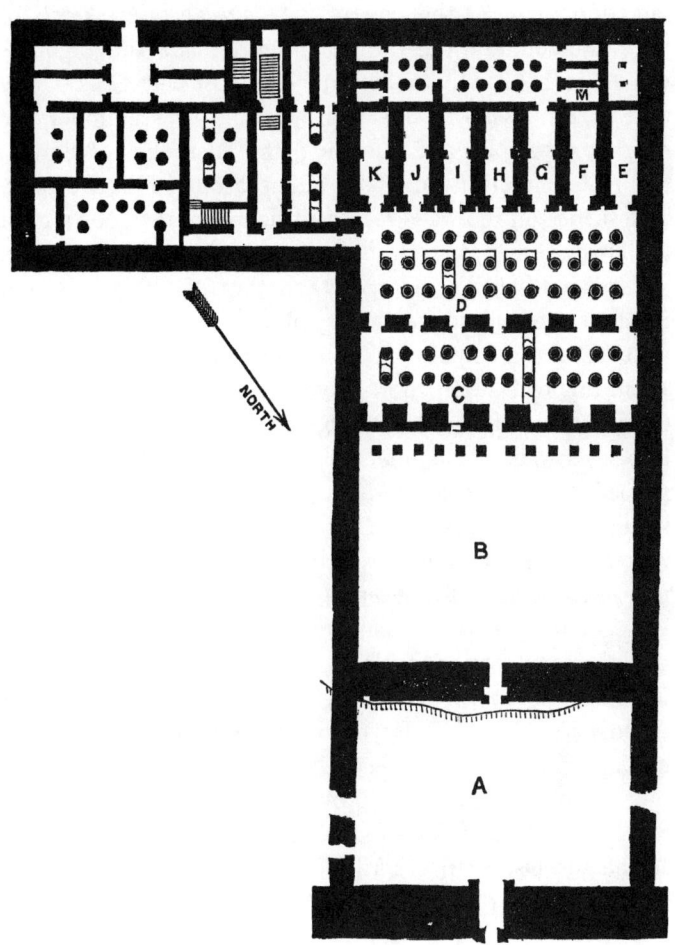

Plan of the Temple of Seti I. at Abydos.

him at Thebes and Memphis, and how he built up the sacred doors. At the end of it he gives a brief sketch of his childhood, and the various grades of rank and dignities which he held. In the interior the first hall, C, is of the time of Rameses II., but it is possible to see under the rough hieroglyphics of this king, the finer ones of Seti I.; this hall contains twenty-four pillars arranged in two rows. The scenes on the walls represent figures of the gods and of the king offering to them, the names of the nomes, etc., etc. The second hall, D, is larger than the first, the style and finish of the sculptures are very fine, the hieroglyphics are in relief, and it contains 36 columns, arranged in three rows. From this hall seven short naves dedicated to Horus, Isis, Osiris, Amen, Harmachis, Ptah, and Seti I. respectively, lead into seven vaulted chambers, E, F, G, H, I, J, K, beautifully shaped and decorated, which are dedicated to the same beings. The scenes on the walls of six of these chambers represent the ceremonies which the king ought to perform in them ; those in the seventh refer to the apotheosis of the king. At the end of chamber G is a door which leads into the sanctuary of Osiris, L, and in the corridor M is the famous TABLET OF ABYDOS, which gives the names of seventy-six kings of Egypt, beginning with Menes and ending with Seti I. The value of this most interesting monument has been pointed out on p. 3.

The **Temple of Rameses II.** was dedicated by this king to the god Osiris ; it lies a little to the north of the temple of Seti I. Many distinguished scholars thought that this was the famous shrine which all Egypt adored, but the excavations made there by M. Mariette proved that it was not. It would seem that during the French occupation of Egypt in the early part of this century this temple stood almost intact; since that time, however, so much damage has been wrought upon it, that the portions of wall which now remain are only about eight or nine feet

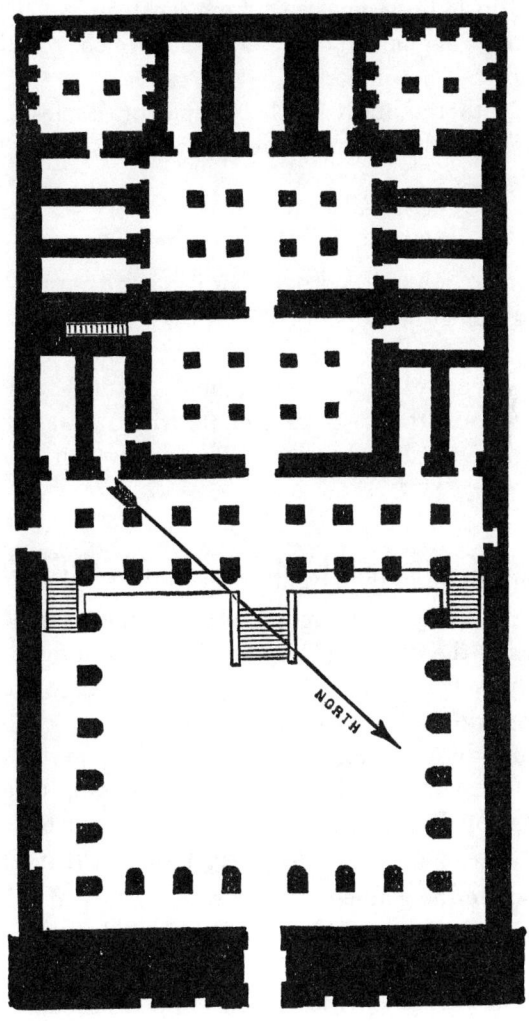

Plan of the Temple of Rameses II. at Abydos.

high. The fragment of the second Tablet of Abydos, now in the British Museum, came from this temple. The few scenes and fragments of inscriptions which remain are interesting but not important.

A little to the north of the temple of Rameses II. is a Coptic monastery, the church of which is dedicated to Amba Musas.

FARSHÛT AND ḲAṢR EṢ-ṢAYYÂD.

FARSHÛT, 368 miles from Cairo, on the west bank of the river, called in Coptic Ⲃⲉⲣⲥ̅ⲟⲟⲧⲧ, contains a sugar factory.

ḲAṢR EṢ-ṢAYYÂD, or "the hunter's castle," 376 miles from Cairo, on the east bank of the river, marks the site of the ancient Chenoboscion. The Copts call the town ϣⲉⲛⲉⲥⲏⲧ.

ḲENEH AND THE TEMPLE OF DENDERAH.*

Keneh, 405½ miles from Cairo, on the east bank of the river, is the capital of the province of the same name. This city is famous for its dates, and the trade which it carries on with the Arabian peninsula.

A short distance from the river, on the west bank, a little to the north of the village of Denderah, stands the **Temple of Denderah**, which marks the site of the classical Tentyra or Tentyris, called Ⲧⲉⲛⲧⲱⲣⲉ by the Copts, where the goddess Hathor was worshipped. During the Middle Empire quantities of flax and linen fabrics

---

* The Greek Tentyra, or Tentyris, is derived from the Egyptian

Ta-en-ta-rert; the name is also written

were produced at Tentyra, and it gained some reputation thereby. In very ancient times Chufu or Cheops, a king of the IVth dynasty, founded a temple here, but it seems never to have become of much importance,* probably because it lay so close to the famous shrines of Abydos and Thebes. The wonderfully preserved Temple now standing there is probably not older than the beginning of our era; indeed, it cannot, in any case, be older than the time of the later Ptolemies: hence it must be considered as the architectural product of a time when the ancient Egyptian traditions of sculpture were already dead and nearly forgotten. It is, however, a majestic monument, and worthy of careful examination.† Strabo says (Bk. xvii., ch. i. 44) of this town and its inhabitants: "Next to Abydos is . . . . . . the city Tentyra, where the crocodile is held in peculiar abhorrence, and is regarded as the most odious of all animals. For the other Egyptians, although acquainted with its mischievous disposition, and hostility towards the human race, yet worship it, and abstain from doing it harm. But the people of Tentyra track and destroy it in every way. Some, however, as they say of the Psyllians of Cyrenæa, possess a certain natural antipathy to snakes, and the people of Tentyra have the same dislike to crocodiles, yet they suffer no injury from them, but dive and cross the river when no other person ventures to do so. When crocodiles were brought to Rome to be exhibited, they were attended by some of the Tentyritæ.

* M. Mariette thought that a temple to Hathor existed at Denderah during the XIIth, XVIIIth and XIXth dynasties.

† "Accessible comme il l'est aujourd'hui jusque dans la dernière de ses chambres, il semble se présenter au visiteur comme un livre qu'il n'a qu'à ouvrir et à consulter. Mais le temple de Dendérah est, en somme, un monument terriblement complexe. . . . Il faudrait plusieurs années pour copier tout ce vaste ensemble, et il faudrait vingt volumes du format (folio !) de nos quatre volumes de planches pour le publier."
—Mariette, *Dendérah, Description Générale*, p. 10.

A reservoir was made for them with a sort of stage on one of the sides, to form a basking place for them on coming out of the water, and these persons went into the water, drew them in a net to the place, where they might sun themselves and be exhibited, and then dragged them back again to the reservoir. The people of Tentyra worship Venus. At the back of the fane of Venus is a temple of Isis; then follow what are called Typhoneia, and the canal leading to Coptos, a city common both to the Egyptians and Arabians." (Falconer's translation.) It will be remembered that Juvenal witnessed a fight between the crocodile worshippers of Kom Ombo and the crocodile haters of Tentyra.

On the walls and on various other parts of the temples are the names of several of the Roman Emperors; the famous portraits of Cleopatra and Cæsarion her son are on the end wall of the exterior. Passing along a dromos for about 250 feet, the portico, A, open at the top, and supported by twenty-four Hathor-headed columns, arranged in six rows, is reached. Leaving this hall by the doorway facing the entrance, the visitor arrives in a second hall, B, having six columns and three small chambers on each side. The two chambers C and D have smaller chambers on the right and left, E was the so-called sanctuary, and in F the emblem of the god worshipped in the temple was placed. From a room on each side of C a staircase led up to the roof. The purposes for which the chambers were used are stated by M. Mariette in his *Dendérah, Descrip. Gén. du Grand Temple de cette ville.* On the ceiling of the portico is the famous "Zodiac," which was thought to have been made in ancient Egyptian times; the Greek inscription=A.D. 35, written in the twenty-first year of Tiberius, and the names of the Roman Emperors, have clearly proved that, like that at Esneh, it belongs to the Roman time. The Zodiac from Denderah, now at Paris, was cut out, with the permis-

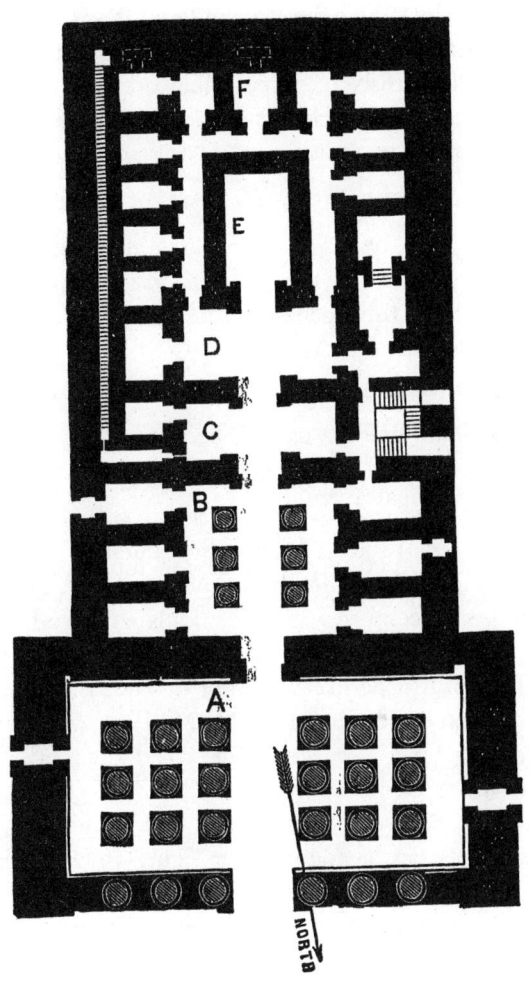

Plan of the Temple at Denderah.

sion of Muḥammad 'Ali, in 1821, from the small temple of Osiris, generally called the "Temple on the Roof."

The **Iseium** is situated to the south of the temple of Hathor, and consists of three chambers and a corridor; near by is a pylon which was dedicated to Isis in the 31st year of Cæsar Augustus.

The **Mammisi,** ⌐⌐ 𓅓, *Pa-mestu,* or "house of giving birth," also built by Augustus, is the name given to the celestial dwelling where the goddess was supposed to have brought forth the third person of the triad which was adored in the temple close by.

The **Typhonium** stands to the north of the Temple of Hathor, and was so named because the god Bes 𓀀, figures of whom occur on its walls, was confused with Typhon; it measures about 120 feet × 60 feet, and is surrounded by a peristyle of twenty-two columns.

The Temple of Denderah was nearly buried among the rubbish which centuries had accumulated round about it, and a whole village of wretched mud-huts actually stood upon the roof! The excavation of this fine monument was undertaken and completed by M. Mariette, who published many of the texts and scenes inscribed upon its walls in his work mentioned above.

The crocodile was worshipped at Kom Ombo, and Juvenal gives an account of a fight which took place between the people of this place and those of Denderah, in which one of the former stumbled, while running along, and was caught by his foes, cut up, and eaten.

A few miles beyond Denderah, on the east bank of the river, lies the town of **Koft,** the 𓄿𓏛𓊖 *Qebt* of the hieroglyphics, and ⲕⲉϥⲧ of the Copts; it was the principal city in the Coptites nome, and was the Thebaïs Secunda of the Itineraries. From Ḳoft the road which crossed the desert to Berenice on the Red Sea started, and the merchandise which passed through the town from the east, and the stone from the famous porphyry quarries in the Arabian desert must have made it wealthy and important. It held the position of a port on the Nile for merchandise from a very early period ; and there is no doubt that every Egyptian king who sent expeditions to Punt, and the countries round about, found Ḳofṭ most usefully situated for this purpose. A temple dedicated to the ithyphallic god Amsu, Isis and Osiris, stood here. It was nearly destroyed by Diocletian A.D. 292. A copy of a medical papyrus in the British Museum states that the work was originally dis covered at Coptos during the time of Cheops, a king of the IVth dynasty ; it is certain then that the Egyptians considered this city to be of very old foundation.

NAKÂDAH (NAGADA).

NAKÂDAH, 428 miles from Cairo, on the west bank of the river, nearly opposite the island of Maṭarah, was the home of a large number of Copts in early Christian times, and several monasteries were situated there. The four which now remain are dedicated to the Cross, St. Michael, St. Victor, and St. George respectively, and tradition says that they were founded by the Empress Helena ; the most important of them is that of St. Michael. The church in this monastery "is one of the most remarkable Christian structures in Egypt, possessing as it does some unique peculiarities. There are four churches, of which three stand side by side in such a manner that they have a single continuous western wall. Two of the four have an apsidal haikal with rectagular side chapels, while the other two are entirely rectangular ; but the two apses differ from all other apses in Egyptian churches by projecting . . . beyond the eastern wall and by showing an outward curvature. They form a solitary exception to the rule that the Coptic apse is

merely internal, and so far belong rather to Syrian architecture than to Coptic. The principal church shows two
other features which do not occur elsewhere in the Christian
buildings of Egypt, namely, an external atrium surrounded
with a cloister, and a central tower with a clerestory . . . . .
Possibly the same remark may apply to the structure of the
iconostasis, which has two side-doors and no central
entrance, though this arrangement is not quite unparalleled
in the churches of Upper Egypt, and may be a later alteration. It will be noticed that the church has a triple
western entrance from the cloisters." (Butler, *Ancient Coptic
Churches of Egypt*, Vol. I., p. 361.)

LUXOR (EL-ḲUṢÛR) AND THEBES.

Luxor, 450 miles from Cairo, on the east bank of the river, is a small town with a few thousand inhabitants, and owes its importance to the fact that it is situated close to the ruins of the temples of the ancient city of Thebes. The name Luxor is a corruption of the Arabic name of the place, El-Ḳuṣûr, which means "the palaces." Ancient Thebes stood on both sides of the Nile, and was generally called in hieroglyphics Uast; that part of the city which was situated on the east bank of the river, and included the temples of Karnak and Luxor, appears to have been called Âptet, whence the Coptic Ⲧⲁⲡⲉ and the name Thebes have been derived. The cuneiform inscriptions and Hebrew Scriptures call it No (Ezek. xxx. 14) and No-Amon* (Nahum iii. 8), and the Greek and Roman writers Diospolis Magna. When or by whom Thebes was founded it is impossible to say. Diodorus says that it is the most ancient city of Egypt; some say that, like Memphis, it was founded by Menes, and others, that it was a colony from Memphis. It is certain, however, that it did not become a city of the first importance until after the decay of Memphis, and as the progress of Egyptian civilization was from north to south, this is only what was to be expected. During the early dynasties no mention is made of Thebes, but we know that as early as the XIIth dynasty some kings were buried there.

The spot on which ancient Thebes stood is so admirably adapted for the site of a great city, that it

* No-amon in Revised Version.

would have been impossible for the Egyptians to over look it. The mountains on the east and west side of the river sweep away from it, and leave a broad plain on each bank of several square miles in extent. It has been calculated that modern Paris could stand on this space of ground. We have, unfortunately, no Egyptian description of Thebes, or any statement as to its size; it may, however, be assumed from the remains of its buildings which still exist, that the descriptions of the city as given by Strabo and Diodorus are on the whole trustworthy. The fame of the greatness of Thebes had reached the Greeks of Homer's age, and its "hundred gates" and 20,000 war chariots are referred to in Iliad IX, 381. The city must have reached its highest point of splendour during the rule of the XVIIIth and XIXth dynasties over Egypt, and as little by little the local god Âmen-Râ became the great god of all Egypt, his dwelling-place Thebes also gained in importance and splendour. The city suffered severely at the hands of Cambyses, who left nothing in it unburnt that fire would consume. Herodotus appears never to have visited Thebes, and the account he gives of it is not satisfactory; the account of Diodorus, who saw it about B.C. 57, is as follows: "Afterwards reigned Busiris, and eight of his posterity after him; the last of which (of the same name with the first) built that great city which the Egyptians call Diospolis, the Greeks Thebes; it was in circuit 140 stades (about twelve miles), adorned with stately public buildings, magnificent temples, and rich donations and revenues to admiration; and that he built all the private houses, some four, some five stories high. And to sum up all in a word, made it not only the most beautiful and stateliest city of Egypt, but of all others in the world. The fame therefore of the riches and grandeur of this city was so noised abroad in every place, that the poet Homer takes notice of it. . . . . . Although there are some that say it had not a hundred gates; but that there were many large porches to the temples, whence the city was called *Hecatompylus*, a hundred gates, for many gates: yet that it was certain they had in it 20,000 chariots of war; for there were a hundred stables all along the river from Memphis to Thebes towards Lybia, each of which was capable to hold two hundred horses, the marks and signs of which are visible at this day. And we have it related, that not only this king, but the succeeding princes from time to time, made it their business to beautify this city; for that there was no city under the sun so adorned with so many and stately monuments of gold, silver, and ivory, and multitudes of colossi and obelisks, cut out of one entire stone. For there were there four temples built, for beauty and greatness to be admired, the most ancient of which was in circuit thirteen furlongs (about two miles), and five and forty cubits high, and had a wall twenty-four feet broad. The ornaments of this temple were suitable to its magnificence, both for cost and workmanship. The fabric hath continued to our time, but the silver and the gold, and ornaments of ivory and precious stones were carried away by the Persians when Cambyses burnt the temples of Egypt. . . . There, they say, are the wonderful sepulchres of the ancient kings, which for state and grandeur far exceed all that posterity can attain unto at this day. The Egyptian priests say that in their sacred registers there are 47 of these sepulchres; but in the reign of Ptolemy Lagus there remained only 17, many of which were ruined and destroyed when I myself came into those parts." (Bk. I., caps. 45, 46, Booth's translation, pp. 23, 24.)

Strabo, who visited Thebes about B.C. 24, says :—" Next to the city of Apollo is Thebes, now called Diospolis, 'with her hundred gates, through each of which issue 200 men, with horses and chariots,' according to Homer, who mentions also its wealth; 'not all the wealth the palaces of Egyptian Thebes contain.' Other writers use the same language, and consider Thebes as the metropolis of Egypt. Vestiges of its magnitude still exist, which extend 80 stadia (about nine miles) in length. There are a great number of temples, many of which Cambyses mutilated. The spot is at present occupied by villages. One part of it, in which is the city, lies in Arabia ; another is in the country on the other side of the river, where is the Memnonium. Here are two colossal figures near one another, each consisting of a single stone. One is entire; the upper parts of the other, from the chair, are fallen down, the effect, it is said, of an earthquake. It is believed that once a day a noise as of a slight blow issues from the part of the statue which remains in the seat and on its base. When I was at those places with Ælius Gallus, and numerous friends and soldiers about him, I heard a noise at the first hour (of the day), but whether proceeding from the base or from the colossus, or produced on purpose by some of those standing around the base, I cannot confidently assert. For from the uncertainty of the cause, I am disposed to believe anything rather than that stones disposed in that manner could send forth sound. Above the Memnonium are tombs of kings in caves, and hewn out of the stone, about forty in number ; they are executed with singular skill, and are worthy of notice. Among the tombs are obelisks with inscriptions, denoting the wealth of the kings of that time, and the extent of their empire, as reaching to the Scythians, Bactrians, Indians, and the present Ionia ; the amount of tribute also, and the number of soldiers, which composed an army of about a million of men. The priests there are said to be, for the most part, astronomers and philosophers. The former compute the days, not by the moon, but by the sun, introducing into the twelve months, of thirty days each, five days every year. But in order to complete the whole year, because there is (annually) an excess of a part of a day, they form a period

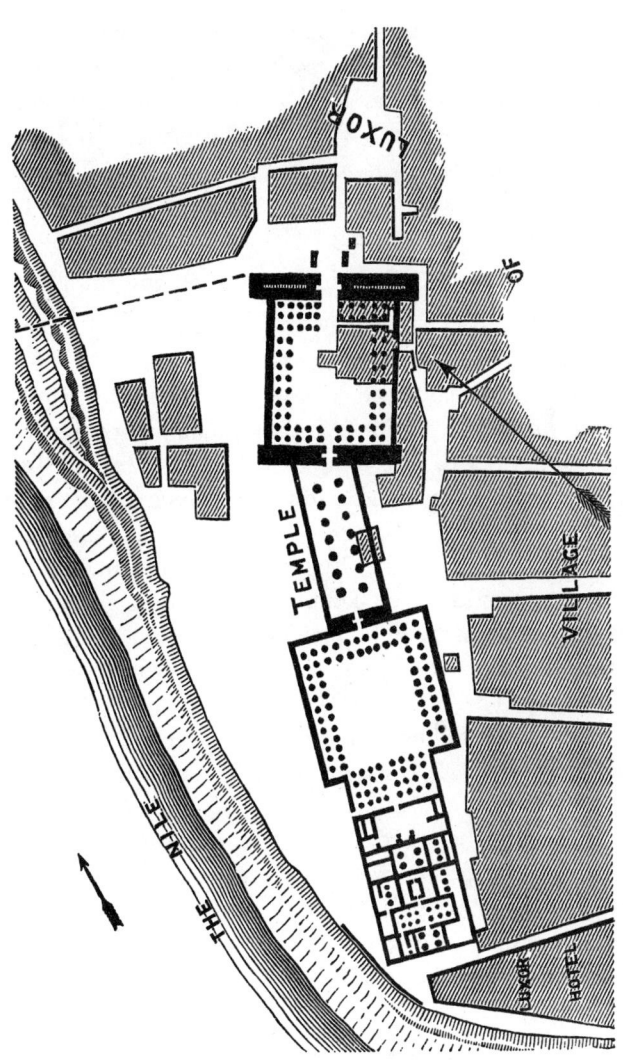

The Temple of Luxor.

from out of whole days and whole years, the supernumerary portions of which in that period, when collected together, amount to a day.*   They ascribe to Mercury (Thoth) all knowledge of this kind.   To Jupiter, whom they worship above all other deities, a virgin of the greatest beauty and of the most illustrious family (such persons the Greeks call pallades) is dedicated " . . . .   (Bk. XVII, chap. 1, sec. 46, translated by Falconer.)

The principal objects of interest on the east or right bank of the river are :—

I. The **Temple of Luxor.**   Compared with Karnak the temple of Luxor is not of any great interest.   Until very recently a large portion of the buildings, connected in ancient days with the temple, were quite buried by the accumulated rubbish and earth upon which a large number of houses stood.   During the last five years excavations have been made by the Egyptian Government, and some interesting results have been obtained.   Among the antiquities thus brought to light may be mentioned a fine granite statue of Rameses II., the existence of which was never imagined.   The temple of Luxor was built on an irregular plan caused by following the course of the river, out of the waters of which its walls, on one side, rose ; it was founded by Amenophis III., about B.C. 1500.   About forty years after, Ḥeru-em-ḥeb added the great colonnade, and as the name of Seti I., B.C. 1366, occurs in places, it is probable that he executed some repairs to the temple.   His son Rameses II., B.C. 1333, set up two obelisks together with the colossi and the large pylon ; the large court, nearly 200 feet square, behind the pylon, was surrounded by a double row of columns.   The **Obelisk** now standing there records the names, titles, etc., of Rameses II., and stands about 82 feet high ; it is one of the finest specimens of sculpture

* See page 70.

known. Its fellow obelisk stands in the Place de la Concorde, Paris.

After the burning and sacking of this temple by the Persians, some slight repairs, and rebuilding of certain chambers, were carried out by some of the Ptolemies, the name of one of whom (Philopator) is found inscribed on the temple. Certain parts of the temple appear to have been used by the Copts as a church, for the ancient sculptures have been plastered over and painted with figures of saints, etc.

II. The **Temple at Karnak.** The ruins of the buildings at Karnak are perhaps the most wonderful of any in Egypt, and they merit many visits from the traveller. It is probable that this spot was "holy ground" from a very early to a very late period, and we know that a number of kings from Thothmes III. to Euergetes II. lavished much wealth to make splendid the famous shrine of Âmen in the Âpts, and other temples situated there. The temples of Luxor and Karnak were united by an avenue about 6,500 feet long and 80 feet wide, on each side of which was arranged a row of sphinxes; from the fact that these monuments are without names, M. Mariette thought that the avenue was constructed at the expense of the priests or the wealthy inhabitants of the town, just as in later days the pronaos of the temple at Denderah was built by the people of that town. At the end of this avenue, to the right, is a road which leads to the so-called **Temple of Mut,** which was also approached by an avenue of sphinxes. Within the enclosure there stood originally two temples, both of which were dedicated to Âmen, built during the reign of Amenophis III.; Rameses II. erected two obelisks in front of the larger temple. To the north-west of these a smaller temple was built in Ptolemaic times, and the ruins on one side of it show that the small temples which stood there were either founded or restored by Rameses II., Osorkon,

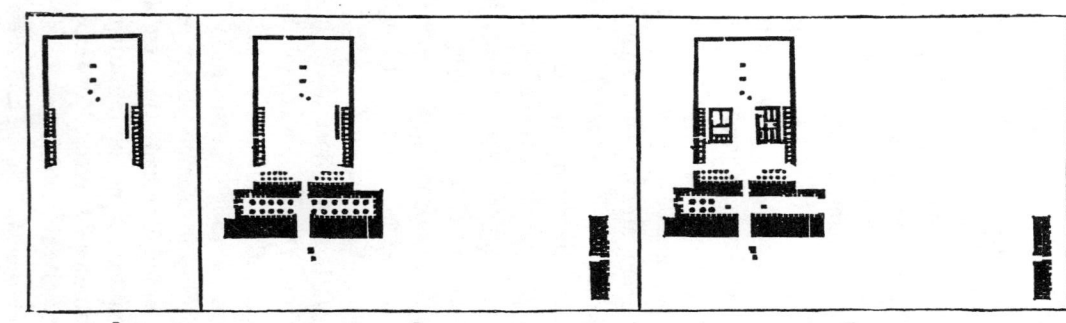

PLANS OF KARNAK—1–3.

1.   2.   3.

1. Karnak before the time of Thothmes I., B.C. 1633.
2. Karnak during the reign of Thothmes I.
3. Karnak during the reign of Queen Hātshepset, B.C. 1600.

From Mariette, *Karnak*, Pl. VI.

Thekeleth, Sabaco, Nectanebus I., and the Ptolemies. Behind the temple enclosure are the remains of a temple dedicated to Ptaḥ of Memphis by Thothmes III.; the three doors behind it and the courts into which they lead were added by Sabaco, Tirhakah, and the Ptolemies.

Returning to the end of the avenue of sphinxes which leads from Luxor to Karnak, a second smaller avenue ornamented with a row of ram-headed sphinxes on each side is entered; at the end of it stands the splendid pylon built by Ptolemy Euergetes II. Passing through the door, a smaller avenue of sphinxes leading to the temple built by Rameses III. is reached; the small avenue of sphinxes and eight of its columns were added by Rameses XIII. This temple was dedicated to Chonsu, and appears to have been built upon the site of an ancient temple of the time of Amenophis III. To the west of this temple is a smaller temple built by Ptolemy IX. Euergetes II.

The great Temple of Karnak fronted the Nile, and was approached by means of a small avenue of ram-headed sphinxes which were placed in position by Rameses II. Passing through the first propylon, a court or hall, having a double row of pillars down the centre, is entered; on each side is a corridor with a row of columns. On the right hand (south) side are the ruins of a temple built by Rameses III., and on the left are those of another built by Seti II. This court or hall was the work of Shashanq, the first king of the XXIInd dynasty. On each side of the steps leading through the second pylon was a colossal statue of Rameses II.; that on the right hand has now disappeared. Passing through this pylon, the famous " Hall of Columns" is entered. The twelve columns forming the double row in the middle are about sixty feet high and about thirty-five feet in circumference; the other columns, 122 in number, are about forty feet high and twenty-seven feet in circumference. Rameses I. set up one column,

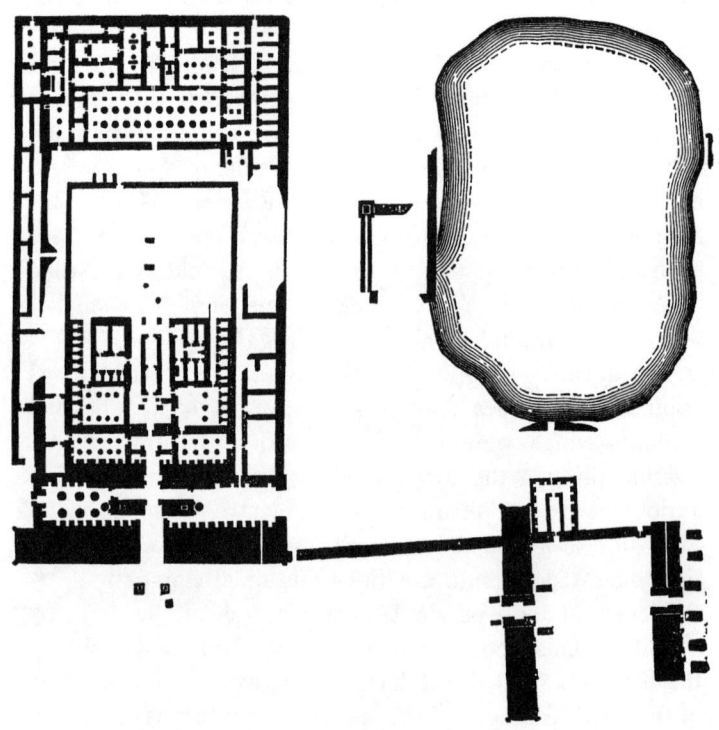

Karnak during the reign of Thothmes III., B.C. 1600.
From Mariette, *Karnak*, Pl. VI.

Seti I., the builder of this hall, set up seventy-nine, and the remaining fifty-four were set up by Rameses II. It is thought that this hall was originally roofed over. At the end of it is the third propylon, which was built by Amenophis III., and served as the entrance to the temple until the time of Rameses I. Between this and the next pylon is a narrow passage, in the middle of which stood two obelisks which were set up by Thothmes I.; the southern one is still standing, and bears the names of this king, but the northern one has fallen,* and its fragments show that Thothmes III. caused his name to be carved on it. At the southern end of this passage are the remains of a gate built by Rameses IX. The fourth and fifth pylons were built by Thothmes I. Between them stood fourteen columns, six of which were set up by Thothmes I., and eight by Amenophis II., and two granite obelisks; one of these still stands. These obelisks were hewn out of the granite quarry by the command of Ḥātshepset,† the daughter of Thothmes I., and sister of Thothmes II. and Thothmes III. This able woman set them up in honour of "father Åmen," and she relates in the inscriptions on the base of the standing obelisk that she covered their tops with *smu* metal, or copper, that they could be seen from a very great distance, and that she had them hewn and brought down to Thebes in about seven months, These obelisks were brought into their chamber from the south side, and were 98 and 105 feet high respectively; the masonry round their bases is of the time of Thothmes III. The sixth pylon and the two walls which

---

* It was standing when Pococke visited Egypt in 1737–1739.

† "Scarcely had the royal brother and husband of Hashop (*sic*) closed his eyes, when the proud queen threw aside her woman's veil, and appeared in all the splendour of Pharaoh, as a born king. For she laid aside her woman's dress, clothed herself in man's attire, and adorned herself with the crown and insignia of royalty." (Brugsch's *Egypt under the Pharaohs*, Vol. I., p. 349.)

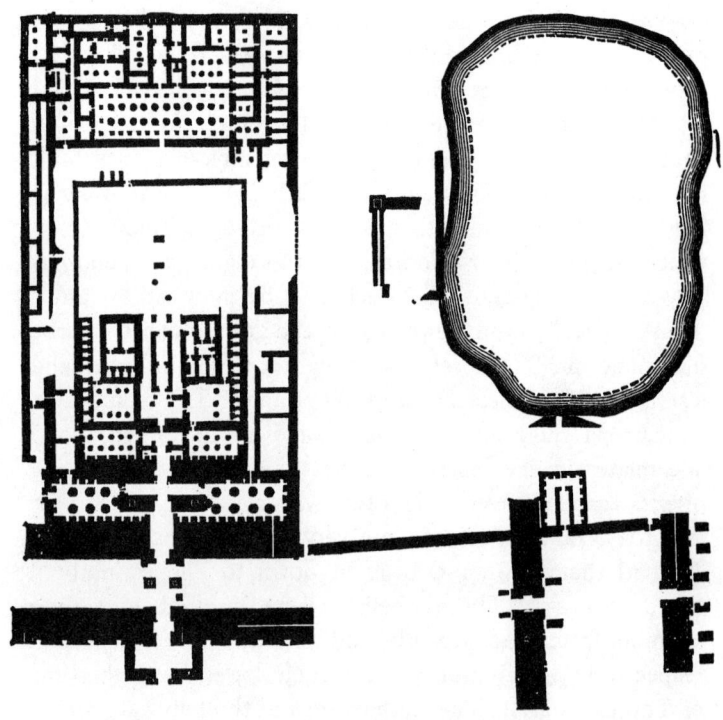

Karnak during the reign of Amenophis III., B.C. 1500.
From Mariette, *Karnak*, Pl. VI.

flank it on the north and south are the work of Thothmes III.,
but Seti II., Rameses III., and Rameses IV. have added
their cartouches to them. On this pylon are inscribed a
large number of geographical names of interest. Passing
through it, the visitor finds himself in a vestibule which
leads into a red granite oblong chamber, inscribed with the
name of Philip III. of Macedon, which is often said to have
formed the sanctuary. In the chambers on each side of it
are found the names of Amenophis I., Thothmes I., Thothmes
II., Ḥātshepset, and Thothmes III. The sanctuary stood
in the centre of the large court beyond the two oblong red
granite pedestals. In ancient days, when Thebes was
pillaged by her conquerors, it would seem that special care
was taken to uproot not only the shrine, but the very
foundations upon which it rested. Some fragments of
columns inscribed with the name of Usertsen I. found
there prove, however, that its foundation dates from
the reign of this king. Beyond the sanctuary court is
a large building of the time of Thothmes III. In it was
found the famous Tablet of Ancestors, now in Paris,
where this king is seen making offerings to a number of his
royal ancestors. On the north side of the building is
the chamber in which he made his offerings, and on the east
side is a chamber where he adored the hawk, the emblem
of the Sun-god Rā; this latter chamber was restored by
Alexander IV. Behind the great temple, and quite distinct
from it, was another small temple. On the south side of
the great temple was a lake which was filled by infiltration
from the Nile; it appears only to have been used for
processional purposes, as water for ablutionary and other
purposes was drawn from the well on the north side of the
interior of the temple. The lake was dug during the reign
of Thothmes III., and its stone quays probably belong to
the same period.

Passing through the gate at the southern end of the

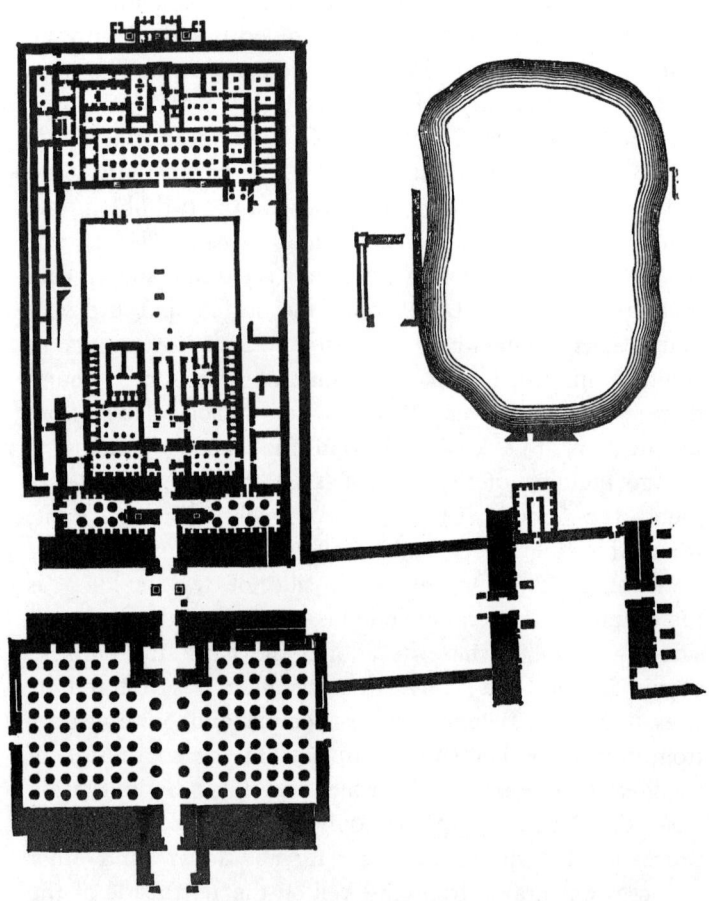

Karnak under Rameses II., B.C. 1333.
From Mariette, *Karnak*, Pl. VII.

passage in which stands the obelisk of Ḥātshepset, a long avenue with four pylons is entered; the first was built by Thothmes III., the second by Thothmes I., and the third and fourth by Ḥeru-em-ḥeb. Between these last two, on the east side stood a temple built by Amenophis II. On the north side of the Great Temple are the ruins of two smaller buildings which belong to the time of the XXVIth dynasty.

The outside of the north wall of the Great Hall of Columns is ornamented with some interesting scenes from the battles of Seti I. against the peoples who lived to the north-east of Syria and in Mesopotamia, called Shasu, Rutennu, and Charu. The king is represented as having conquered all these people, and returning to Thebes laden with much spoil and bringing many captives. It is doubtful if the events really took place in the order in which they are depicted; but the fidelity to nature, and the spirit and skill with which these bas-reliefs have been executed, make them some of the most remarkable sculptures known. The scene in which Seti I. is shown grasping the hair of the heads of a number of people, in the act of slaying them, is symbolic.

The outside of the south wall is ornamented with a large scene in which Shashanq (Shishak), the first king of the XXIInd dynasty, is represented smiting a group of kneeling prisoners; the god Âmen, in the form of a woman, is standing by presenting him with weapons of war. Here also are 150 cartouches, surmounted with heads, in which are written the names of the towns captured by Shishak. The type of features given to these heads by the sculptor shows that the vanquished peoples belonged to a branch of the great Semitic family. The hieroglyphics in one of the cartouches were supposed to read "the king of Judah," and to represent Jeroboam, who was vanquished by Shishak; it has now been proved conclusively that they form the name of a place called Iuta-melek. Passing along to the

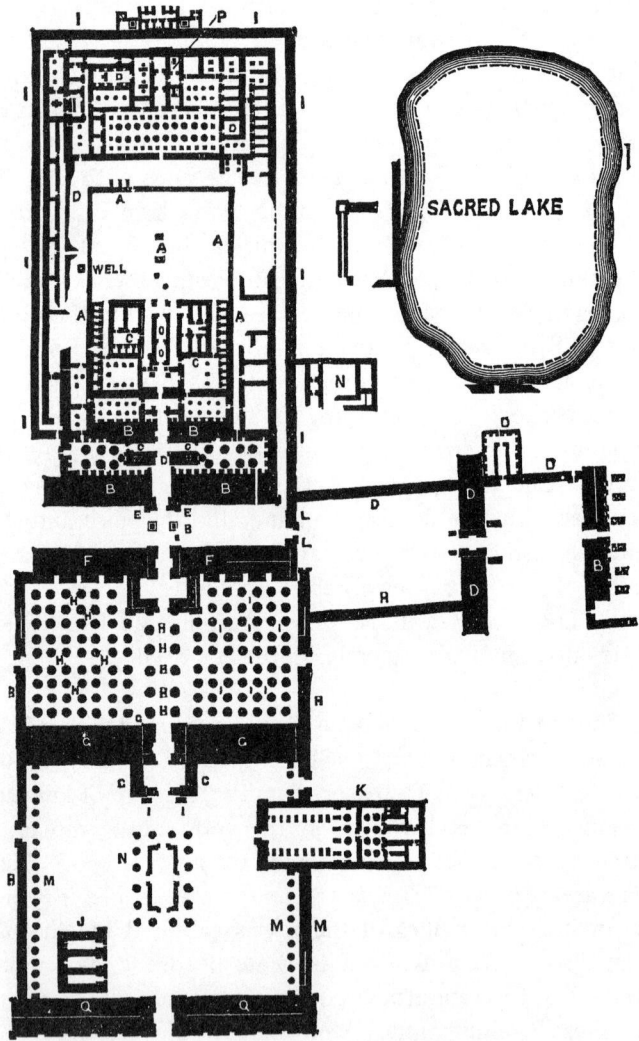

Karnak under the Ptolemies. From Mariette, *Karnak*, Pl. VII.

A. Walls standing before the time of Thothmes I.
B. Pylons built by Thothmes I.
O. Walls and obelisks of Hatshepset.
D. Walls, pylon, etc., of Thothmes III.
E. Gateway of Thothmes IV.
F. Pylon of Amenophis III.
G. Pylon of Rameses I.
H. Walls and columns of Seti I.
I. Columns, walls, and statues of Rameses II.

J. Temple of Seti II.
K. Temple of Rameses III.
L. Gateway of Rameses IX.
M. Pillars and walls of the XXIInd dynasty.
N. Pillars of Tirhakah.
O. Corridor of Philip III. of Macedon.
P. Chamber and shrine of Alexander II.
Q. Pylon built by the Ptolemies.

east, the visitor comes to a wall at right angles to the first, upon which is inscribed a copy of the poem of Pen-ta-urt, celebrating the victory of Rameses II. over the Cheta, in the fifth year of his reign; and on the west side of the wall is a stele on which is set forth a copy of the offensive and defensive treaty between this king and the prince of the Cheta.

The inscriptions on the magnificent ruins at Karnak show that from the time of Usertsen I., B.C. 2433, to that of Alexander IV., B.C. 312 (?), the religious centre* of Upper Egypt was at Thebes, and that the most powerful of the kings of Egypt who reigned during this period spared neither pains nor expense in adding to and beautifying the temples there.

The fury of the elements, the attacks of Egypt's enemies, and above all the annual inundation of the Nile, have helped to throw down these splendid buildings. The days are not far distant when, unless energetic measures are taken meanwhile, a large number of the columns in the wonderful hall of Seti I. must fall, and in their fall will do irreparable damage to the other parts of the building. It is much to be hoped that the public opinion of the civilized world will not allow these deeply interesting relics of a mighty nation to perish before their eyes. Steps should at once be taken to keep out the inundation, and if possible the tottering columns and walls should be strengthened.

---

* The short-lived heresy of the worship of the disk of the Sun instead of that of Åmen-Rā would not interfere with the general popularity of Theban temples.

On the west bank of the river the following are the most interesting antiquities :—

I. The **Temple of Ḳûrnah.** This temple was built by Seti I. in memory of his father Rameses I. ; it was completed by Rameses II., by whom it was re-dedicated to the memory of his father Seti I. Two pylons stood before it, and between them was an avenue of sphinxes. This temple was to all intents and purposes a cenotaph, and as such its position on the edge of the desert, at the entrance to a necropolis, is explained. In the temple were six columns, and on each side were several small chambers. The sculptures on the walls represent Rameses II. making offerings to the gods, among whom are Rameses I. and Seti I. According to an inscription there, it is said that Seti I. went to heaven and was united with the Sun-god before this temple was finished, and that Rameses II. made and fixed the doors, finished the building of the walls, and decorated the interior. The workmanship in certain parts of this temple recalls that of certain parts of Abydos ; it is probable that the same artists were employed.

II. The **Ramesseum.** This temple, called also the MEMNONIUM and the tomb of Osymandyas (Diodorus I., iv), was built by Rameses II., in honour of Ámen-Rā. As at Ḳûrnah, two pylons stood in front of it. The first court had a double row of pillars on each side of it ; passing up a flight of steps, and through the second pylon, is a second court, having a double row of round columns on the east and west sides, and a row of pilasters, to which large figures of Rameses II. under the form of Osiris, are attached on the north and south sides. Before the second pylon stood a colossal statue of Rameses II., at least sixty feet high, which has been thrown down (by Cambyses ?), turned over on its back, and mutilated. In the hall are twelve huge columns, arranged in two rows, and thirty-six smaller ones arranged in six rows. On the

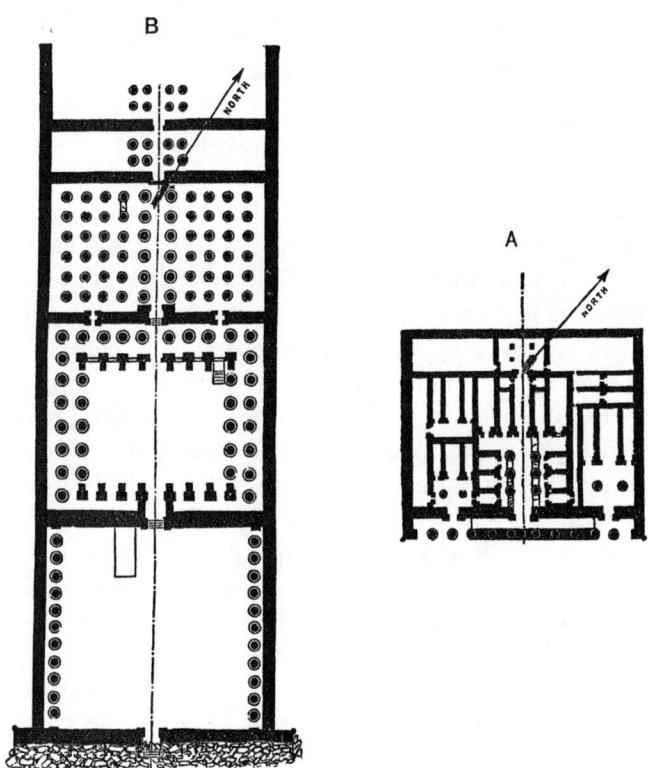

A. Plan of the Temple at Ḳûrnah.

B. Plan of the Ramesseum at Ḳûrnah.

interior face of the second pylon are sculptured scenes in the war of Rameses II. against the Cheta, which took place in the fifth year of his reign ; in them he is represented slaying the personal attendants of the prince of the Cheta. Elsewhere is the famous scene in which Rameses, having been forsaken by his army, is seen cutting his way through the enemy, and hurling them one after the other into the Orontes near Kadesh. The walls of the temple are ornamented with small battle scenes and reliefs representing the king making offerings to the gods of Thebes. On the ceiling of one of the chambers is an interesting astronomical piece on which the twelve Egyptian months are mentioned.

III. The **Colossi.**—These two interesting statues were set up in honour of Amenophis III., whom they represent ; they stood in front of the pylon of a calcareous stone temple which was built by this king; this has now entirely disappeared. They were hewn out of a hard grit-stone, and the top of each was about sixty feet above the ground ; originally each was monolithic. The statue on the north is the famous **Colossus of Memnon,** from which a sound was said to issue every morning when the sun rose. The upper part of it was thrown down by an earthquake, it is said, about B.C. 27 ; the damage was partially repaired during the reign of Septimus Severus, who restored the head and shoulders of the figure by adding to it five layers of stone. When Strabo was at Thebes with Ælius Gallus he heard "a noise at the first hour of the day, but whether proceeding from the base or from the colossus, or produced on purpose by some of those standing round the base, I cannot confidently assert." It is said that after the colossus was repaired no sound issued from it. Some think that the noise was caused by the sun's rays striking upon the stone, while others believe that a priest hidden in the colossus produced it by striking a stone. The inscriptions show that many distinguished Romans visited the "vocal Memnon" and heard the sound; one Petronianus, of a poetical turn of mind, stated that it made a sighing sound in complaining to its mother, the dawn, of the injuries inflicted upon it by Cambyses. The inscriptions on the back of the colossi give the names of Amenophis III.

IV. **Medînet Habû.**—This village lies to the south of the colossi, and its foundation dates from Coptic times. The early Christians established themselves around the ancient Egyptian temple there, and having carefully plastered over the wall sculptures in one of its chambers, they used it as a chapel. Round and about this temple many Greek and Coptic inscriptions have been found, which prove that the Coptic community here was one of the largest and most important in Upper Egypt. The temple here is actually composed of two temples; the older was built by Thothmes III., and the later by Rameses III. The first court of the temple of Thothmes III. was built during the time of the Roman occupation of Egypt, and the names of Titus, Hadrian, Antoninus, etc., are found on various parts of its walls. The half-built pylon at the end of this court is of the same period, although the door between them bears the names of Ptolemy X. Soter II. (Lathyrus) and Ptolemy XIII., Neos Dionysos (Auletes). The little court and pylon beyond are inscribed with the names of Tirhakah, B.C. 693, and Nectanebus II., B.C. 358. Passing through this last court and its pylon, the temple proper is reached. The oldest name found here is that of Thothmes II. The work begun by this king was completed by Thothmes III., and several subsequent kings restored or added new parts to it.

Before the Temple of Rameses III. there stood originally a building consisting of two square towers, the four sides of which were symmetrically inclined to a common centre. The interior chambers were ornamented with sculptures, on which were depicted scenes in the domestic (?) life of the

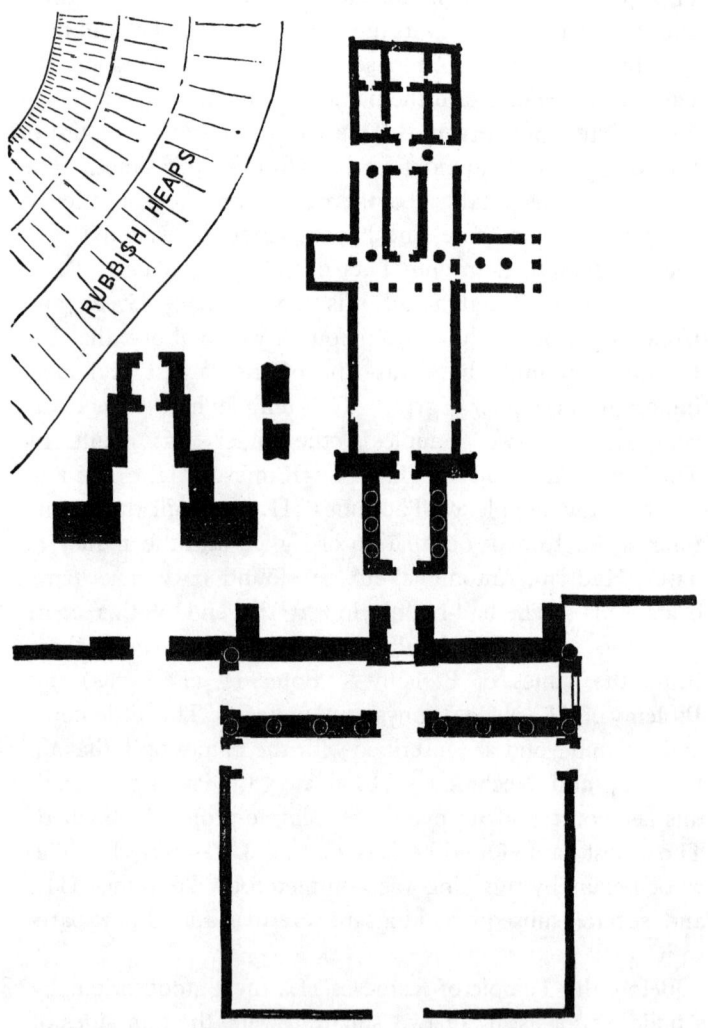

The Temple of Thothmes II. at Medinet Habu.

king, and from this it has been concluded that the building formed the PALACE OF RAMESES III. Elsewhere the king is shown smiting his enemies, and from the features and dress of many of them it is possible to tell generally what nations they represent; it is quite clear that the sculptor intended his figures to be typical portraits. It is a noticeable fact that the cartouches of Rameses III. are the only ones found in this building.

V. The **Temple of Rameses III.** is entered by passing through the first pylon, the front of which is ornamented with scenes from the wars of this king against the people of Arabia and Phœnicia. The weapons of the king are presented to him by Åmen-Rā the Sun-god. In the first court is a row of seven pillars, to which are attached figures of the king in the form of Osiris; M. Mariette was of opinion that these declared the funereal nature of the building. The second pylon is built of red granite, and the front is ornamented with scenes in which Rameses III. is leading before the gods Åmen and Mut a number of prisoners, whom he has captured in Syria and along the coasts of the Mediterranean; from these scenes it is evident that he was able to wage war by sea as well as land. The second court, which, according to M. Mariette, is one of the most precious which Egyptian antiquity has bequeathed to us, has a portico running round its four sides; it is supported on the north and south sides by eight Osiris columns, and on the east and west by five circular columns. The Copts disgraced this splendid court by building a sandstone colonnade in the middle, and destroyed here, as elsewhere, much else that would have been of priceless value. Beyond the second court was a hall of columns, on each side of which were several small chambers, and beyond that were other chambers and corridors and the sanctuary.

The scenes sculptured on the inside of the second court represent the wars of Rameses III. against the Libyans, in

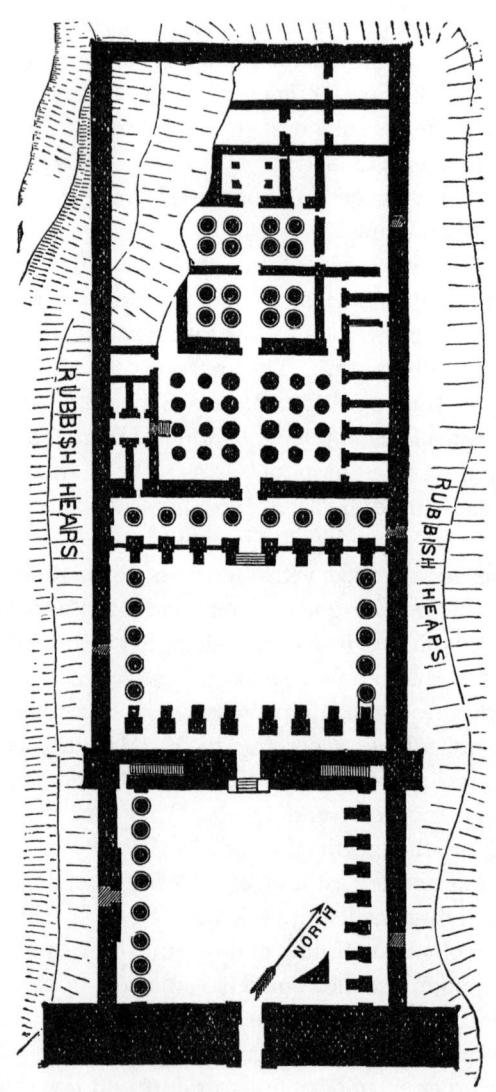

The Great Temple of Rameses III. at Medinet Habu.

which the generals and officers of the Egyptian king lead crowds of prisoners into his presence, whence they are brought in triumph to Thebes to be offered to the gods of that town. Elsewhere Rameses is making offerings to the various gods of Thebes and performing certain ceremonies. The procession, coronation of the king, musicians, and the sending off of four birds to announce to the ends of the world that Rameses III. was king, are among the many interesting scenes depicted here.

Outside the building, on the south wall, is a list of religious festivals, and on the north wall are ten scenes, of which the following are the subjects : 1. The king and his army setting out to war. 2. Battle of the Egyptians against the Libyans, and defeat of the latter. 3. Slaughter of the enemy by thousands, and the prisoners led before the king. 4. The king addresses his victorious army, and an inventory is made of the spoil captured. 5. The march continued. 6. Second encounter and defeat of the enemy called Takare ; their camp is captured, and women and children flee away in all directions. 7. The march continued. On the way one lion is slain and another wounded. The country passed through is probably northern Syria. 8. Naval battle scene. The fight takes place near the sea-shore, and Rameses and his archers distress the enemy by shooting at them from the shore. 9. Return towards Egypt. The number of the slain is arrived at by counting the hands which have been cut off the bodies on the field of battle. 10. Return to Thebes. The king presents his prisoners to the gods Åmen-Rā, Mut, and Chonsu. Speech of the prisoners, who beg the king to allow them to live that they may proclaim his power and glory.

The temple of Rameses III. is one of the most interesting of the Egyptian temples, and is worthy of several visits.

VI. **Dêr el-Medînet.** This small temple, which stands between the Colossi and Medînet Habû, was begun by

Ptolemy IV. Philopator and finished by Ptolemy IX. Euergetes II.; in one of its chambers is the judgment scene which forms the vignette of the 125th chapter of the Book of the Dead, hence the funereal nature of the building may be inferred.

VII. **Dêr el-Baḥari.** This temple was built by Ḥātshepset, the sister and wife of Thothmes II., B.C. 1600. The finest marble limestone was used in its construction, and its architect seems to have been an able man called Senmut, who was honoured with the friendship of the queen, and promoted by her to be chief clerk of the works. Before the temple was an avenue of sandstone sphinxes and two obelisks. It was built in stages on the side of a hill, and its courts were connected by means of flights of steps. As early as the XXIInd dynasty the temple had fallen into disuse, and soon after this time its chambers appear to have been used for sepulchres. The wall sculptures are beautiful specimens of art, and depict the return of Egyptian soldiers from some military expedition, and the scenes which took place during the expedition which the queen organized and sent off to Punt. This latter expedition was most successful, and returned to Egypt laden with things the "like of which had never before been seen in that land." The prince of Punt came to Egypt with a large following, and became a vassal of Ḥātshepset.

THE DISCOVERY OF THE ROYAL MUMMIES AT DÊR EL-BAHARI.*

In the summer of the year 1871 an Arab, a native oi Ḳûrnah, discovered a large tomb filled with coffins heaped one upon the other. On the greater number of them were visible the cartouche and other signs which indicated that

* A minute and detailed account of this discovery is given by Maspero in "Les Momies Royales de Déïr el Bahari" (Fasc. I., t. IV., of the *Mémoires* of the French Archæological Mission at Cairo).

the inhabitants of the coffins were royal personages. The native who was so fortunate as to have chanced upon this remarkable "find," was sufficiently skilled in his trade of antiquity hunter to know what a valuable discovery he had made ; his joy must however have been turned into mourning, when it became evident that he would need the help of many men even to move some of the large royal coffins which he saw before him, and that he could not keep the knowledge of such treasures locked up in his own breast. He revealed his secret to his two brothers and to one of his sons, and they proceeded to spoil the coffins of *ushabti** figures, papyri, scarabs and other antiquities which could be taken away easily and concealed in their *abbas* (ample outer garments) as they returned to their houses. These precious objects were for several winters sold to chance tourists on the Nile, and the lucky possessors of this mine of wealth replenished their stores from time to time by visits made at night to the tomb. As soon as the objects thus sold reached Europe, it was at once suspected that a "find" of more than ordinary importance had been made. An English officer called Campbell showed M. Maspero a hieratic Book of the Dead written for Pi-net'em ; M. de Saulcy sent him photographs of the hieroglyphic papyrus of Net'emet ; M. Mariette bought at Suez a papyrus written for the Queen Ḥent-taiu, and Rogers Bey exhibited at Paris a wooden tablet upon which was written a hieratic text relating to the *ushabti* figures which were to be buried with the princess Nesi-Chensu. All these interesting and most valuable objects proved that the natives of Thebes had succeeded

---

* *Ushabti* figures made of stone, green or blue glazed Egyptian porcelain, wood, &c., were deposited in the tombs with the dead, and were supposed to perform for them any field labours which might be decreed for them by Osiris, the king of the under-world, and judge of the dead.

in unearthing a veritable "Cave of Treasures," and M. Maspero, the Director of the Bûlâk Museum, straightway determined to visit Upper Egypt with a view of discovering whence came all these antiquities. Three men were implicated, whose names were learnt by M. Maspero from the inquiries which he made of tourists who purchased antiquities.

In 1881 he proceeded to Thebes, and began his investigations by causing one of the dealers, 'Abd er-Rasûl Aḥmad, to be arrested by the police, and an official inquiry into the matter was ordered by the Mudîr of Ḳeneh. In spite of threats and persuasion, and many add tortures, the accused denied any knowledge of the place whence the antiquities came. The evidence of the witnesses who were called to testify to the character of the accused, tended to show that he was a man of amiable disposition, who would never dream of pillaging a tomb, much less do it. Finally, after two months' imprisonment, he was provisionally set at liberty. The accused then began to discuss with his partners in the secret what plans they should adopt, and how they should act in the future. Some of them thought that all trouble was over when 'Abd er-Rasûl Aḥmad was set at liberty, but others thought, and they were right, that the trial would be recommenced in the winter. Fortunately for students of Egyptology, differences of opinion broke out between the parties soon after, and 'Abd er-Rasûl Aḥmad soon perceived that his brothers were determined to turn King's evidence at a favourable opportunity. To prevent their saving themselves at his expense, he quietly travelled to Ḳeneh, and there confessed to the Mudîr that he was able to reveal the place where the coffins and papyri were found. Telegrams were sent to Cairo announcing the confession of 'Abd er-Rasûl Aḥmad, and when his statements had been verified, despatches containing fuller particulars were sent to Cairo from Ḳeneh. It was decided that a small expedition to Thebes should at once be made to take possession of and bring to Cairo the antiquities which were to be revealed to the world by 'Abd er-Rasûl Aḥmad, and the charge of bringing this work to a successful issue was placed in the hands of M. Émil Brugsch. Although the season was summer, and the heat very great, the start for Thebes was made on July 1. At Ḳeneh M. Brugsch found a number of papyri and other valuable antiquities which 'Abd er-Rasûl had sent there as an earnest of the truth of his promise to reveal the hidden treasures. A week later M. Brugsch and his companions were shown the shaft of the tomb, which was most carefully hidden in the north-west part of the natural circle which opens to the south of the valley of Dêr el-Baḥari, in the little row of hills which separates the Bibân el-Mulûk from the Theban plain. According to M. Maspero *, the royal mummies were removed here from their tombs in the Bibân el-Mulûk by Āauputh, the son of Shashanq, about B.C. 966, to prevent them being destroyed by the thieves, who were sufficiently numerous and powerful to defy the government of the day. The pit which led to the tomb was about forty feet deep, and the passage, of irregular level, which led to the tomb was about 220 feet long; at the end of this passage was a nearly rectangular chamber about twenty-five feet long, which was found to be literally filled with coffins, mummies, funereal furniture, boxes, *ushabti* figures, Canopic jars, † bronze vases, etc., etc. A large number of men were

* *Histoire Ancienne des Peuples de L'Orient*, 4ième ed., p. 360.

† The principal intestines of a deceased person were placed in four jars, which were placed in his tomb under the bier; the jars were dedicated to the four children of Horus, who were called Ȧmset, Ḥāpi, Tuamāutef and Qebḥsenuf. The name "Canopic" is given to them by those who follow the opinion of some ancient writers that Canopus, the pilot of Menelaus, who is said to have been buried at Canopus in Egypt, was worshipped there under the form of a jar with small feet, a thin neck, a swollen body, and a round back.

at once employed to exhume these objects, and for eight
and forty hours M. Brugsch and Aḥmad Effendi Kamal
stood at the mouth of the pit watching the things brought
up. The heavy coffins were carried on the shoulders of
men to the river, and in less than two weeks everything had
been sent over the river to Luxor. A few days after this
the whole collection of mummies of kings and royal personages was placed upon an Egyptian Government steamer
and taken to the Museum at Bûlâk.

When the mummies of the ancient kings of Egypt
arrived at Cairo, it was found that the Bûlâk Museum was
too small to contain them, and before they could be ex-
posed to the inspection of the world, it was necessary for
additional rooms to be built. Finally, however, M. Maspero
had glass cases made, and, with the help of some cabinets
borrowed from his private residence attached to the
Museum, he succeeded in exhibiting, in a comparatively
suitable way, the mummies in which such world-wide
interest had been taken. Soon after the arrival of the
mummies at Bûlâk M. Brugsch opened the mummy of
Thothmes III., when it was found that the Arabs had
attacked it and plundered whatever was valuable upon it.
In 1883 the mummy of Queen Mes-Ḥent-Themeḥu,
, emitted unpleasant odours, and by
M. Maspero's orders it was unrolled. In 1885 the mummy
of Queen Åḥmes Nefertâri, , was un-
rolled by him, and as it putrified rapidly and stank, it
had to be buried. Finally, when M. Maspero found that
the mummy of Seqenen-Râ, , was also
decaying, he decided to unroll the whole collection, and
Rameses II. was the first of the great kings whose features
were shown again to the world after a lapse of 3,200 years.

Such are the outlines of the history of one of the

greatest discoveries ever made in Egypt. It will ever be regretted by the Egyptologist that this remarkable collection of mummies was not discovered by some person who could have used for the benefit of scholars the precious information which this "find" would have yielded, before so many of its objects were scattered; as it is, however, it would be difficult to over-estimate its historical value.

The following is a list of the names of the principal kings and royal personages which were found on coffins at Dêr el-Baḥari and of their mummies :—

XVIIth Dynasty, before B.C. 1700.

King Seqenen-Rā, coffin and mummy.
Nurse of Queen Nefertâri Râā, coffin only. This coffin contained the mummy of a queen whose name is read Ȧn-Ḥāpi.

XVIIIth Dynasty, B.C. 1700–1400.

King Ȧḥmes (Amāsis I.), coffin and mummy.
Queen Ȧḥmes Nefertâri, coffin.
King Ȧmenḥetep I., coffin and mummy.
The Prince Se-Ȧmen, coffin and mummy.
The Princess Set-Ȧmen, coffin and mummy.
The Scribe Senu, chief of the house of Nefertâri, mummy.
Royal wife Set-ka-mes, mummy.
Royal daughter Meshentthemḥu, coffin and mummy.
Royal mother Ȧāḥ-ḥetep, coffin.
King Thothmes I., coffin usurped by Pi-net'em.
King Thothmes II., coffin and mummy.
King Thothmes III., coffin and mummy.
Coffin and mummy of an unknown person.

XIXth Dynasty, B.C. 1400–1200.

King Rameses I., part of coffin.
King Seti I., coffin and mummy.
King Rameses II., coffin and mummy.

XXth Dynasty, B.C. 1200–1100.

King Rameses III., mummy found in the coffin of Nefertàri.

XXIst Dynasty, B.C. 1100–1000.

Royal mother Net'emet.
High-priest of Âmen, Masaherthà, coffin and mummy.
High-priest of Âmen, Pai-net'em III., coffin and mummy.
Priest of Âmen, T'eṭ-Ptaḥ-àuf-ānch, coffin and mummy.
Scribe Nebseni, coffin and mummy.
Queen Māt-ka-Rā, coffin and mummy.
Princess Uast-em-chebit, coffin and mummy.
Princess Nesi-Chensu.

VIII. The Tombs of the Kings, called in Arabic Bibân el-Mulûk, are hewn out of the living rock in a valley, which is reached by passing the temple at Ḳûrnah ; it is situated about three or four miles from the river. This valley contains the tombs of the kings of the XIXth and XXth dynasties, and is generally known as the Eastern Valley ; a smaller valley, the Western, contains the tombs of the last kings of the XVIIIth dynasty.   These tombs consist of long inclined planes with a number of chambers or halls receding into the mountain sometimes to a distance of 500 feet.   Strabo gives the number of these royal tombs as 40, 17 of which were open in the time of Ptolemy Lagus ; in 1835 21 were known, but the labours of M. Mariette were successful in bringing four more to light.   The most important of these tombs are :—

No. 17. **Tomb of Seti I.**, B.C. 1366, commonly called 'Belzoni's Tomb," because it was discovered by that brave traveller in the early part of this century ; it had already been rifled, but the beautiful alabaster sarcophagus, which is now preserved in the Soane Museum in London, was still lying in its chamber at the bottom of the tomb.   The inscriptions and scenes sculptured on the walls form parts of

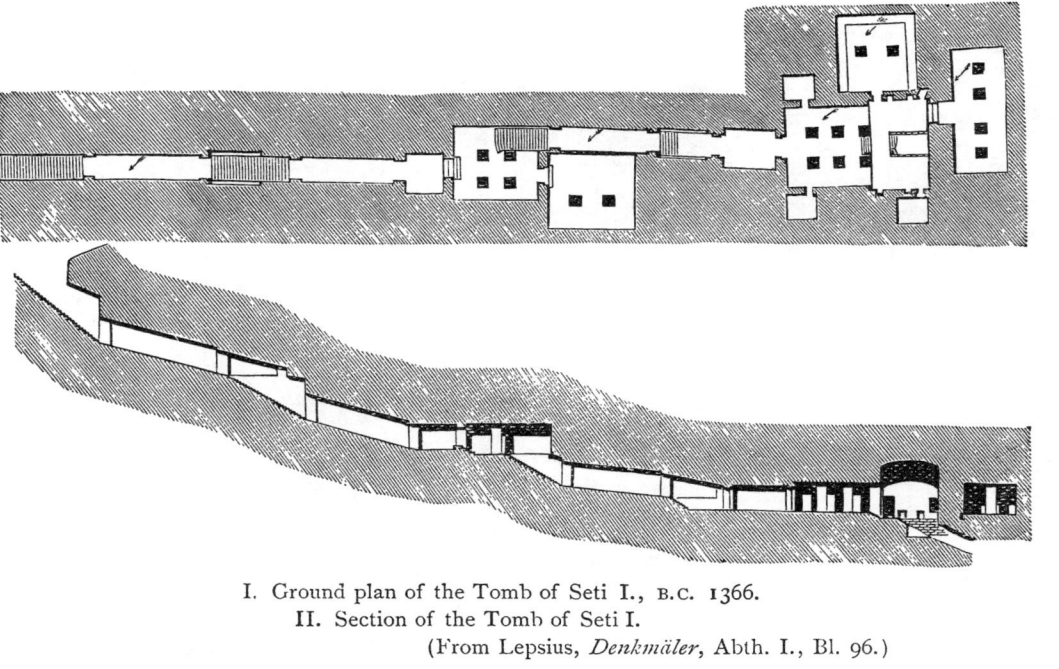

I. Ground plan of the Tomb of Seti I., B.C. 1366.
II. Section of the Tomb of Seti I.
(From Lepsius, *Denkmäler*, Abth. I., Bl. 96.)

the "Book of being in the under-world;" it is quite impossible to describe them here, for a large number of pages would be required for the purpose. It must be sufficient to draw attention to the excellence and beauty of the paintings and sculptures, and to point out that the whole series refers to the life of the king in the under-world. The tomb is entered by means of two flights of steps, at the bottom of which is a passage terminating in a small chamber. Beyond this are two halls having four and two pillars respectively, and to the left are the passages and small chambers which lead to the large six-pillared hall and vaulted chamber in which stood the sarcophagus of Seti I. Here also is an inclined plane which descends into the mountain for a considerable distance; from the level of the ground to the bottom of this incline the depth is about 150 feet; the length of the tomb is nearly 500 feet. The designs on the walls were first sketched in outline in red, and the alterations by the master designer or artist were made in black; it would seem that this tomb was never finished. The mutilations and destruction which have been committed here during the last twenty-five years are truly lamentable. The mummy of Seti I., found at Dêr el-Baḥari, is preserved in the Gîzeh Museum.

No. 11. **Tomb of Rameses III.**, B.C. 1200, commonly called "Bruce's Tomb," because it was discovered by this traveller, and the "Tomb of the Harper," on account of the scene in it in which men are represented playing harps. The architect did not leave sufficient space between this and a neighbouring tomb, and hence after excavating passages and chambers to a distance of more than 100 feet, he was obliged to turn to the right to avoid breaking into it. The flight of steps leading into the tomb is not as steep as that in No. 17, the paintings and sculptures are not so fine, and the general plan of ornamentation differs. The scenes on the walls of the first passage resemble those in the first passage of No. 17, but in the other passages and chambers warlike, domestic, and agricultural scenes and objects are depicted. The body of the red granite sarcophagus of Rameses III. is in Paris, the cover is in the Fitzwilliam Museum, Cambridge, and the mummy of this king is at Gîzeh. The length of the tomb is about 400 feet.

No. 2. The **Tomb of Rameses IV.**, about B.C. 1166, though smaller than the others, is of considerable interest; the granite sarcophagus, of colossal proportions, still stands *in situ* at the bottom. Having seen the beautiful sculptures and paintings in the Tomb of Seti I., the visitor will probably not be disposed to spend much time in that of Rameses IV.

No. 9. The **Tomb of Rameses VI.**, or "Memnon's Tomb," was considered of great interest by the Greeks and Romans who visited it in ancient days; the astronomical designs on some of the ceilings, and the regular sequence of its passages and rooms are interesting. The fragments of the granite sarcophagus of this king lie at the bottom of the tomb.

No. 6. The **Tomb of Rameses IX.**, is remarkable for the variety of sculptures and paintings of a nature entirely different from those found in the other royal tombs; they appear to refer to the idea of resurrection after death and of immortality, which is here symbolized by the principle of generation.

The **Tomb of Rameses I.**, father of Seti I., is the oldest in this valley; it was opened by Belzoni.

The **Tomb* of Rechmàrā** is situated in the hill behind the Ramesseum called Shêkh 'Abd el-Ḳûrnah; it is one of the most interesting of all the private tombs found at Thebes. The scenes on the walls represent a procession of tribute bearers from Punt carrying apes, ivory, etc.,

---

* No. 35, according to Wilkinson, and No. 15, according to Champollion.

and of people from parts of Syria and the shores of the Mediterranean bringing to him gifts consisting of the choicest products of their lands, which Rechmârā receives for Thothmes III. The countries can in many cases be identified by means of the articles depicted. The scenes in the inner chamber represent brickmaking, ropemaking, smiths' and masons' work, etc., etc., superintended by Rechmârā, prefect of Thebes; elsewhere are domestic scenes and a representation of Rechmârā sailing in a boat, lists of offerings, etc.

The most ancient necropolis at Thebes is Drah abu'l Neḳḳah, where tombs of the XIth, XVIIth, and XVIIIth dynasties are to be found. The coffins of the Ȧntef kings (XIth dynasty), now in the Louvre and the British Museum, were discovered here, and here was made the marvellous "find" of the jewellery of Ȧḥ-ḥetep,* wife of Kames, a king of the XVIIth dynasty, about B.C. 1750. A little more to the south is the necropolis of Assassîf, where during the XIXth, XXIInd, and XXVIth dynasties many beautiful tombs were constructed. If the visitor has time, an attempt should be made to see the fine tomb of Peṭā-Ȧmen-ȧpt.

ARMANT (ERMENT).

Armant, or Erment, 458½ miles from Cairo, on the west bank of the river, was called in Egyptian ⬚⬚ Menth, and ⬚⬚ Ȧnnu qemāt, "Heliopolis of the South"; it marks the site of the ancient Hermonthis, where, according to Strabo, "Apollo and Jupiter are both worshipped."

The ruins which remain there belong to the Iseion built during the reign of the last Cleopatra (B.C. 51–29). The stone-lined tank which lies near this building was probably used as a Nilometer.

* Now preserved at Gîzeh.

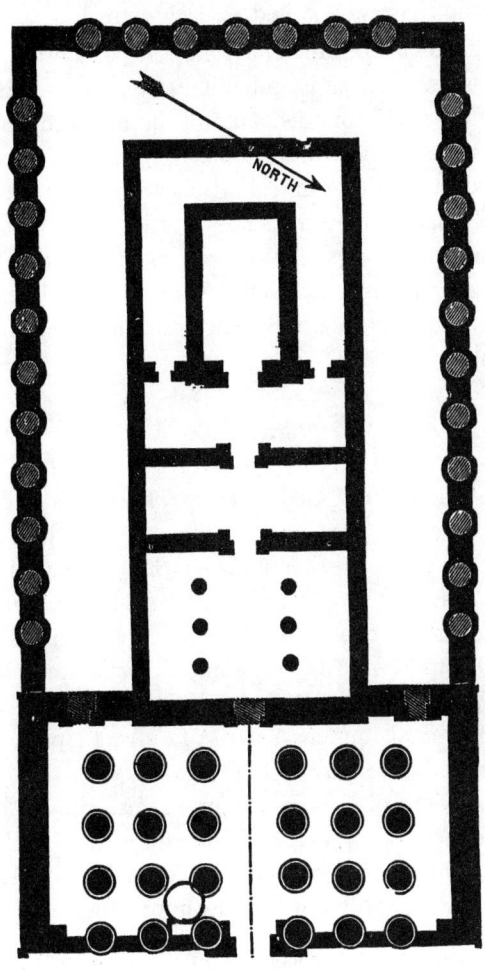

Plan of the Temple of Esneh, with restorations by Grand Bey.

ESNEH.

Esneh, or Asneh, 484½ miles from Cairo, on the west bank of the river, was called in Egyptian 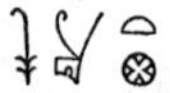 Senet; it marks the site of the ancient Latopolis, and was so called by the Greeks, because its inhabitants worshipped the Latus fish. Thothmes III. founded a temple here, but the interesting building which now stands almost in the middle of the modern town is of late date, and bears the names of several of the Roman emperors. The portico is supported by twenty-four columns, each of which is inscribed; their capitals are handsome. The Zodiac here, like that at Denderah, belongs to a late period, but is interesting.

El-Kâb.

El-Kâb, 502 miles from Cairo, on the east bank of the river, was called in Egyptian 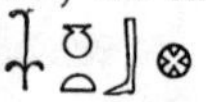 Necheb; it marks the site of the ancient Eileithyias. There was a city here in very ancient days, and ruins of temples built by Thothmes IV., Ȧmenḥetep III., Seti I., Rameses II., Rameses III., Ptolemy IX. Euergetes II. are still visible. A little distance from the town, in the mountain, is the tomb of Ȧḥmes (Amāsis), the son of Abana, an officer born in the reign of Seqenen Rā, who fought against the Hyksos, and who served under Amāsis I., Amenophis I., and Thothmes I. The inscription on the walls of his tomb gives an account of the campaign against some Mesopota mian enemies of Egypt and of the siege of their city. Amāsis was the "Captain-General of Sailors." The tomb of his daughter's son Pahir lies just above his.

UṬFÛ (EDFÛ).

Edfû, 515½ miles from Cairo, on the west bank of the river was called in Egyptian 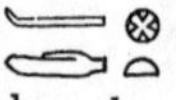 Beḥuṭet, and in Coptic ⲁⲃⲧⲱ; it was called by the Greeks Apollino-

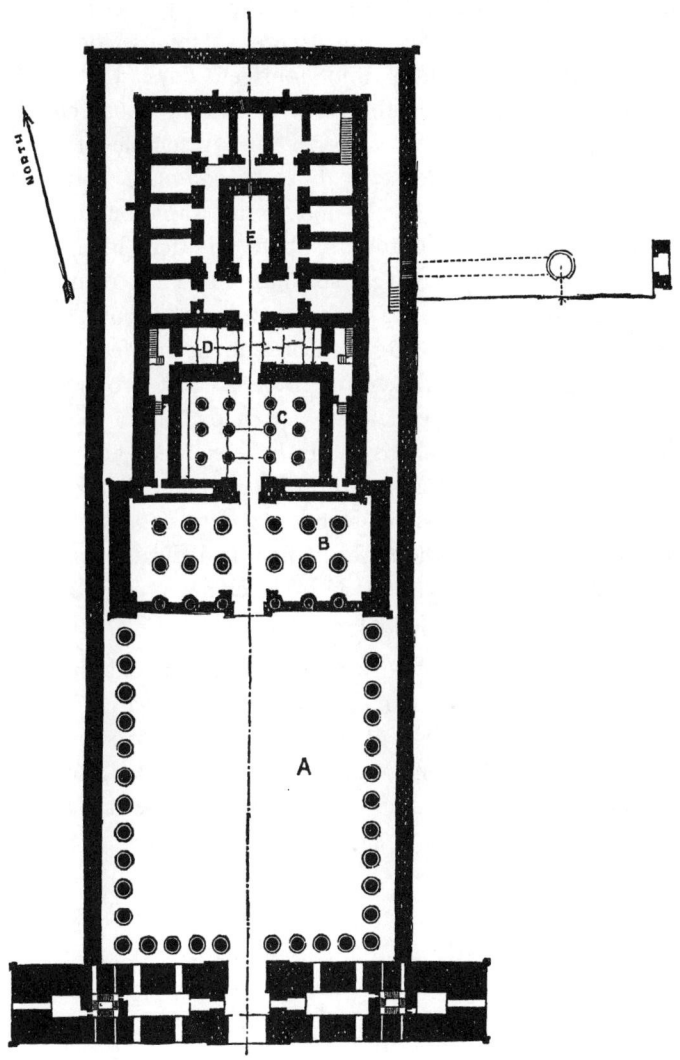

Plan of the Great Temple of Edfû.

polis Magna, where the crocodile and its worshippers were detested. The **Temple of Edfû,** for which alone both the ancient and modern towns were famous, occupied 180 years three months and fourteen days, that is to say it was begun during the reign of Ptolemy Euergetes I., B.C. 237, and finished B.C. 57. It resembles that ot Denderah in many respects, but its complete condition marks it out as one of the most remarkable buildings in Egypt, and its splendid towers, about 112 feet high, make its general magnificence very striking. The space enclosed by the walls measures 450 × 120 feet; the front of the propylon from side to side measures about 252 feet. Passing through the door the visitor enters a court, around three sides of which runs a gallery supported on thirty-two pillars. The first and second halls, A, B, have eighteen and twelve pillars respectively; passing through chambers C and D, the shrine E is reached, where stood a granite naos in which a figure of Horus, to whom the temple is dedicated, was preserved. This naos was made by Nectanebus I., a king of the XXXth dynasty, B.C. 378.

The pylons are covered with battle scenes, and the walls are inscribed with the names and sizes of the various chambers in the building, lists of names of places, etc.; the name of the architect, Î-em-ḥetep, or Imouthis, has also been inscribed. From the south side of the pylons, and from a small chamber on each side of the chamber C, staircases ascended to the roof.

The credit of clearing out the temple of Edfû belongs to M. Mariette. Little more than twenty-five years ago the mounds of rubbish outside reached to the top of its walls, and certain parts of the roof were entirely covered over with houses and stables.

HAGAR SILSILEH.

Hagar (or Gebel) **Silsileh,** 541½ miles from Cairo, on the east and west banks of the river, derives its name probably not from the Arabic word of like sound meaning "chain," but from the Coptic ⲭⲱⲗⲭⲉⲗ, meaning "stone wall"; the place is usually called 𓈖 *Chennu* in hieroglyphic texts. The ancient Egyptians here quarried the greater part of the sandstone used by them in their buildings, and the names of the kings inscribed in the caves here show that these quarries were used from the earliest to the latest periods. The most extensive of these are to be found on the east bank of the river, but those on the west bank contain the interesting tablets of Âmen-em-ḥeb, a king of the XVIIIth dynasty, who is represented conquering the Ethiopians, Seti I., Rameses II. his son, Meneptaḥ, etc. At Silsileh the Nile was worshipped, and the little temple which Rameses II. built in this place seems to have been dedicated chiefly to it. At this point the Nile narrows very much, and it is generally thought that a cataract once existed here; there is, however, no evidence to show when the Nile broke through and swept such a barrier, if it ever existed, away.

KOM OMBO.

Kom Ombo, 556½ miles from Cairo, on the east bank of the Nile, was an important place at all periods of Egyptian history; it was called by the Egyptians 𓉐𓎡, Pa-Sebek, "the temple of Sebek" (the crocodile god), and 𓎡, Nubit, and ⲛⲟⲩⲃⲱ by the Copts. The oldest object here is a sandstone gateway which Thothmes III. dedicated to the god Sebek. The larger temple was begun by Ptolemy VII. Philometor, and the building was continued by his immediate successors; it has two entrances, and is dedicated to Horus and Sebek. Unlike other Egyptian temples, it has neither dromos nor propylon; the portico was supported by fifteen pillars, thirteen of which are still standing, and the hall contained ten. This temple measured about 185 feet × 114 feet; all its walls and columns were covered with coloured hieroglyphics, and the cornice which ran round the portico and hall was exceedingly fine. To the north-west of this temple is a smaller sandstone temple which was dedicated to Isis (?) Both temples stood in an enclosure which measured about 460 × 400 yards, on each side of which was a thick crude brick wall; on the south and south-east sides there was a door.

ASWAN.

Aswân (or Uswân), the southern limit of Egypt proper, 583 miles from Cairo, on the east bank of the river, called in Egyptian ⌐ 🜂 , Coptic ⲤⲞⲨⲀⲚ, was called by the Greeks Syene, which stood on the slope of a hill to the south-west of the present town. Properly speaking Syene was the island of Elephantine. In the earliest Egyptian inscriptions it is called ⌐ , or ⌐ , Âbu, *i.e.*, "the district of the elephant," and it formed the metropolis of the first nome of Upper Egypt. As we approach the time of the Ptolemies, the name Sunnu, *i.e.*, the town on the east bank of the Nile, from whence comes the Arabic name Aswân, takes the place of Âbu. The town obtained great notoriety among the ancients from the fact that Eratosthenes and Ptolemy considered it to lie on the tropic of Cancer, and to be the most northerly point where, at the time of the summer solstice, the sun's rays fell vertically; as a matter of fact, however, the town lies 0' 37' 23" north of the tropic of Cancer. There was a famous well there, into which the sun was said to shine at the summer solstice, and to illuminate it in every part. In the time of the Romans three cohorts were stationed here,* and the town was of considerable importance. In the twelfth century of our era it was the seat of a bishop. Of its size in ancient days

---

* It is interesting to observe that the Romans, like the British, held Egypt by garrisoning three places, viz. Aswân, Babylon (Cairo), and Alexandria. The garrison at Aswân defended Egypt from foes on the south, and commanded the entrance of the Nile; the garrison at Babylon guarded the end of the Nile valley and the entrance to the Delta; and the garrison at Alexandria protected the country from invasion by sea.

nothing definite can be said, but Arabic writers describe it as a flourishing town, and they relate that a plague once swept off 20,000 of its inhabitants. Aswân was famous for its wine in Ptolemaic times. The town has suffered greatly at the hands of the Persians, Arabs, and Turks on the north, and the Nubians, by whom it was nearly destroyed in the twelfth century, on the south. The oldest ruins in the town are those of a Ptolemaic temple, which are still visible.

The island of **Elephantine** * lies a little to the north of the cataract just opposite Aswân, and has been famous in all ages as the key of Egypt from the south; the Romans garrisoned it with numerous troops, and it represented the southern limit of their empire. The island itself was very fertile, and it is said that its vines and fig-trees retained their leaves throughout the year. The kings of the Vth dynasty sprang from Elephantine. The gods worshipped here by the Egyptians were called Chnemu, Sati and Sept, and on this island Amenophis III. built a temple, remains of which were visible in the early part of this century. Of the famous Nilometer which stood here, Strabo says : " The Nilometer is a well upon the banks of the Nile, constructed of close-fitting stones, on which are marked the greatest, least, and mean risings of the Nile ; for the water in the well and in the river rises and subsides simultaneously. Upon the wall

---

* " A little above Elephantine is the lesser cataract, where the boatmen exhibit a sort of spectacle to the governors. The cataract is in the middle of the river, and is formed by a ridge of rocks, the upper part of which is level, and thus capable of receiving the river, but terminating in a precipice, where the water dashes down. On each side towards the land there is a stream, up which is the chief ascent for vessels. The boatmen sail up by this stream, and, dropping down to the cataract, are impelled with the boat to the precipice, the crew and the boats escaping unhurt." (Strabo, Bk. xvii. chap. i., 49, Falconer's translation.) Thus it appears that "shooting the cataract" is a very old amusement.

of the well are lines, which indicate the complete rise of the river, and other degrees of its rising. Those who examine these marks communicate the result to the public for their information. For it is known long before, by these marks, and by the time elapsed from the commencement, what the future rise of the river will be, and notice is given of it. This information is of service to the husbandmen with reference to the distribution of the water; for the purpose also of attending to the embankments, canals, and other things of this kind. It is of use also to the governors, who fix the revenue; for the greater the rise of the river, the greater it is expected will be the revenue." According to Plutarch the Nile rose at Elephantine to the height of 28 cubits; a very interesting text at Edfû states that if the river rises 24 cubits 3¼ hands at Elephantine, it will water the country satisfactorily.

To the south-west of Atrûn island, in a sandy valley, lie the ruins of an ancient building of the sixth or seventh century of our era, half convent, half fortress. A dome, ornamented with coloured representations of Saints Michael, George, and Gabriel, and the twelve Apostles, still remains in a good state of preservation. To the east of the convent is the cemetery, where some interesting stelæ and linen fragments were found.

A mile or so to the north of the convent stands the bold hill in the sides of which are hewn the tombs which General Sir F. W. Grenfell excavated; this hill is situated in Western Aswân, the ⲥⲟⲧⲁⲛ ⲇⲉ ⲛⲉⲥⲥⲉⲛⲧ of the Copts, and is the Contra Syene of the classical authors. The tombs are hewn out of the rock, tier above tier, and the most important of these were reached by a stone staircase, which to this day remains nearly complete, and is one of the most interesting antiquities in Egypt. The tombs in this hill may be roughly divided into three groups. The first group was hewn in the best and thickest layer of stone in the top of the hill, and was made for the rulers of Elephantine who lived during the VIth and XIIth dynasties. The second group is composed of tombs of different periods; they are hewn out of a lower layer of stone, and are not of so much importance. The third group, made during the Roman occupation of Egypt, lies a comparatively short height above the river. All these tombs were broken into at a very early period, and the largest of them formed a common sepulchre for people of all classes from the XXVIth dynasty downwards. They were found filled with broken coffins and mummies and sepulchral stelæ, etc., etc., and everything showed how degraded Egyptian funereal art had become when these bodies were buried there. The double tomb at the head of the staircase was made for Sabben and Mechu; the former was a dignitary of high rank who lived during the reign of Pepi II., a king of the VIth dynasty, whose prenomen Nefer-ka-Rā is inscribed on the left hand side of the doorway; the latter was a *smer*, prince and inspector, who appears to have lived during the XIIth dynasty. The paintings on the walls and the proto-Doric columns which support the roof are interesting, and its fine state of preservation and position makes it one of the most valuable monuments of that early period. A little further northward is the small tomb of Ḥeqȧb, and beyond this is the fine, large tomb hewn originally for Se-Renput, one of the old feudal hereditary governors of Elephantine, but which was appropriated by Nub-kau-Rā-necht. He was the governor of the district of the cataract, and the general who commanded a lightly-armed body of soldiers called "runners;" he lived during the reign of Usertsen I., the second king of the XIIth dynasty, and his tomb must have been one of the earliest hewn there during that period. Further excavations in this hill will no doubt bring to light many other interesting tombs now unknown; it is much to be hoped that Sir Francis Grenfell will see his way to causing his work to be continued.

Aswân was as famous for its granite, as Silsileh was for its sandstone. The Egyptian kings were in the habit of sending to Aswân for granite to make sarcophagi, temples, obelisks, etc., and it will be remembeaed that Unà was sent there to bring back in barges granite for the use of Pepi II., a king of the VIth dynasty. It is probable that the granite slabs which cover the pyramid of Mycerinus (IVth dynasty) were brought from Aswân. The undetached obelisk, which still lies in one of the quarries, is an interesting object.

Near the quarries are two ancient Arabic cemeteries, in which are a number of sandstone grave-stones, many of them formed from stones taken from Ptolemaic buildings, inscribed in Cufic * characters with the names of the Muḥammedans buried there, and the year, month, and day on which they died. We learn from them that natives of Edfû and other parts of Egypt were sometimes brought here and buried.

The first **Cataract**, called Shellâl by the Arabs, begins a little to the south of Aswân, and ends a little to the north of the island of Philæ ; eight cataracts are reckoned on the Nile, but this is the most generally known. Here the Nile becomes narrow and flows between two mountains, which descend nearly perpendicularly to the river, the course of which is obstructed by huge boulders and small rocky islands and barriers, which stand on different levels, and cause the falls of water which have given this part of the river its name. On the west side the obstacles are not so

---

* A kind of Arabic writing in which very old copies of the Ḳor'ân, etc., are written: it takes its name from Kûfah, الكوفة El-Kûfa, a town on the Euphrates. Kûfah was one of the chief cities of 'Irâḳ, and is famous in the Muḥammedan world because Muḥammad and his immediate successors dwelt there. Enoch lived here, the ark was built here, the boiling waters of the Flood first burst out here, and Abraham had a place of prayer set apart here.

numerous as on the east, and sailing and rowing boats can
ascend the cataract on this side when the river is high.
The noise made by the water is at times very great, but it
has been greatly exaggerated by both ancient and modern
travellers, some of whom ventured to assert that the "water
fell from several places in the mountain more than two
hundred feet." Some ancient writers asserted that the
fountains of the Nile were in this cataract, and Herodotus
believed that the source of the Nile was here. Many of the
rocks here are inscribed with the names of kings who
reigned during the Middle Empire; in many places on the
little islands in the cataract quarries were worked. The
island of Sehêl should be visited on account of the numerous
inscriptions left there by princes, generals, and others who
passed by on their way to Nubia; the village of Mahâtah,
on the east bank of the river, is prettily situated, and worth a
visit.

PHILÆ.

Philæ is the name given by the Greeks and Romans to
two islands situated at the head of the first cataract, about
six miles above Aswân; the larger one is called Biggeh, and
the smaller Philæ. Inscriptions found on rocks in the larger
island show that as far back as the time of Amenophis II.
an Egyptian temple stood here; the greater number of
these inscriptions were cut by Egyptian officials on their
way to and from Nubia. The smaller island, to which the
name Philæ is generally confined, consists of a granite rock,
the sides of which, having been scarped, have had walls
built on them; it measures 417 yards long and 135 yards
wide. The name of this island in Egyptian was ⌂𓏤
P-āa-lek, Coptic ΠΙⲖⲀⲔ, *i.e.*, 'the frontier.' The monuments on this island are numerous and interesting, but they
belong to a comparatively late date, none that have yet been
found being older than the time of Nectanebus, the last native

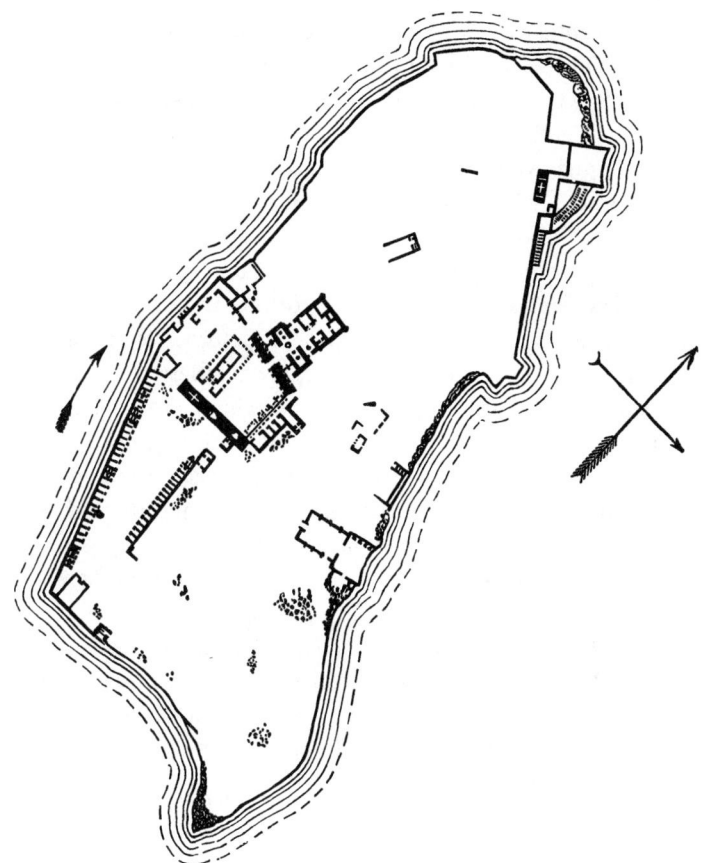

Plan of the Buildings on the Island of Philæ.

king of Egypt. On the south-west corner are the remains of the small temple which this king dedicated to Isis. The most important ruins are those of the Temple of Isis, which was begun by Ptolemy II. Philadelphus and Arsinoë, and was added to and completed by the Ptolemies and Roman emperors who came after. On each side of the path which led to the temple is a corridor: that on the west has thirty-two pillars and that on the east sixteen; at the north end of the east corridor is the so-called chapel of Æsculapius, which was built by Ptolemy V. Epiphanes and Cleopatra. The towers of the first propylon are about 65 feet high, and their southern faces are ornamented with sculptures representing Ptolemy VII. Philometor triumphing over his enemies. On the east side of the large court, which is entered through the propylon, is a portico with ten columns, and on the west side are the three chambers forming the so-called mammisi, on the walls of which are representations of the birth of Horus. In this courtyard there is a copy of the famous Rosetta Stone inscription, given, unfortunately, without the Greek text. Passing through the second propylon, a portico having ten beautifully painted capitals is entered, and north of this are three chambers, in the last of which is the monolith shrine. Round and about are several small chambers and passages with secret openings. When Strabo visited the island he saw the hawk which was worshipped there, and which was said to have been brought from Ethiopia; it was very sick and nearly dead.*

---

* "A little above the cataract is Philæ, a common settlement, like Elephantina, of Ethiopians and Egyptians, and equal in size, containing Egyptian temples, where a bird, which they call hierax (the hawk), is worshipped; but it did not appear to me to resemble in the least the hawks of our country nor of Egypt, for it was larger, and very different in the marks of its plumage. They said that the bird was Ethiopian, and is brought from Ethiopia when its predecessor dies, or before its death. The one shown to us when we were there was sick and nearly dead."—(Strabo, xvii., 1–49, Falconer's translation.)

On the western side of the island stands the beautiful little temple usually called Pharaoh's bed, and a little to the north of it is a small temple built by Ptolemy IX. Euergetes II.; the other ruins on the island are not of importance, but if time permits, a visit should be paid to the Nilometer built in a staircase leading down to the river. Philæ was said to be one of the burial places of Osiris, and as such was held in the greatest esteem by both Egyptians and Ethiopians; it was considered a most holy place, and only priests were allowed to live there unmolested. An oath sworn by Osiris of Philæ was inviolable, and the worship of this god flourished here until A.D. 453, that is to say, seventy years after the proclamation of the famous edict of Theodosius against the religion of Egypt. In the time of the Romans a strong garrison was stationed here. In Coptic times a Christian church, remains of which are still visible, was built on the northern end of Philæ. The picturesque scenery at Philæ is too well known to need comment.

THE NILE BETWEEN THE FIRST AND SECOND CATARACTS.

The country which is entered on leaving Philæ is generally known by the name of Ethiopia, or Nubia ; the latter name has been derived by some from *nub*, the Egyptian word for gold, because in ancient days much gold was brought into Egypt from that land. In the hieroglyphics, Nubia or Ethiopia, is generally called 🏛 ⌇⌇ Kesh (the Cush of the Bible) and ⟹ 🔯 ⌇⌇ Ta-kenset; from the latter name the Arabic El-kenûs is derived. It is known that as far back as the VIth dynasty, the Egyptians sent to this country for certain kinds of wood, and that all the chief tribes which lived round about Korosko, hastened to help the Egyptian officer Unà in the mission which he undertook for King Pepi II. It seems pretty certain too, if we may trust Unà's words, that the whole country was made to acknowledge the sovereignty of the Egyptian king. From the VIIth to the XIth dynasty nothing is known of the relations which existed between the two countries, but in the time of Usertsen I., the second king of the XIIth dynasty, an expedition was undertaken by the Egyptians for the purpose of fixing the boundaries of the two countries, and we know from a stele set up at Wâdi Ḥalfah by this king, that his rule extended as far south as this place. Two reigns later the inhabitants of Nubia or Ethiopia had become so troublesome, that Usertsen III. found it necessary to build fortresses at Semneh and Kummeh, south of the second cataract, and to make stringent laws forbidding the passage of any negro ship unless it was laden with cattle or mer chandise.

The Hyksos kings appear not to have troubled greatly about Nubia. When the XVIIIth dynasty had obtained full power in Egypt, some of its greatest kings, such as Thothmes III. and Åmenḥetep III., marched into Nubia and built temples there; under the rulers of the XIXth dynasty, the country became to all intents and purposes a part of Egypt. Subsequently the Nubians appear to have acquired considerable power, and as Egypt became involved in conflicts with more Northern countries, this power increased until Nubia was able to declare itself independent. For several hundreds of years the Nubians had the benefit of Egyptian civilization, and all that it could teach them, and they were soon able to organize war expeditions into Egypt with success. As early as the XXVth dynasty, the territory to the north of Syene or Aswân was a part of the Nubian or Ethiopian kingdom, the second capital of which, towards the north, was Thebes. About B.C. 730 a rebellion, headed by Tafnecht, chief of Saïs, broke out, and it was so successful, that the rebels marched into middle Egypt, i.e., the tract of land which lay between the Delta and the Ethiopian terri-tory, and overthrew the Ethiopian governors. When Piānchi king of Ethiopia heard this, he prepared an army, and marching northwards captured the whole of Egypt as far as Memphis. The kings of Egypt of the XXVth dynasty were Ethiopians, and their capital city was Napata or Gebel Barkal; Tirhakah, the last of the dynasty, is thought to have built the pyramids at Meroë. Cambyses undertook an ill-directed expedition into Ethiopia, but he met with no success, and the result of his labour was only to open up the country to travellers. Under the rule of the Ptolemies many cities were founded in Ethiopia. In the reign of Augustus, the Ethiopians, under their Queen Candace, were repulsed, and their capital city destroyed by C. Petronius, the successor of the prefect of Egypt, Aelius Gallus, who placed a Roman garrison in Ibrîm, about B.C. 22. Candace

sued for peace. In the reign of Diocletian the greater part
of the country south of Philæ was ceded to the Nubians or
Ethiopians. The principal tribes of the Ethiopians in
ancient days were 1. Blemmyes and Megabari, 2. Icthyo-
phagi, 3. Macrobii, and 4. Troglodytæ.

After leaving Philæ, the first place of interest passed is
Dabôd, on the west bank of the river, 599½ miles from
Cairo. At this place, called ⌂ 𓄿 𓊪 𓎼 Ta-ḥet in the
inscriptions, are the ruins of a temple founded by Àt′a-char-
Àmen,* a king of Ethiopia, who reigned about the middle
of the third century B.C. The names of Ptolemy VII.
Philometor and Ptolemy IX. Physcon are found engraved
upon parts of the building. Dabôd probably stands ·on the
site of the ancient Parembole, a port or castle on the borders
of Egypt and Ethiopia, and attached alternately to each
kingdom. During the reign of Diocletian it was ceded to the
Nubæ by the Romans, and it was frequently attacked by the
Blemmyes from the east bank of the river. At **Kardâsh,**
on the west bank of the river, 615 miles from Cairo, are the
ruins of a temple and a quarry; seven miles further south,
on the west bank of the river, is **Wâdi Tâfah,** where
there are also some ruins; they are however of little
ínterest.

KALÂBSHÎ.

Kalâbshî, on the west bank of the river, 629 miles from
Cairo, stands on the site of the classical Talmis, called in
hieroglyphics 𓈖𓏏𓊖 Thermeset, and 𓎛𓊪𓄿𓅱𓆊

* (𓇋𓏏𓄿𓊪𓏏𓂋𓏏𓈖𓇋𓏠𓈖) "*Àt′a-char-Àmen,* living for
ever, beloved of Isis," with the prenomen (𓇳𓈖𓏏𓇳 𓈖𓏤)
Àt-nu-Rā, setep-en-neteru.

Ka-ḥefennu; it stands immediately on the Tropic of Cancer. The god of this town was called ☰ ⚲ ‖ ⚏ Merul or Melul, the Mandulis or Malulis of the Greeks. At Kalâbshî there are the ruins of two temples of considerable interest. The larger of these, which is one of the largest temples in Nubia, appears to have been built upon the site of an ancient Egyptian temple founded by Thothmes III., B.C. 1600, and Amenophis II., B.C. 1566, for on the pronaos this latter monarch is representing offering to the god Âmsu and the Ethiopian god Merul or Melul. It seems to have been restored in Ptolemaic times, and to have been considerably added to by several of the Roman emperors—Augustus, Caligula, Trajan, etc. From the appearance of the ruins it would seem that the building was wrecked either immediately before or soon after it was completed ; some of the chambers were plastered over and used for chapels by the early Christians. A large number of Greek and Latin inscriptions have been found engraved on the walls of this temple, and from one of them we learn that the Blemmyes were frequently defeated by Silco, king of the Nubæ and Ethiopians, about the end of the third century of our era.

At **Bêt el-Walî,** a short distance from the larger temple, is the interesting rock-hewn temple which was made to commemorate the victories of Rameses II. over the Ethiopians. On the walls of the court leading into the small hall are some beautifully executed sculptures, representing the Ethiopians bringing before the king large quantities of articles of value, together with gifts of wild and tame animals, after their defeat. Many of the objects depicted must have come from a considerable distance, and it is evident that in those early times Talmis was the great central market to which the products and wares of the Sûdân were brought for sale and barter. The sculptures are executed with great freedom and spirit, and when the colours upon them were fresh they must have formed one of the most striking sights in Nubia. Some years ago casts of these interesting sculptures were taken by Mr. Bonomi, at the expense of Mr. Hay, and notes on the colours were made; these two casts, painted according to Mr. Bonomi's notes, are now set up on the walls in the Fourth Egyptian Room in the British Museum (Northern Gallery), and are the only evidences extant of the former beauty of this little rock-hewn temple, for nearly every trace of colour has vanished from the walls. The scenes on the battle-field are of great interest.

Between Kalâbshî and **Dendûr,** on the west bank of the river, 642 miles from Cairo, there is nothing of interest to be seen; at Dendûr are the remains of a temple built by Augustus, (☐) Pa-āa, where this emperor is shown making offerings to Âmen, Osiris, Isis, and Sati. At **Gerf Hussên,** on the west bank of the river, 651 miles from Cairo, are the remains of a rock-hewn temple built by Rameses II. in honour of Ptah, Hathor, and Aneq; the work is poor and of little interest. This village marks the site of the ancient Tutzis.

Dakkeh, on the west bank of the river, $662\frac{1}{2}$ miles from Cairo, marks the site of the classical Pselcis, the ☐ P-selket of the hieroglyphics. About B.C. 23 the Ethiopians attacked the Roman garrisons at Philæ and Syene, and having defeated them, overran Upper Egypt. Petronius, the successor of Ælius Gallus, marching with less than 10,000 infantry and 800 horse against the rebel army of 30,000 men, compelled them to retreat to Pselcis, which he afterwards besieged and took. "Part of the insurgents were driven into the city, others fled into the uninhabited country; and such as ventured upon the passage of the river, escaped to a neighbouring island, where there were not many crocodiles on account of the current. Among the fugitives were the generals of Candace,* queen of the Ethiopians in our time, a masculine woman, and who had lost an eye. Petronius, pursuing them in rafts and ships, took them all, and despatched them immediately to Alexandria." (Strabo, XVII., 1, 54.) From Pselcis Petronius advanced to Premnis (Ibrîm), and afterwards to Napata, the royal seat of Candace, which he razed to the ground. As long as the Romans held Ethiopia, Pselcis was a garrison town.

The temple at Dakkeh was built by *Arq-Amen ānch t'etta mer Auset,* "Àrq-Àmen, living for ever, beloved of Isis," having the prenomen "*Amen ṭet ānch àt Rā.*" In the sculptures on the ruins which remain Àrq-Àmen is shown standing between Menthu-Rā, lord of Thebes, and Àtmu the god of Heliopolis, and sacrificing to Thoth, who promises to give him a long and prosperous life as king. Àrq-Àmen is called the "beautiful god, son of Chnemu and Osiris, born of Sati and Isis, nursed by Aneq and Nephthys," etc. According to Diodorus, the priests of Meroë in Ethiopia were in the habit of sending, "whensoever they please, a messenger to the king, commanding him to put himself to death ; for that such is the pleasure of the gods ; . . . and so in former ages, the kings without force or compulsion of arms, but merely bewitched by a fond superstition, observed the custom; till Ergamenes (Àrq-Àmen), a king of Ethiopia, who reigned in the time of Ptolemy II., bred up in the Grecian discipline and philosophy, was the first that was so bold as to reject and despise such commands. For this prince . . . marched with a considerable body of men to the sanctuary, where stood the golden temple of the Ethiopians, and there cut the throats of all the priests."

* Candace was a title borne by all the queens of Meroë.

(Bk. III., chap. vi.)   Many of the Ptolemies appear to have made additions to the temple at Dakkeh.

On the east bank of the river opposite Dakkeh is **Kubân,** called ⸢𓁹𓆖𓏏𓃒𓃀⸣ Baka, in the hieroglyphics, a village which is said to mark the site of Tachompso or Metachompso, "the place of crocodiles."   As Pselcis increased, so Tachompso declined, and became finally merely a suburb of that town ; it was generally called Contra-Pselcis.   During the XVIIIth and XIXth dynasties this place was well fortified by the Egyptians, and on many blocks of stone close by are found the names of Thothmes III., Ḥeru-em-heb, and Rameses II.   It appears to have been the point from which the wretched people condemned to labour in the gold mines in the desert of the land of Akita set out ; and an interesting inscription on a stone found here relates that Rameses II., having heard that much gold existed in this land, which was inaccessible on account of the absolute want of water, bored a well in the mountain, twelve cubits deep, so that henceforth men could come and go by this land.   His father Seti I. had bored a well 120 cubits deep, but no water appeared in it.

About 20 miles from Dakkeh, and 690 from Cairo, on the west bank of the river, is **Wâdi Sebûa,** or the "Valley of the Lions," where there are the remains of a temple partly built of sandstone, and partly excavated in the rock ; the place is so called on account of the dromos of sixteen sphinxes which led up to the temple.   On the sculptures which still remain here may be seen Rameses II., the builder of the temple, " making an offering of incense to father Âmen, the king of the gods," who says to him, "I give to thee all might, and I give the world to thee, in peace." Elsewhere the king is making offerings to Tefnut, lady of heaven Nebt-ḥetep, Horus and Thoth, each of whom promises to bestow some blessing upon him.   On another part is a boat containing a ram-headed god, and Harmachis, seated in a shrine, accompanied by Horus, Thoth, Isis, and Māt; the king kneels before him in adoration, and the god says that he will give him myriads of years and festivals; on each side is a figure of Rameses II. making an offering. Beneath this scene is a figure of a Christian saint holding a key, and an inscription on each side tells us that it is meant to represent Peter the Apostle. This picture and the remains of plaster on the walls show that the chambers of the temple were used by the early Christians as chapels.

Korosko, on the east bank of the river, 703 miles from Cairo, was from the earliest times the point of departure for merchants and others going to and fro from the Sûdân; from the western bank there was a caravan route across into north Africa. In ancient days the land which lay to the east of Korosko was called 𓄿𓅓𓄿𓅓 Uaua, and as early as the VIth dynasty the officer Unà visited it in order to obtain blocks of acacia wood for his king Pepi II. An inscription, found a few hundred yards to the east of the town, records that the country round about was conquered in the XIIth dynasty by Ámenemḥāt I. ⟨𓇳𓏏𓈗𓋴⟩. About seven miles off is the battle-field of Toski, on the west bank of the Nile. A capital idea of the general character of Nubian scenery can be obtained by ascending the mountain, which is now, thanks to a good path, easily accessible.

At **Amada,** on the west bank of the river, 711 miles from Cairo, is a small but interesting temple, which appears to have been founded in the XIIth dynasty by Usertsen II., who conquered Nubia by setting fire to standing crops, by carrying away the wives and cattle, and by cutting down the men on their way to and from the wells. This temple was repaired by Thothmes III. and other kings of the XVIIIth dynasty.

At **Dêrr,** on the east bank of the river, 715 miles from Cairo, is a small, badly executed rock-hewn temple of the time of Rameses II., where the usual scenes representing the defeat of the Ethiopians are depicted. The king is accompanied by a tame "lion which follows after his majesty, 〔hieroglyphs〕 ———, *maàu śesi en ḥen-f,* to slay . . . . . ." Close to the temple is the rock stele of the prince Ȧmen-em-ḥeb of the same period; the temple was dedicated to Ȧmen-Rā. The Egyptian name of the town was 〔hieroglyphs〕, *Pa-Rā pa ṭemài,* "the town of the temple of the sun."

Thirteen miles beyond Dêrr, 728 miles from Cairo, also on the east bank of the river, stands **Ibrîm,** which marks the site of the ancient Primis, or Premnis, called in the Egyptian inscriptions 〔hieroglyphs〕, Mȧāmam. This town was captured during the reign of Augustus by Petronius on his victorious march upon Napata. In the first and third naos at Primis are representations of Neḥi, the governor of Nubia, with other officers, bringing gifts before Thothmes III., which shows that these caves were hewn during the reign of this king; and in another, Rameses II. is receiving adorations from Setau, prince of Ethiopia, and a number of his officers. At Anibe, just opposite Ibrîm, is the grave of Penni, the governor of the district, who died during the reign of Rameses VI.

ABÛ SIMBEL.*

Abû Simbel, on the west bank of the river, 762 miles from Cairo, is the classical Aboccis, and the place called 〔hieroglyphs〕 Ȧbshek in the Egyptian inscriptions. Around, or near the temple, a town of considerable size

* The spelling of this name is doubtful.

I. Plan of the Temple of Rameses II. at Abû Simbel.
II. The seated Colossi and front of the Temple at Abû Simbel.

From Lepsius' *Denkmäler*, Bd. iii., Bl. 185.

once stood; all traces of this have, however, disappeared. To the north of the great temple, hewn in the living rock, is a smaller temple, about 84 feet long, which was dedicated to the goddess Hathor by Rameses II. and his wife Nefert-Åri. The front is ornamented with statues of the king, his wife, and some of his children, and over the door are his names and titles. In the hall inside are six square Hathor-headed pillars also inscribed with the names and titles of Rameses and his wife. In the small chamber at the extreme end of the temple is an interesting scene in which the king is making an offering to Hathor in the form of a cow; she is called the "lady of Åbshek," and is standing behind a figure of the king.

The chief object of interest at Abû Simbel is the Great Temple built by Rameses II. to commemorate his victory over the Cheta in north-east Syria; it is the largest and finest Egyptian monument in Nubia, and for simple grandeur and majesty is second to none in all Egypt. This temple is hewn out of the solid grit-stone rock to a depth of 185 feet, and the surface of the rock, which originally sloped down to the river, was cut away for a space of about 90 feet square to form the front of the temple, which is ornamented by four colossal statues of Rameses II., 66 feet high, seated on thrones, hewn out of the living rock. The cornice is, according to the drawing by Lepsius, decorated with twenty-one cynocephali, and beneath it, in the middle, is a line of hieroglyphics, , *ṭå-nå nek ānch usr neb*, "I give to thee all life and strength," on the right side of which are four figures of Rā, , and eight cartouches containing the prenomen of Rameses II., with a uræus on each side; on the left side are four figures of Åmen, , and eight cartouches as on the right. The line of boldly cut hieroglyphics below reads, "The living Horus, the mighty bull, beloved of Māt, king of the North and

South, Usr-Māt-Rā setep en-Rā, son of the Sun, Rameses, beloved of Ȧmen, beloved of Harmachis the great god." Over the door is a statue of Harmachis, and on each side of him is a figure of the king offering . Each of the four colossi had the name of Rameses II. inscribed upon each shoulder and breast. On the leg of one of these are several interesting Greek inscriptions, which were thought to have been written by the Egyptian troops who marched into Ethiopia in the days of Psammetichus I.

The interior of the temple consists of a large hall, in which are eight columns with large figures of Osiris about 17 feet high upon them, and from which eight chambers open; a second hall having four square columns; and a third hall, without pillars, from which open three chambers. In the centre chamber is an altar and four seated figures, viz., Harmachis, Rameses II., Ȧmen-Rā, and Ptaḥ; the first two are coloured red, the third blue, and the fourth white. In the sculptures on the walls Rameses is seen offering to Ȧmen-Rā, Sechet, Harmachis, Ȧmsu, Thoth, and other deities; a list of his children occurs, and many small scenes of considerable importance. The subjects of the larger scenes are, as was to be expected, representations of the principal events in the victorious battles of the great king, in which he appears putting his foes to death with the weapons which Harmachis has given to him. The accompanying hieroglyphics describe these scenes with terse accuracy.

One of the most interesting inscriptions at Abû Simbel is that found on a slab, which states that in the fifth year of the reign of Rameses II., his majesty was in the land of T'ah, not far from Kadesh on the Orontes. The outposts kept a sharp look-out, and when the army came to the south of the town of Shabtûn, two of the spies of the Shasu came into the camp and pretended that they had been sent by the chiefs of their tribe to inform Rameses II. that they had forsaken the chief of the Cheta,* and that they wished to make an alliance with his majesty and become vassals of his. They then went on to say that the chief of the Cheta was in the land of Chirebu to the north of Tunep, some distance off, and that they were afraid to come near the Egyptian king. These two men were giving false information, and they had actually been sent by the Cheta chief to find out where Rameses and his army was ; the Cheta chief and his army were at that moment drawn up in battle array behind Kadesh. Shortly after these men were dismissed, an Egyptian scout came into the king's presence bringing with him two spies from the army of the chief of the Cheta; on being questioned, they informed Rameses that the chief of the Cheta was encamped behind Kadesh, and that he had succeeded in gathering together a multitude of soldiers and chariots from the countries round about. Rameses summoned his officers to his presence, and informed them of the news which he had just heard ; they listened with surprise, and insisted that the newly-received information was untrue. Rameses blamed the chiefs of the intelligence department seriously for their neglect of duty, and they admitted their fault. Orders were straightway issued for the Egyptian army to march upon Kadesh, and as they were crossing an arm of the river near that city the hostile forces fell in with each other. When Rameses saw this, he " growled at them like his father Menthu, lord of Thebes," and having hastily put on his full armour, he mounted his chariot and drove into the battle. His onset was so sudden and rapid that before he knew where he was he

---

* The Cheta have, during the last few years, been identified with the Hittites of the Bible ; there is no ground for this identification beyond the slight similarity of the names. The inscriptions upon the sculptures found at Jerâbîs still remain undeciphered.

found himself surrounded by the enemy, and completely isolated from his own troops. He called upon his father Ȧmen-Rā to help him, and then addressed himself to a slaughter of all those that came in his way, and his prowess was so great that the enemy fell in heaps, one over the other, into the waters of the Orontes. He was quite alone, and not one of his soldiers or horsemen came near him to help him. It was only with great difficulty he succeeded in cutting his way through the ranks of the enemy. At the end of the inscription he says, "Every thing that my majesty has stated, that did I in the presence of my soldiers and horsemen." This event in the battle of the Egyptians against the Cheta was made the subject of an interesting poem by Pen-ta-urt; this composition was considered worthy to be inscribed upon papyri, and upon the walls of the temples which Rameses built.

A little to the south of the Great Temple is a small building of the same date, which was used in connexion with the services, and on the walls of which are some interesting scenes. It was re-opened a few years ago by Miss Edwards and her party.

The village of Wâdi Ḥalfah, on the east bank of the Nile, 802 miles from Cairo, marks the site of a part of the district called ⌇ Buhen in the hieroglyphic inscription, where, as at Dêrr and Ibrîm, the god Harmachis was worshipped. On the plain to the east of the village some interesting flint weapons have been found, and a few miles distant are the fossil remains of a forest. On the western bank of the river, a little further south, are the remains of a temple which, if not actually built, was certainly restored by Thothmes III. It was repaired and added to by later kings of Egypt, but it seems to have fallen into disuse soon after the Romans gained possession of Egypt. A few miles south of Wâdi Ḥalfah begins the second cataract, a splendid view of which can be obtained from the now famous rock of Abûṣîr on the west bank of the river. Nearly every traveller who has visited Abû Simbel has been to this rock and inscribed his name upon it ; the result is an interesting collection of names and dates, the like of which probably exists nowhere else.

A narrow gauge railway from Wâdi Ḥalfah to Sarras was laid down by the English a few years ago to carry troops and stores above the Second Cataract, and until quite recently about eighteen miles of it, passing through wild scenery, remained *in situ.* The other part of it had been torn up by the dervishes, who threw the iron rails into the cataract, used the sleepers to boil their kettles, and twisted lengths of the telegraph wires together to form spears. This line has again been restored by the Egyptian army.

The remains of Egyptian temples, etc., at Semneh above the second cataract are of interest, but it is probable that they would not repay the traveller who was not specially concerned with archæology, for the fatigue of the journey and the expense which he must necessarily incur to reach them.

LIST OF EGYPTIAN KINGS.

DYNASTY I., FROM THINIS, B.C. 4400.

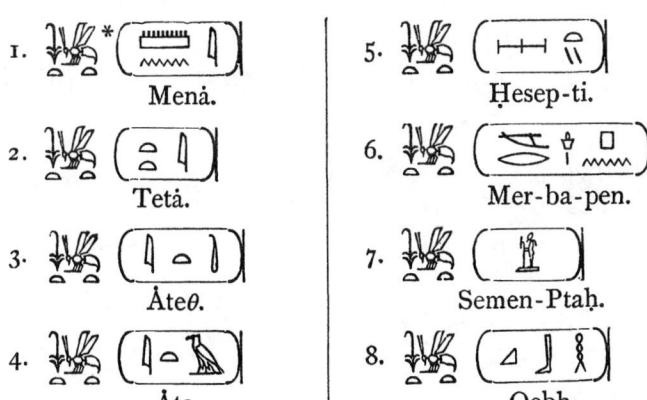

1. Menà.
2. Tetà.
3. Àteθ.
4. Àta.
5. Ḥesep-ti.
6. Mer-ba-pen.
7. Semen-Ptaḥ.
8. Qebḥ.

DYNASTY II., FROM THINIS, B.C. 4133.

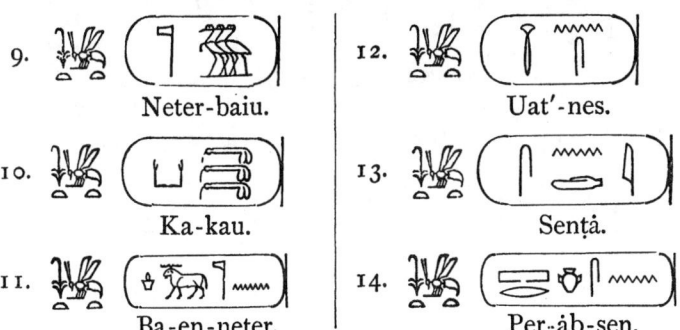

9. Neter-baiu.
10. Ka-kau.
11. Ba-en-neter.
12. Uat'-nes.
13. Sentà.
14. Per-àb-sen.

* = *suten net*, " King of the North and South."

15. Nefer-ka-Rā.*

16. Nefer-ka-seker.

17. Ḥet'efa.

DYNASTY III., FROM MEMPHIS, B.C. 3966.

18. T'at'ai.

22. Set'es.

19. Neb-ka.

23. Sertetâ.

20. Ser.

24. Âḥtes.

21. Tetâ.

25. Nub-ka-Rā.

26. Nefer-ka-Rā, son of the Sun, Ḥuni.

DYNASTY IV., FROM MEMPHIS, B.C. 3766.

27. Seneferu.

28. χufu.
(Cheops.)

* Though ☉ Rā is generally placed first in the cartouche, it is generally to be read last.

† 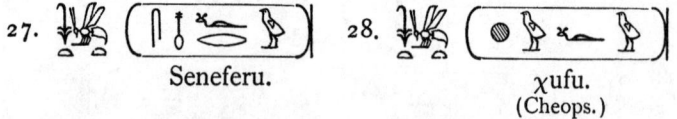 = *se Rā*, "son of the Sun."

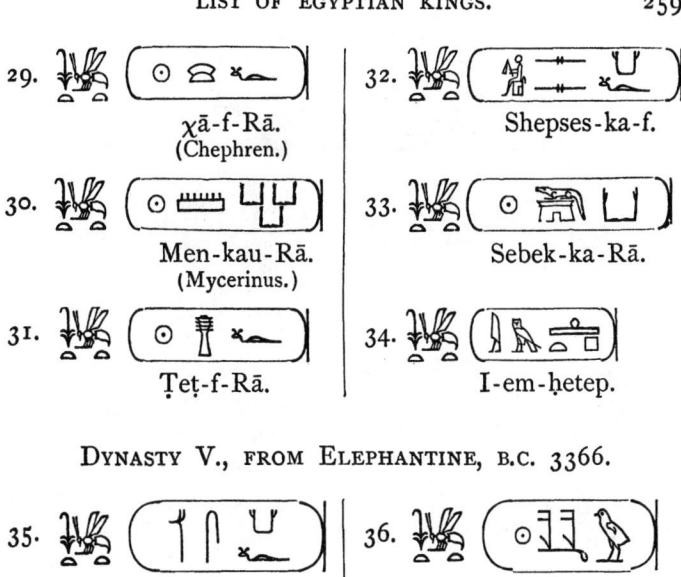

29. χā-f-Rā.
(Chephren.)

30. Men-kau-Rā.
(Mycerinus.)

31. Teṭ-f-Rā.

32. Shepses-ka-f.

33. Sebek-ka-Rā.

34. I-em-ḥetep.

DYNASTY V., FROM ELEPHANTINE, B.C. 3366.

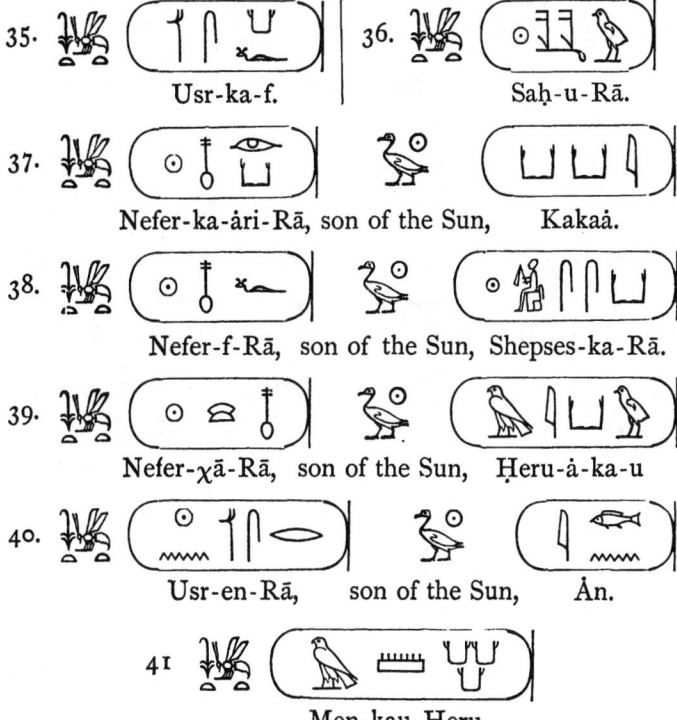

35. Usr-ka-f.

36. Saḥ-u-Rā.

37. Nefer-ka-ȧri-Rā, son of the Sun, Kakaȧ.

38. Nefer-f-Rā, son of the Sun, Shepses-ka-Rā.

39. Nefer-χā-Rā, son of the Sun, Ḥeru-ȧ-ka-u

40. Usr-en-Rā, son of the Sun, Ȧn.

41 Men-kau-Ḥeru.

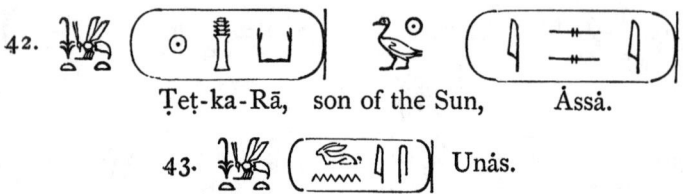

42. Ṭeṭ-ka-Rā, son of the Sun, Ȧssȧ.

43. Unȧs.

DYNASTY VI, FROM MEMPHIS, B.C. 3266.

44. Tetȧ.   **or**   Tetȧ-mer-en-Ptaḥ.
(Teta beloved of Ptaḥ.)

45. 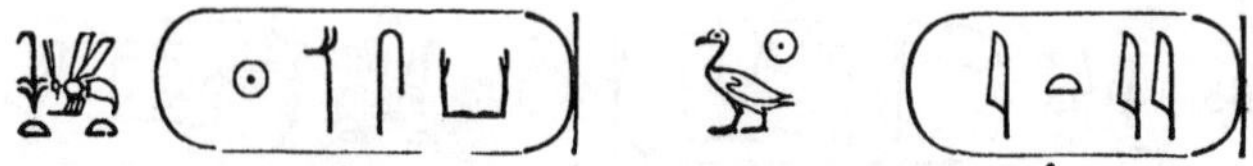 Usr-ka-Rā,   son of the Sun,   Ȧti.

46.  Meri-Rā,   son of the Sun,   Pepi (I.).

47.  Mer-en-Rā, son of the Sun,   Ḥeru-em-sa-f.

48.  Nefer-ka-Rā,   son of the Sun,   Pepi (I.).

49.  Rā-mer-en-se (?)-em-sa-f   50.  Neter-ka-Rā.

51.  Men-ka-Rā, son of the Sun,   Netȧqerti.
(Nitocris.)

DYNASTIES VII. AND VIII., FROM MEMPHIS; DYNASTIES IX. AND X., FROM HERACLEOPOLIS, B.C. 3100.

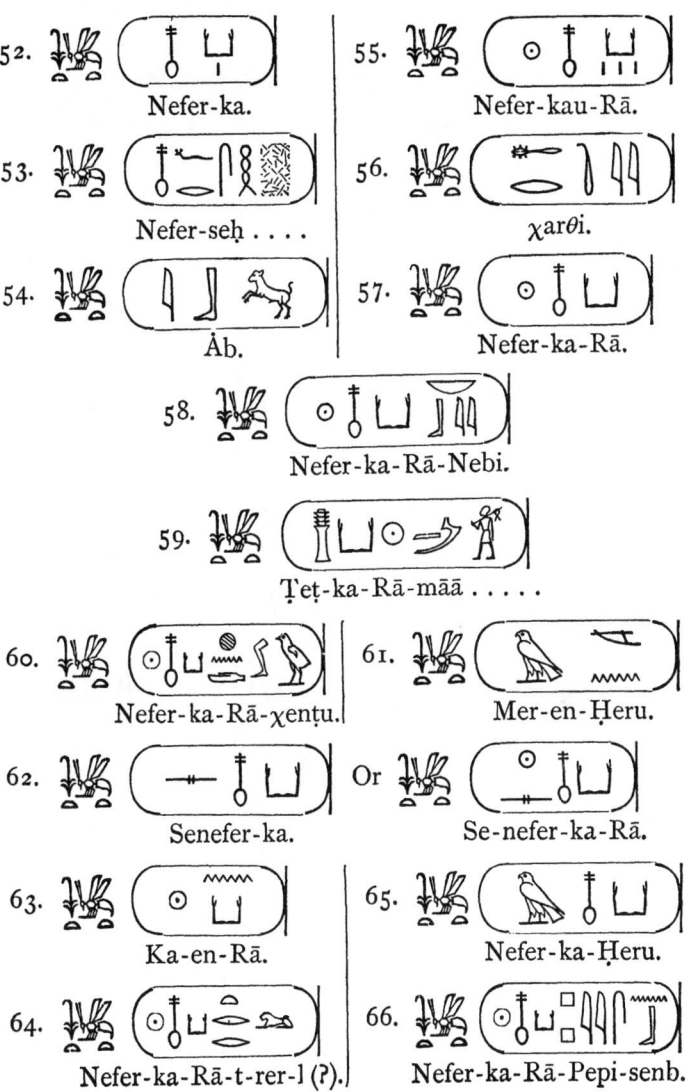

52. Nefer-ka.

53. Nefer-seḥ . . . .

54. Áb.

55. Nefer-kau-Rā.

56. χarθi.

57. Nefer-ka-Rā.

58. Nefer-ka-Rā-Nebi.

59. Ṭeṭ-ka-Rā-māā . . . . .

60. Nefer-ka-Rā-χenṭu.

61. Mer-en-Ḥeru.

62. Senefer-ka.

Or Se-nefer-ka-Rā.

63. Ka-en-Rā.

64. Nefer-ka-Rā-t-rer-l (?).

65. Nefer-ka-Ḥeru.

66. Nefer-ka-Rā-Pepi-senb.

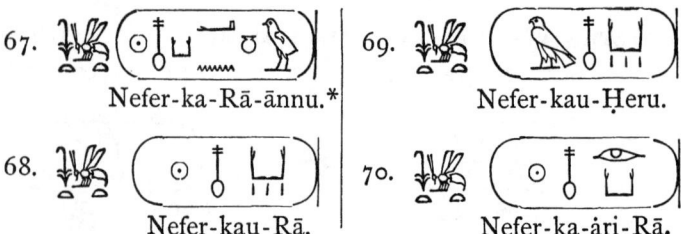

67. Nefer-ka-Rā-ānnu.*

68. Nefer-kau-Rā.

69. Nefer-kau-Ḥeru.

70. Nefer-ka-ȧri-Rā.

DYNASTY XI., FROM THEBES.

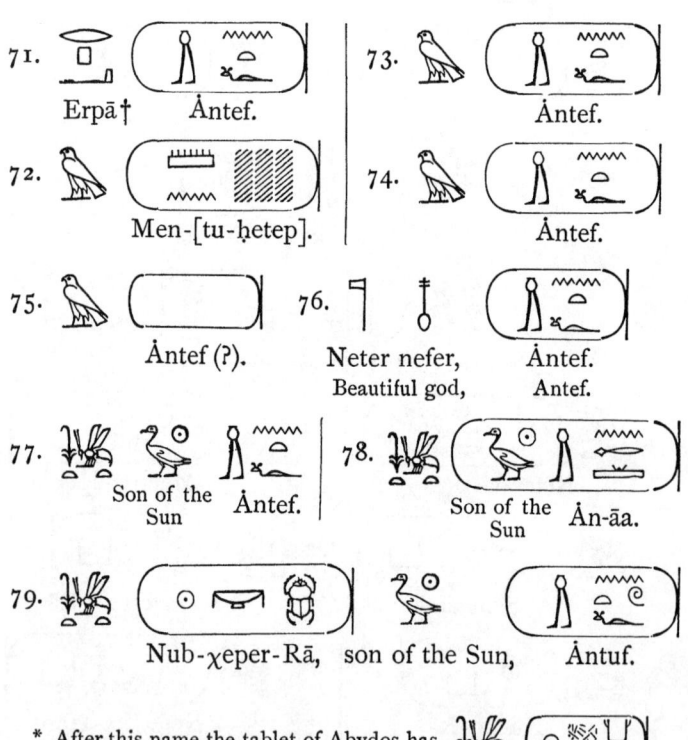

71. Erpā† Ȧntef.

72. Men-[tu-ḥetep].

73. Ȧntef.

74. Ȧntef.

75. Ȧntef (?).

76. Neter nefer, Ȧntef.
Beautiful god, Ȧntef.

77. Son of the Sun Ȧntef.

78. Son of the Sun Ȧn-āa.

79. Nub-χeper-Rā, son of the Sun, Ȧntuf.

* After this name the tablet of Abydos has
.... kau-Ra.

† Erpā, usually translated "hereditary prince" or "duke," is one
of the oldest titles of nobility in Egypt.

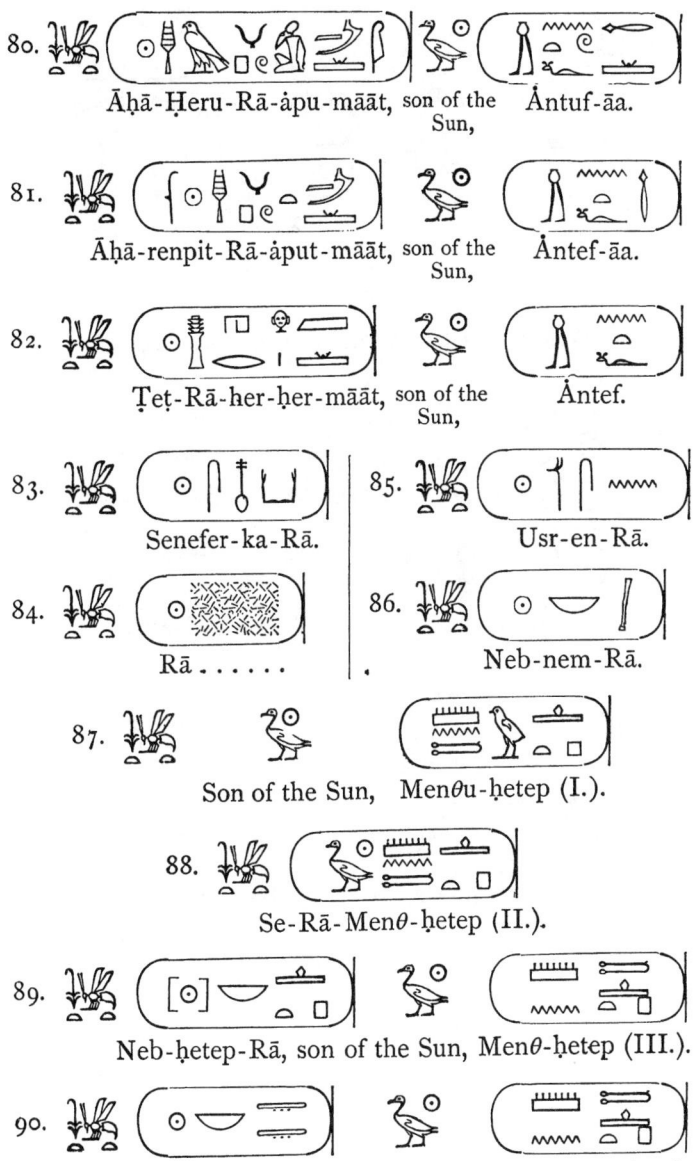

80. Āḥā-Ḥeru-Rā-àpu-māāt, son of the Sun, Àntuf-āa.

81. Āḥā-renpit-Rā-àput-māāt, son of the Sun, Àntef-āa.

82. Ṭeṭ-Rā-her-ḥer-māāt, son of the Sun, Àntef.

83. Senefer-ka-Rā.

84. Rā......

85. Usr-en-Rā.

86. Neb-nem-Rā.

87. Son of the Sun, Menθu-ḥetep (I.).

88. Se-Rā-Menθ-ḥetep (II.).

89. Neb-ḥetep-Rā, son of the Sun, Menθ-ḥetep (III.).

90. Neb-taiu-Rā, son of the Sun, Menθ-ḥetep (IV.).

91.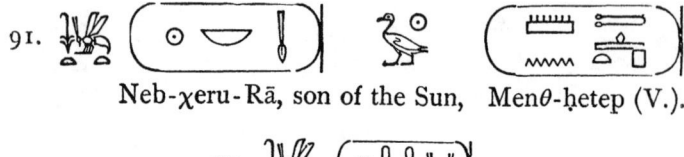

Neb-χeru-Rā, son of the Sun, Menθ-ḥetep (V.).

92.

Se-ānχ-ka-Rā.

DYNASTY XII., FROM THEBES, B.C. 2466.

93.

Seḥetep-áb-Rā, son of the Sun, Åmen-em-ḥāt (I.).

94.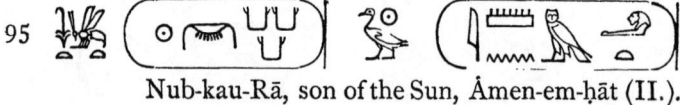

χeper-ka-Rā, son of the Sun, Usertsen (I.).

95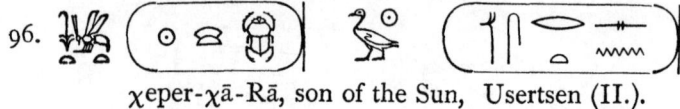

Nub-kau-Rā, son of the Sun, Åmen-em-ḥāt (II.).

96.

χeper-χā-Rā, son of the Sun, Usertsen (II.).

97.

χā-kau-Rā, son of the Sun, Usertsen (III.).

98.

Māāt-en-Rā,   son of the Åmen-em-ḥāt (III.).
              Sun,

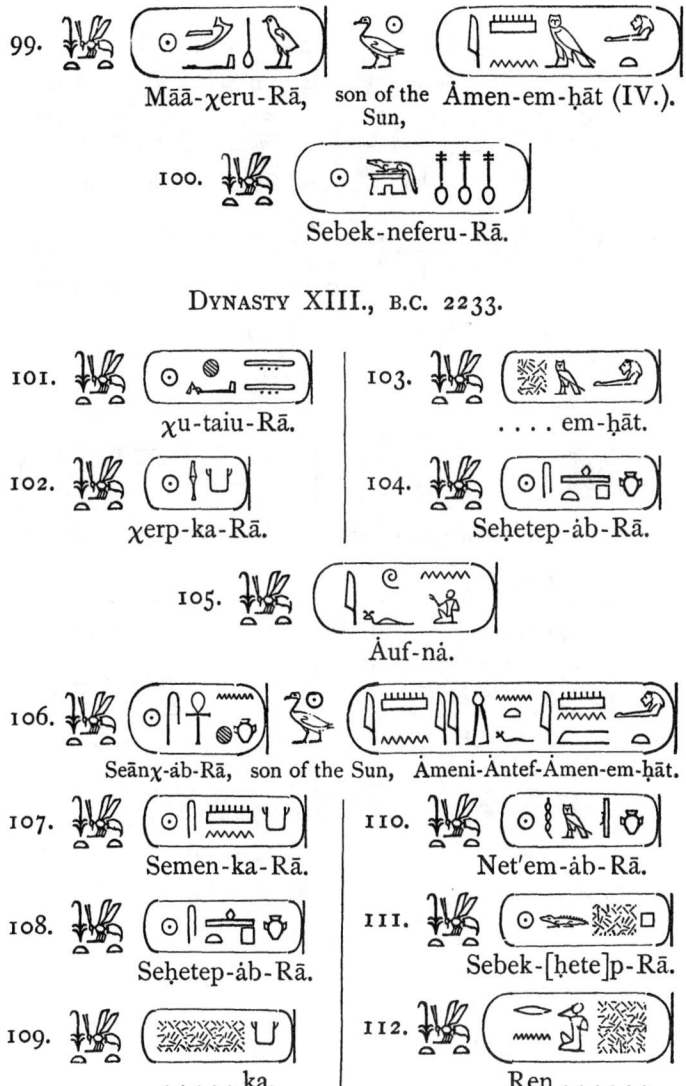

99. Māā-χeru-Rā, son of the Sun, Åmen-em-ḥāt (IV.).

100. Sebek-neferu-Rā.

DYNASTY XIII., B.C. 2233.

101. χu-taiu-Rā.

103. .... em-ḥāt.

102. χerp-ka-Rā.

104. Seḥetep-áb-Rā.

105. Åuf-ná.

106. Seānχ-áb-Rā, son of the Sun, Åmeni-Åntef-Åmen-em-ḥāt.

107. Semen-ka-Rā.

110. Net'em-áb-Rā.

108. Seḥetep-áb-Rā.

111. Sebek-[ḥete]p-Rā.

109. .... ka.

112. Ren ......

113. Set'ef .... Rā.

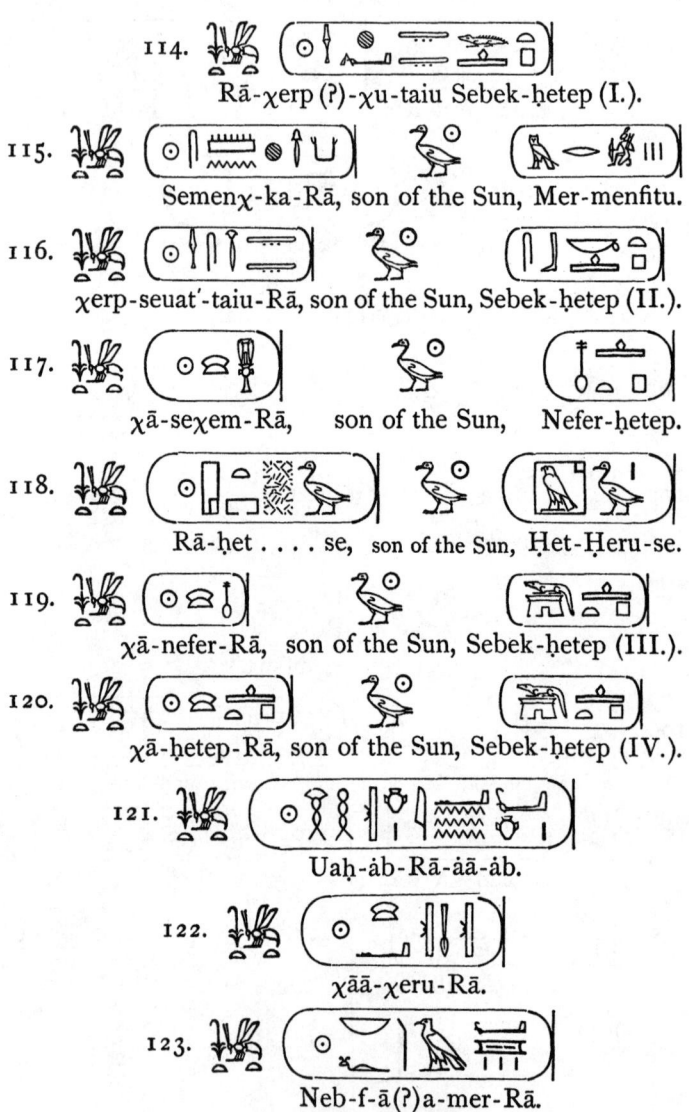

114. Rā-χerp (?)-χu-taiu Sebek-ḥetep (I.).

115. Semenχ-ka-Rā, son of the Sun, Mer-menfitu.

116. χerp-seuat'-taiu-Rā, son of the Sun, Sebek-ḥetep (II.).

117. χā-seχem-Rā,   son of the Sun,   Nefer-ḥetep.

118. Rā-ḥet . . . . se,   son of the Sun,   Ḥet-Ḥeru-se.

119. χā-nefer-Rā, son of the Sun, Sebek-ḥetep (III.).

120. χā-ḥetep-Rā, son of the Sun, Sebek-ḥetep (IV.).

121. Uaḥ-ȧb-Rā-ȧā-ȧb.

122. χāā-χeru-Rā.

123. Neb-f-ā(?)a-mer-Rā.

124. Nefer-ȧb-Rā.

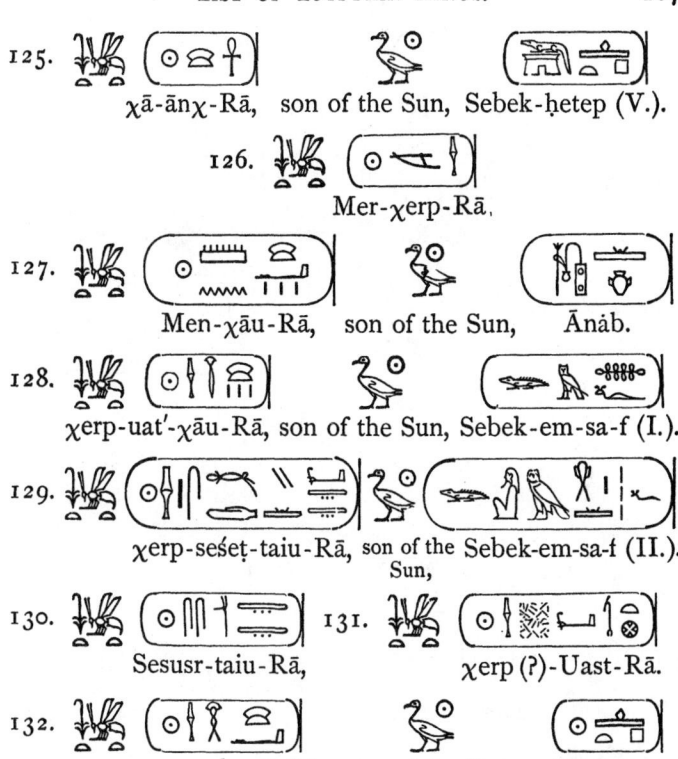

125. χā-ānχ-Rā, son of the Sun, Sebek-ḥetep (V.).

126. Mer-χerp-Rā.

127. Men-χāu-Rā, son of the Sun, Ānáb.

128. χerp-uat'-χāu-Rā, son of the Sun, Sebek-em-sa-f (I.).

129. χerp-seśeṭ-taiu-Rā, son of the Sun, Sebek-em-sa-f (II.).

130. Sesusr-taiu-Rā, 131. χerp (?)-Uast-Rā.

132. χerp-uaḥ-χā-Rā, son of the Sun, Rā-ḥetep.

DYNASTY XIV.

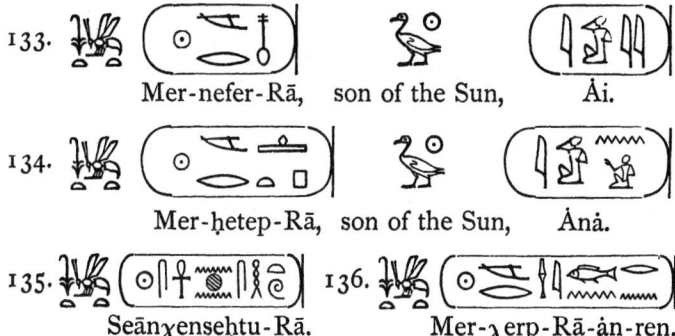

133. Mer-nefer-Rā, son of the Sun, Ái.

134. Mer-ḥetep-Rā, son of the Sun, Áná.

135. Seānχenseḥtu-Rā. 136. Mer-λerp-Rā-án-ren.

137.  Seuat'-en-Rā

138.  χā-ka-Rā.

139.  Ka-meri-Rā    neter nefer    Mer-kau-Rā.

140. 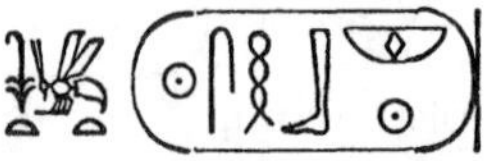 Seḥeb-Rā.

141. 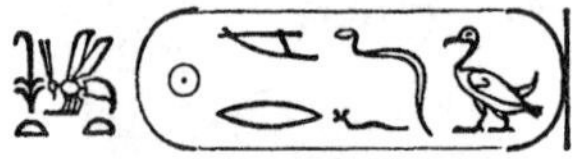 Mer-t'efa-Rā.

142.  Sta-ka-Rā.

143.  Neb-t'efa-Rā Rā (*sic*).

144.  Uben-Rā.

147. 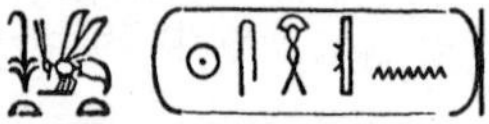 Seuaḥ-en-Rā.

145. Her-āb-Rā.

148.  Seχeper-en-Rā.

146. Neb-sen-Rā.

149. 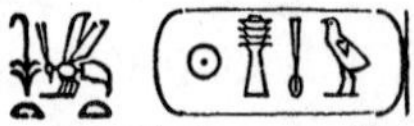 Ṭeṭ-χeru-Rā.

Dynasty XV., "Shepherd Kings."

150.

Āa-peḥ-peḥ-Set, son of the Sun, Nub-Set (?).

151.

. . . Bánān.

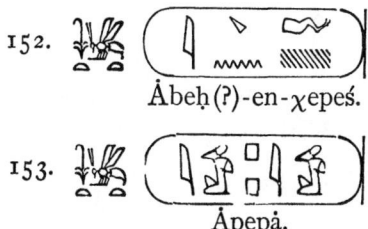

152. Âbeḥ(?)-en-χepeś.

153. Âpepá.

DYNASTY XVI., "SHEPHERD KINGS."

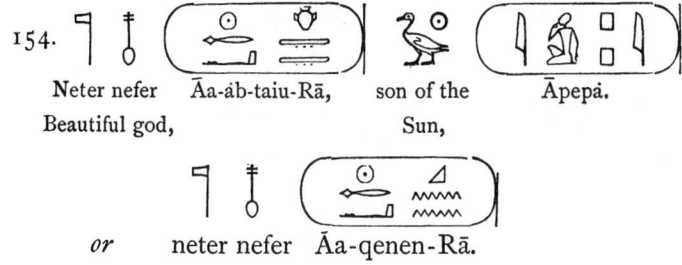

154. Neter nefer   Āa-áb-taiu-Rā,   son of the   Āpepá.
Beautiful god,   Sun,

or   neter nefer   Āa-qenen-Rā.

DYNASTY XVII., FROM THEBES.

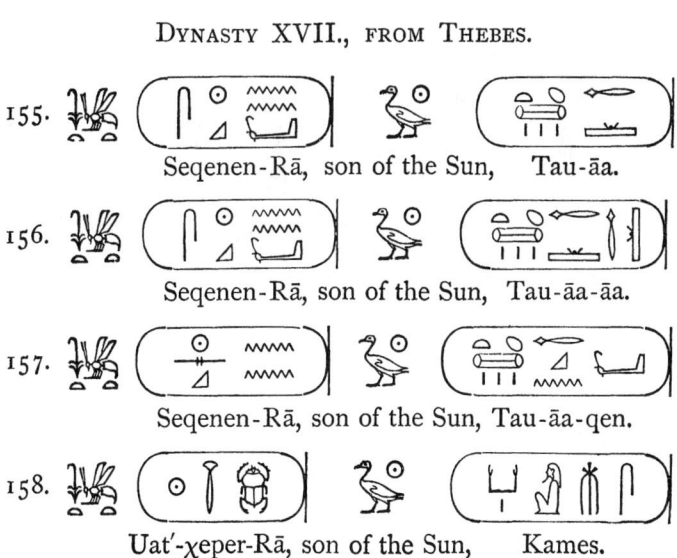

155. Seqenen-Rā, son of the Sun,   Tau-āa.

156. Seqenen-Rā, son of the Sun,   Tau-āa-āa.

157. Seqenen-Rā, son of the Sun,   Tau-āa-qen.

158. Uat'-χeper-Rā, son of the Sun,   Kames.

159.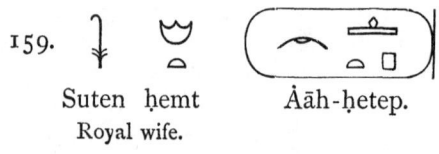

Suten ḥemt   Âāh-ḥetep.
Royal wife.

160.

Âāh-mes-se-pa-âri.

DYNASTY XVIII., FROM THEBES, B.C. 1700.

161.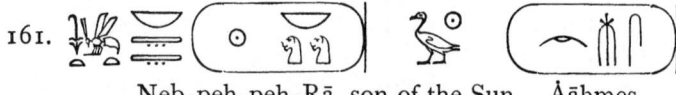

Neb-peḥ-peḥ-Rā, son of the Sun,   Âāḥmes.
             (Amāsis I.)

162.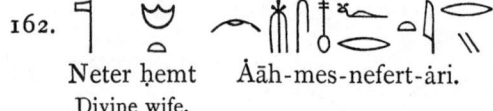

Neter ḥemt   Âāh-mes-nefert-âri.
Divine wife.

163.

Ser-ka-Rā,   son of the Sun,   Âmen-ḥetep.
             (Amenophis I.)

164.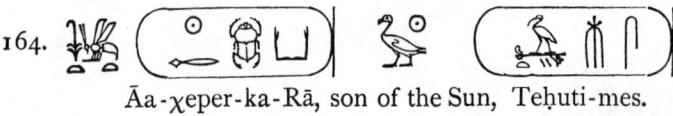

Āa-χeper-ka-Rā, son of the Sun,   Teḥuti-mes.
             (Thothmes I.)

165.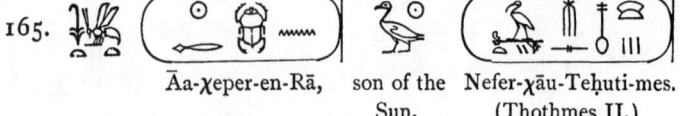

Āa-χeper-en-Rā,   son of the   Nefer-χāu-Teḥuti-mes.
         Sun,   (Thothmes II.)

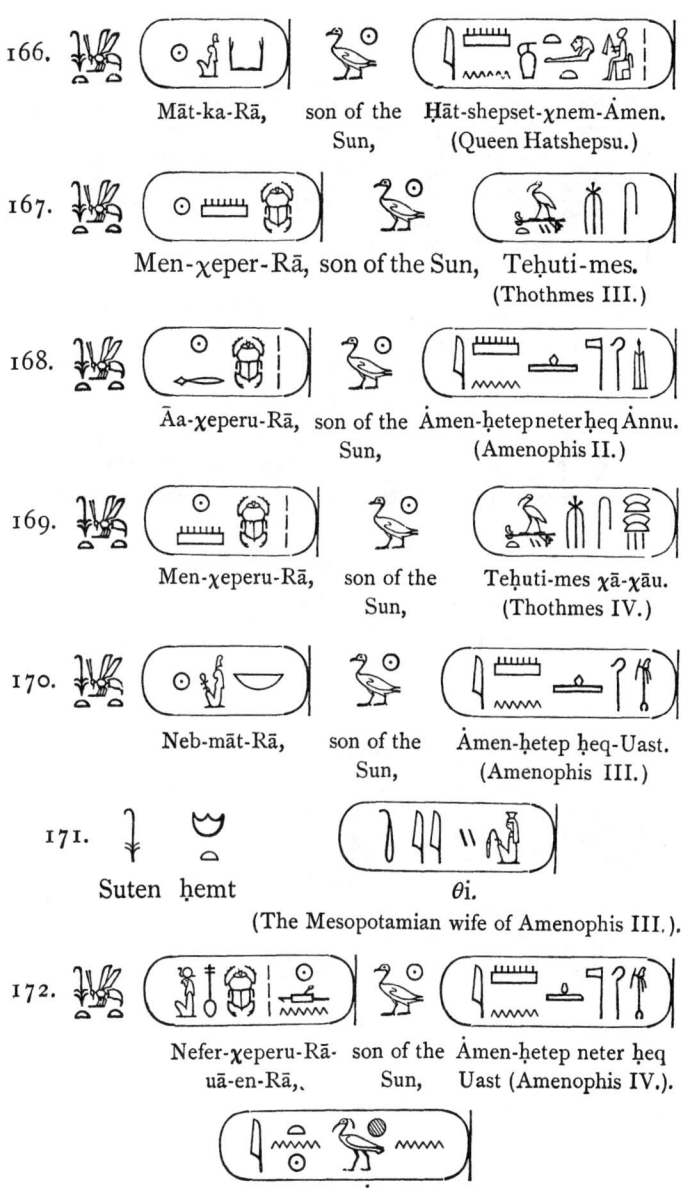

166. Māt-ka-Rā,   son of the   Ḥāt-shepset-χnem-Åmen.
                         Sun,   (Queen Hatshepsu.)

167. Men-χeper-Rā, son of the Sun,   Teḥuti-mes.
                                            (Thothmes III.)

168. Āa-χeperu-Rā,   son of the   Åmen-ḥetepneterḥeqÅnnu.
                        Sun,   (Amenophis II.)

169. Men-χeperu-Rā,   son of the   Teḥuti-mes χā-χāu.
                         Sun,   (Thothmes IV.)

170. Neb-māt-Rā,   son of the   Åmen-ḥetep ḥeq-Uast.
                         Sun,   (Amenophis III.)

171. Suten ḥemt   θi.
(The Mesopotamian wife of Amenophis III.).

172. Nefer-χeperu-Rā-   son of the   Åmen-ḥetep neter ḥeq
     uā-en-Rā,   Sun,   Uast (Amenophis IV.).

or   χu-en-Åten.

173.  Suten ḥemt   urt   Nefer-neferu-áten Neferti-īθ.
Royal wife,   great lady.

174.  Ānχ-χeperu-Rā, son of the   Seāa-ka-neχt-χeperu-Rā
Sun,

175.  Neb-χeperu-Rā, son of the   Tut-ānχ-Åmen ḥeq Ånnu
Sun,   resu (?)

176.  χeper-χeperu-māt-ári-Rā,   son of the   Atf-neter Åi neter
Sun,   ḥeq Uast.

177.  Ser-χeperu-Rā-   son of the   Åmen-meri-en Ḥeru-
setep-en-Rā,   Sun,   em-ḥeb.

DYNASTY XIX., FROM THEBES, B.C. 1400.

178.  Men-peḥtet-Rā, son of the Sun,   Rā-messu.
(Rameses I.)

179.  Men-māt-Rā, son of the Sun,   Ptaḥ-meri-en-Seti.
(Seti I.)

180. Usr-māt-Rā setep-   son of the   Rā-messu-meri-Åmen.
en-Rā,   Sun,   (Rameses II.)

181. 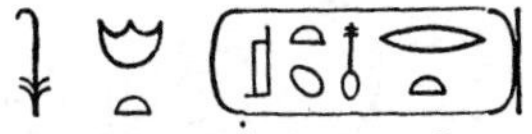 Suten ḥemt Áuset-nefert.
Royal wife.

182.  Suten mut · Tui.
Royal mother.

183.  Ba-Rā-meri-en-Ámen, son of the Sun, Ptaḥ-meri-en-ḥetep-ḥer-māt.
(Meneptah I.)

184.  Men-mȧ-Rȧ setep-en-Rā, son of the Sun, Ȧmen-meses-ḥeq-Uast.
(Amen-meses.)

185.  Usr-χeperu-Rā-meri-Ámen, son of the Sun, Seti-meri-en-Ptaḥ.
(Seti II).

186.  χu-en-Rā setep-en-Rā, son of the Sun, Ptaḥ-meri-en-se-Ptaḥ.
(Meneptah II.)

187.  Usr-χāu-Rā setep-en-Rā meri-Ámen, son of the Sun, Rā-meri Ámen-merer Set-neχt.
(Set-Neχt.)

DYNASTY XX., FROM THEBES, B.C. 1200.

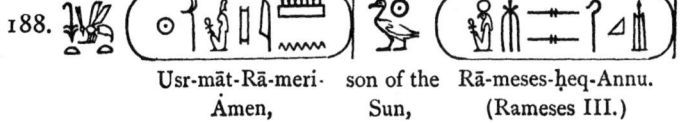

188. Usr-māt-Rā-meri-Ámen, son of the Sun, Rā-meses-ḥeq-Annu.
(Rameses III.)

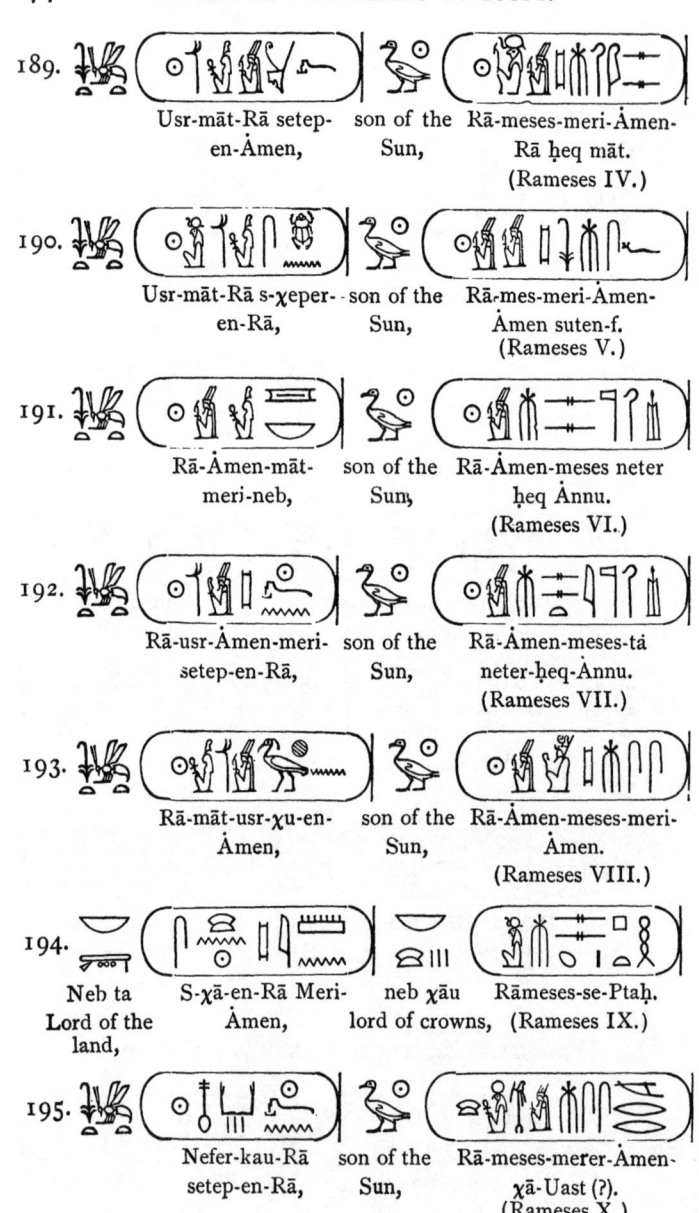

189. Usr-māt-Rā setep-
en-Åmen,
son of the
Sun,
Rā-meses-meri-Åmen-
Rā ḥeq māt.
(Rameses IV.)

190. Usr-māt-Rā s-χeper-
en-Rā,
son of the
Sun,
Rā-mes-meri-Åmen-
Åmen suten-f.
(Rameses V.)

191. Rā-Åmen-māt-
merj-neb,
son of the
Sun,
Rā-Åmen-meses neter
ḥeq Ånnu.
(Rameses VI.)

192. Rā-usr-Åmen-meri-
setep-en-Rā,
son of the
Sun,
Rā-Åmen-meses-tá
neter-ḥeq-Ånnu.
(Rameses VII.)

193. Rā-māt-usr-χu-en-
Åmen,
son of the
Sun,
Rā-Åmen-meses-meri-
Åmen.
(Rameses VIII.)

194. Neb ta
Lord of the
land,
S-χā-en-Rā Meri-
Åmen,
neb χāu
lord of crowns,
Rāmeses-se-Ptaḥ.
(Rameses IX.)

195. Nefer-kau-Rā
setep-en-Rā,
son of the
Sun,
Rā-meses-merer-Åmen-
χā-Uast (?).
(Rameses X.)

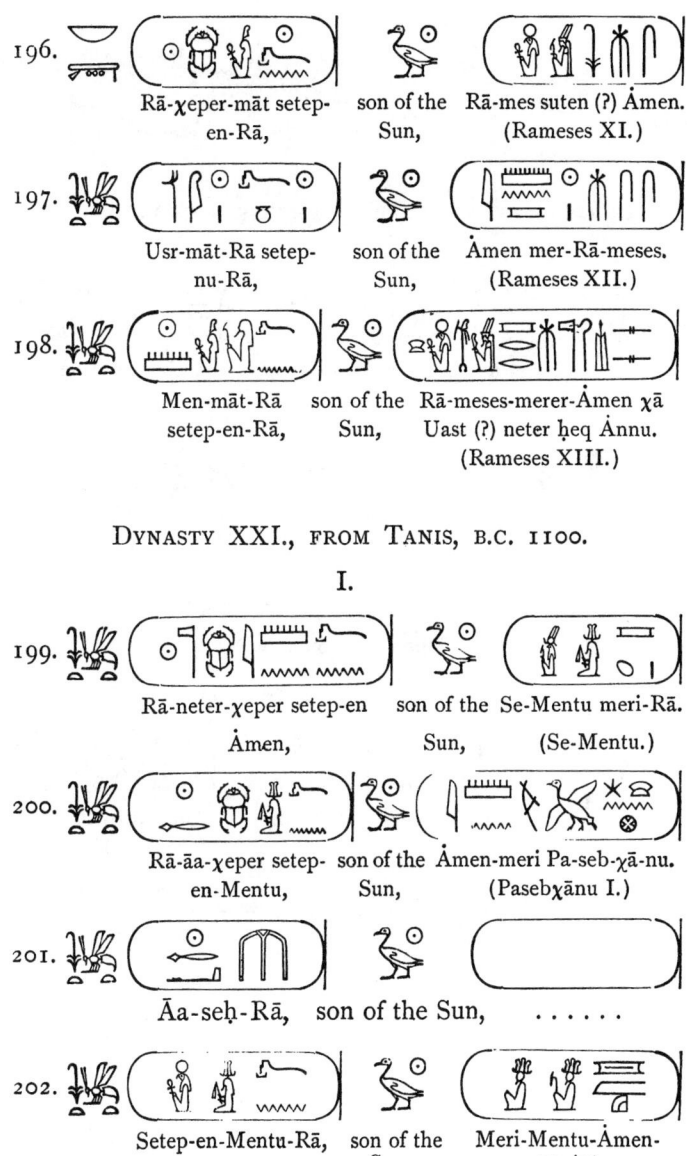

196. Rā-χeper-māt setep-en-Rā,   son of the Sun,   Rā-mes suten (?) Āmen. (Rameses XI.)

197. Usr-māt-Rā setep-nu-Rā,   son of the Sun,   Āmen mer-Rā-meses. (Rameses XII.)

198. Men-māt-Rā setep-en-Rā,   son of the Sun,   Rā-meses-merer-Āmen χā Uast (?) neter ḥeq Ānnu. (Rameses XIII.)

DYNASTY XXI., FROM TANIS, B.C. 1100.

I.

199. Rā-neter-χeper setep-en Āmen,   son of the Sun,   Se-Mentu meri-Rā. (Se-Mentu.)

200. Rā-āa-χeper setep-en-Mentu,   son of the Sun,   Āmen-meri Pa-seb-χā-nu. (Pasebχānu I.)

201. Āa-seḥ-Rā,   son of the Sun, ...

202. Setep-en-Mentu-Rā,   son of the Sun,   Meri-Mentu-Āmen-em-āpt. (Amenemapt.)

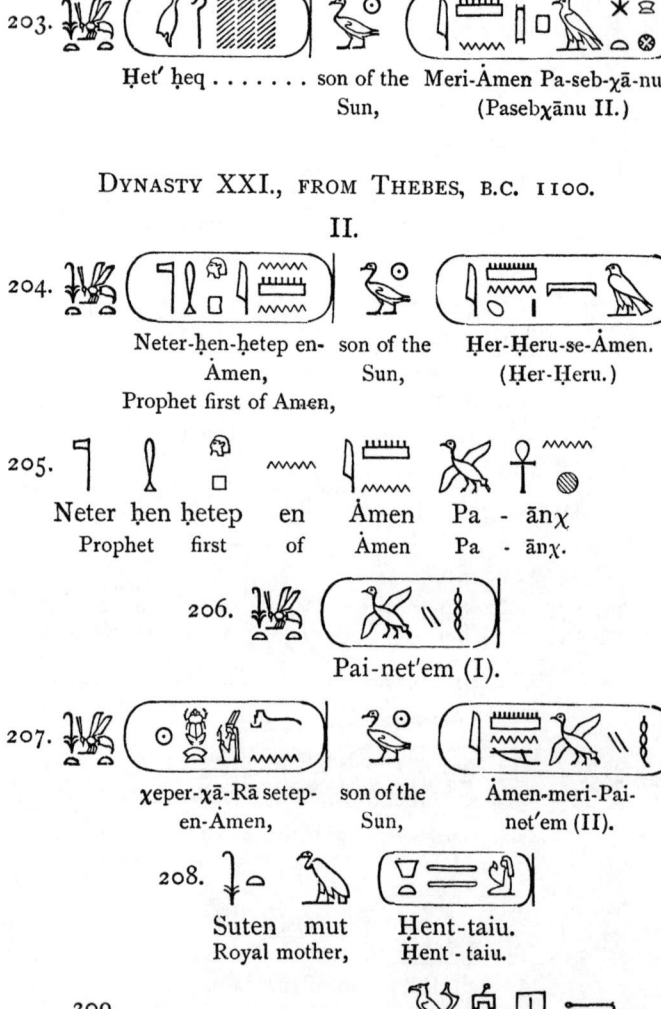

203. Ḥet' ḥeq . . . . son of the   Meri-Ȧmen Pa-seb-χā-nu.
                          Sun,   (Pasebχānu II.)

DYNASTY XXI., FROM THEBES, B.C. 1100.

II.

204. Neter-ḥen-ḥetep en- son of the   Ḥer-Ḥeru-se-Ȧmen.
     Ȧmen,   Sun,   (Ḥer-Ḥeru.)
     Prophet first of Amen,

205. Neter ḥen ḥetep   en   Ȧmen   Pa - ānχ
     Prophet first of   Ȧmen   Pa - ānχ.

206. Pai-net'em (I).

207. χeper-χā-Rā setep- son of the   Ȧmen-meri-Pai-
     en-Ȧmen,   Sun,   net'em (II).

208. Suten   mut   Ḥent-taiu.
     Royal mother, Ḥent - taiu.

209. Prophet first of Amen,   Masaherθ.

210. Prophet first, Men-χeper-Rā, child Royal, Ȧmen-meri Pai-net'em.

211.  Neter ḥen ḥetep en Āmen-Rā, Pai-net'em (III.)
Prophet first of Amen-Rā..

212.  Suten ḥemt Māt-ka-Rā.
Royal wife.

DYNASTY XXII., FROM BUBASTIS, B.C. 966.

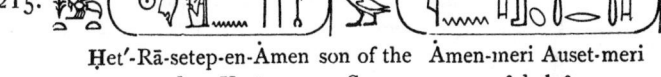

213.  χeper-seχet-Rā setep-en-Rā, son of the Sun, Āmen-meri-Shashanq. (Shashanq I.)

214.  χerp-χeper-Rā setep-en-Rā, son of the Sun, Āmen-meri Uasárken. (Osorkon I.)

215.  Ḥet'-Rā-setep-en-Āmen neter ḥeq Uast, son of the Sun, Āmen-meri Auset-meri θekeleθ. (Takeleth I.)

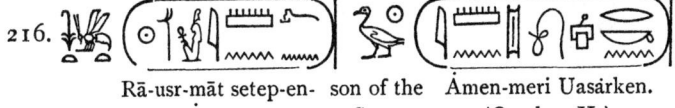

216. Rā-usr-māt setep-en-Āmen, son of the Sun, Āmen-meri Uasárken. (Osorkon II.)

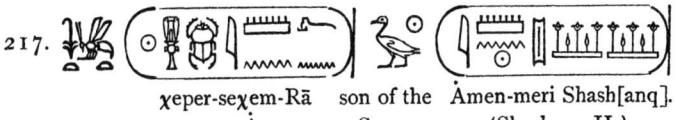

217. χeper-seχem-Rā setep-en-Āmen, son of the Sun, Āmen-meri Shash[anq]. (Shashanq II.)

218.

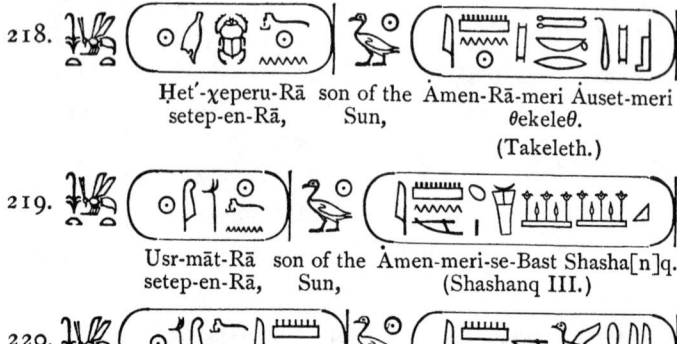

Ḥet'-χeperu-Rā   son of the   Amen-Rā-meri Áuset-meri
setep-en-Rā,   Sun,   θekeleθ.
                                 (Takeleth.)

219.

Usr-māt-Rā   son of the   Ámen-meri-se-Bast Shasha[n]q.
setep-en-Rā,   Sun,   (Shashanq III.)

220.

Usr-māt-Rā setep-   son of the   Ámen-meri Pa-mái.
en-Ámen,   Sun,   (Pa-mai.)

DYNASTY XXIII., FROM TANIS, B.C. 766.

221.

Se-her-áb-Rā, son of the Sun,   Peṭā-se-Bast.

222.

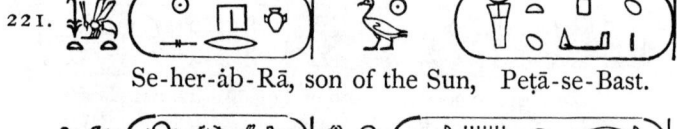

Āa-χeper-Rā   son of the   Rā-Ámen-meri Uasarkená.
setep- en-Ámen, Sun,   (Osorkon III.)

DYNASTY XXIV., FROM SAIS, B.C. 733.

223.

Uaḥ-ka-Rā, son of the Sun,   Bakenrenf.

DYNASTY XXIV., FROM ETHIOPIA, B.C. 733.

224.

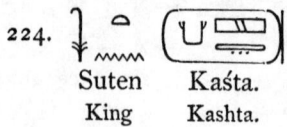

Suten   Kaśta.
King   Kashta.

225. Men-χeper-Rā, son of the Sun, P-ānχi.

226.  Åmen-meri P-ānχi, son of the Sun, P-ānχi.

DYNASTY XXV., FROM ETHIOPIA, B.C. 700.

227.  Nefer-ka-Rā, son of the Sun, Shabaka.
(Sabaco.)

228.  Teṭ-kau-Rā, son of the Sun, Shabataka.

229.  Rā-nefer-tem-χu, son of the Sun, Tahrq.
(Tirhakah.)

230. 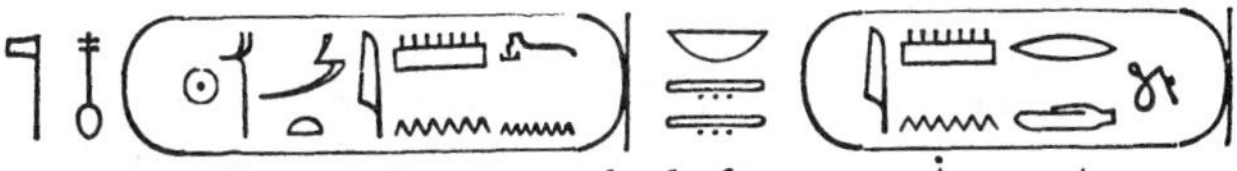 Neter nefer Usr-māt-Rā setep- lord of two Åmenruṭ.
God beautiful, en-Åmen, lands,

DYNASTY XXVI., FROM SAIS, B.C. 666.

231.  Uaḥ-åb-Rā, son of the Sun, Psemθek.
(Psammetichus I.)

232. Nem-âb-Rā,   son of the Sun,   Nekau.
(Necho II.)

233.  Nefer-âb-Rā, son of the Sun,   Psemθek.
(Psammetichus II.)

234. 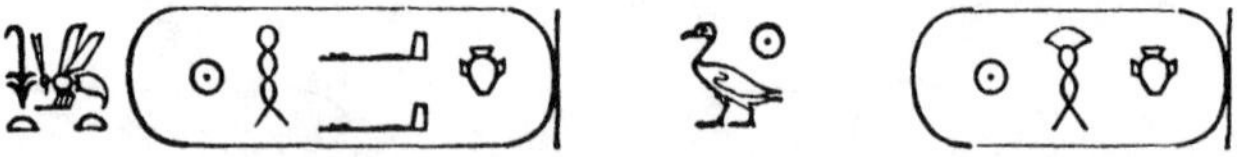 Ḥāā-âb-Rā,   son of the Sun, Uaḥ-âb-Rā.
(Apries.)

235.  χnem-âb-Rā, son of the Sun,   Âḥmes-se-net.
(Amāsis II.)

236.  Ānχ-ka-en-Rā, son of the Sun,   Psemθek.
(Psammetichus III.)

DYNASTY XXVII. (PERSIAN), B.C. 527.

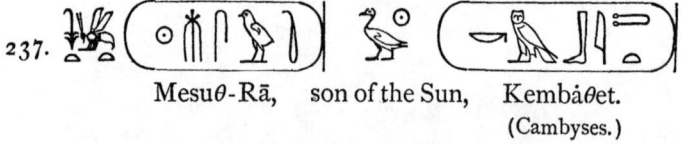

237. Mesuθ-Rā,   son of the Sun,   Kembáθet.
(Cambyses.)

238. Settu,   son of the Sun,   Ântariusha.
(Darius Hystaspes.)

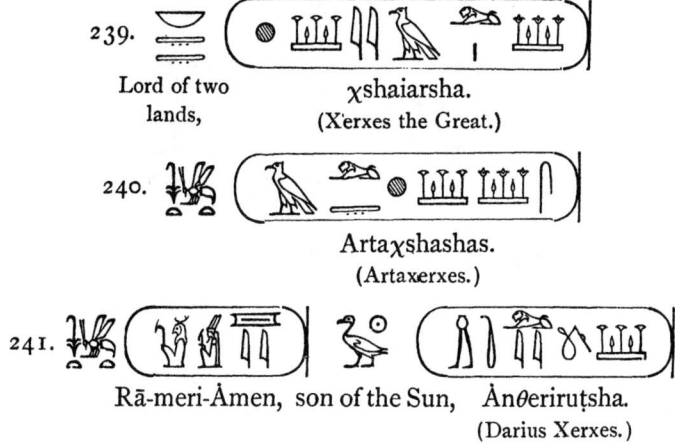

239. Lord of two lands, χshaiarsha. (X'erxes the Great.)

240. Artaχshashas. (Artaxerxes.)

241. Rā-meri-Åmen, son of the Sun, Ånθerirutsha. (Darius Xerxes.)

DYNASTY XXVIII., FROM SAIS.

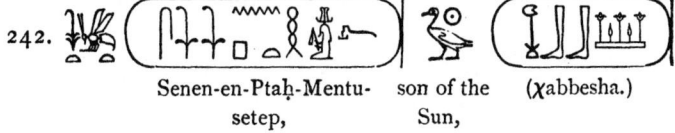

242. Senen-en-Ptaḥ-Mentu-setep, son of the Sun, (χabbesha.)

DYNASTY XXIX., FROM MENDES, B.C. 399.

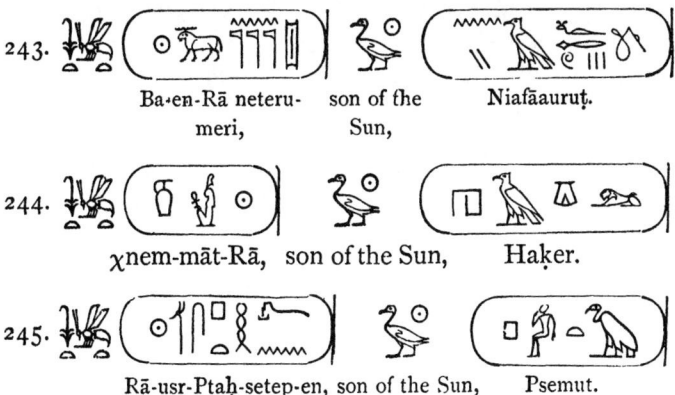

243. Ba·en-Rā neteru-meri, son of the Sun, Niafāauruṭ.

244. χnem-māt-Rā, son of the Sun, Haḳer.

245. Rā-usr-Ptaḥ-setep·en, son of the Sun, Psemut.

DYNASTY XXX., FROM SEBENNYTUS, B.C. 378.

246.

S-net'em-āb-Rā   son of the   Neχt-Ḥeru-ḥebt-meri-
setep-en-Ȧmen,   Sun,   Ȧmen.
(Nectanebus I.)

247.

χeper-ka-Rā,   son of the Sun,   Neχt-neb-f.
(Nectanebus II.)

DYNASTY XXXI.,* PERSIANS.

DYNASTY XXXII., MACEDONIANS, B.C. 332.

248.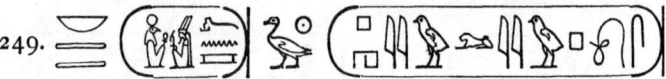

Setep-en-Rā-meri-   son of the   Aleksȧnṭres
Ȧmen,   sun,   (Alexander the Great.)

249.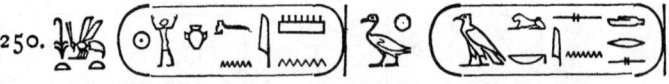

neb taiu Setep-en-Ḳā- son of the   Phiuliupuas
meri-Ȧmen,   Sun,   (Philip Aridaeus.)

250.

Rā-qa-āb-setep-en-Ȧmen, son of the   Aleksantres.
Sun.   (Alexander IV.)

---

* The word "dynasty" is retained here for convenience of classification.

DYNASTY XXXIII., PTOLEMIES, B.C. 305.

251.

Setep-en-Rā-meri- son of the   Ptulmis
   Ȧmen,   Sun,   (Ptolemy I. Soter I.)

252.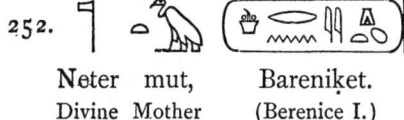

Neter   mut,   Bareniḳet.
Divine Mother   (Berenice I.)

253.

Rā-usr-ka-meri Ȧmen, son of the Sun,   Ptulmis
                  (Ptolemy II. Philadelphus.)

254.

Sutenet   set suten sent suten ḥemt neb taiu   Ȧrsanat
Royal daughter, royal sister, royal wife, lady of the two lands (Arsinoë)

255.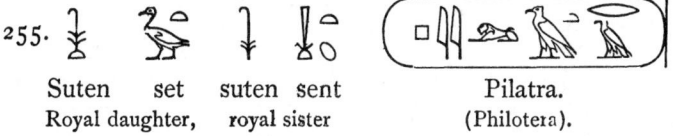

Suten   set   suten sent   Pilatra.
Royal daughter,   royal sister   (Philotera).

256.

Neteru-senu-uā-en-Rā-setep-Ȧmen-χerp (?)-en-ānχ, son of the Son,

Ptualmis ānχ t'etta Ptaḥ meri
Ptolemy (III. Euergetes I.), living for ever, beloved of Ptaḥ.

257.

Ḥeqt   nebt   taiu,   Bārenikat
Princess, lady of the two lands,   (Berenice II.)

258.

Neteru-menχ-uā-[en]-Ptaḥ-setep-en-Rā-usr-ka-Åmen-χerp (?)-ānχ,

son of the Sun   Ptualmis ānχ t'etta Åuset meri
    Ptolemy (IV. Philopator,) living for ever, beloved of Isis.

259.

Suten set suten sent ḥemt urt nebt taiu
Royal daughter, royal sister, wife, great lady, lady of the two lands

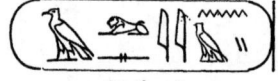

Arsinai.
Arsinoë (III., wife of Philopator I.)

260.

Neteru-meri-uā-en-Ptaḥ-setep-Rā-usr-ka-Åmen-χerp-ānχ,

son of the Sun   Ptualmis ānχ t'etta Ptaḥ meri.
    Ptolemy (V. Epiphanes) living for ever, beloved of Ptaḥ.

261. Ptolemy VI. Eupator, wanting.

262.

Suten set sen ḥemt   Qlauapeṭrat.
Royal daughter, sister, wife,   (Cleopatra I).

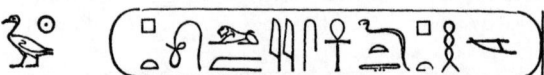

263.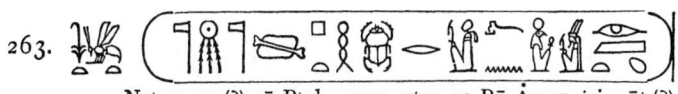

Neteru-χu (?)-uā-Ptaḥ-χeper-setep-en-Rā-Åmen-åri-māt (?),

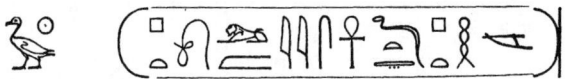

son of the Sun.   Ptualmis ānχ t'etta Ptaḥ meri.

Ptolemy (VII. Philometor I.), living for ever, beloved of Ptaḥ.

264.

Sutenet set   suten sent   ḥemt   suten   mut   neb   taiu

Royal daughter, royal sister, wife, royal mother, lady of the two lands,

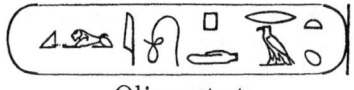

Qlåuapeṭrat.

(Cleopatra II. wife of Philometor I.).

265. Ptolemy VIII. Philopator II. wanting.

266.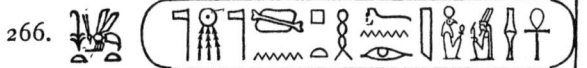

Neteru-χu (?)-uā-en-Ptaḥ-setep-en-Rā-Åmen-åri-māt χerp ānχ

son of the Sun.   Ptualmis ānχ t'etta Ptaḥ meri.

Ptolemy (IX. Euergetes II.), living for ever, beloved of Ptaḥ.

267.

Suten net

King of North and South,   lord of   two lands,

Neteru-menχ-māt-s-meri-net-uā-Ptaḥ-χerp (?)-setep-en-Rā-
Åmen-åri-māt.

Rā-se neb χāu

Son of the Sun, lord of
diadems,

Ptualmis ānχ t'etta Ptaḥ meri.

Ptolemy X. (Soter II. Philometor II.).

268.

Suten net,   Neteru-menχ-uā-Ptaḥ-setep-en-Rā-Amen-ári-māt-
King of North and   senen-Ptaḥ-ānχ-en,
South,

son of the   Ptualmis t'etu-nef Áleksentres ānχ t'etta Ptaḥ meri
Sun.   Ptolemy (XI.) called is he Alexander, living for ever,
beloved of Ptaḥ.

269.

Ḥeqt neb taiu

Princess, lady of two lands,

Erpā-ur-qebḥ-Báaárenekát.

Berenice (III.)

270. Ptolemy XII. (Alexander II.), wanting.

271.

P-neter-n-uā-enti-nehem-Ptaḥ-setep-en-ári-māt-en-
Rā-Ámen-χerp-ānχ

son of the Sun.   Ptualmis ānχ t'etta Ptaḥ Áuset meri.
Ptolemy (XIII.), living for ever, beloved of Isis and Ptaḥ.

272.

Neb taiu

Lady of two lands,

Qlapeṭrat t'eṭtu-nes Ṭrapenet.

Cleopatra (V.), called is she Tryphaena.

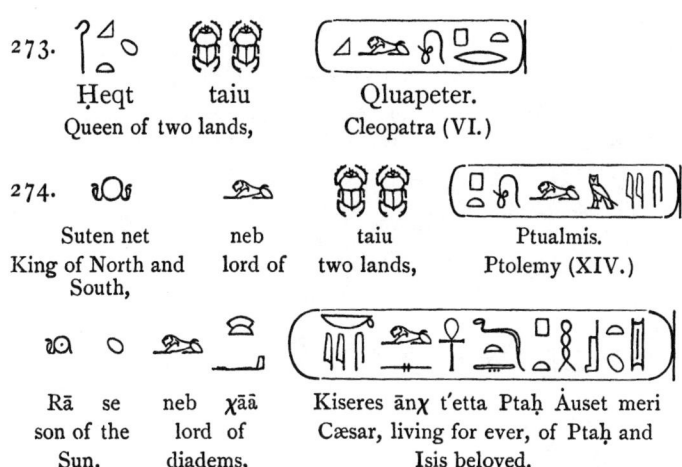

273. Ḥeqt   taiu   Qluapeter.
Queen of two lands,   Cleopatra (VI.)

274. Suten net   neb   taiu   Ptualmis.
King of North and   lord of   two lands,   Ptolemy (XIV.)
South,

Rā   se   neb χāā   Kiseres ānχ t'etta Ptaḥ Ȧuset meri
son of the   lord of   Cæsar, living for ever, of Ptaḥ and
Sun,   diadems,   Isis beloved.

DYNASTY XXXIV. ROMAN EMPERORS. B.C. 27.

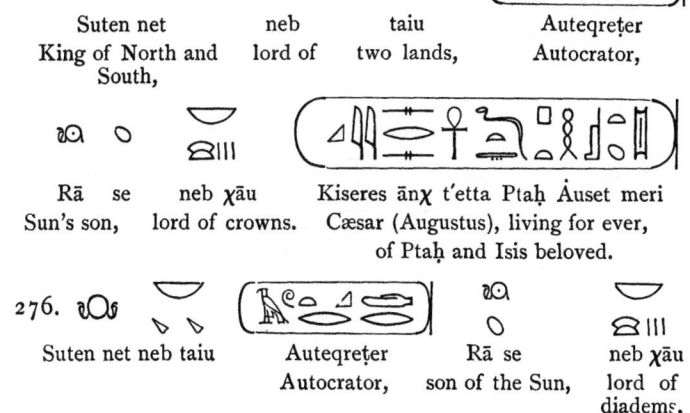

275. Suten net   neb   taiu   Auteqreṭer
King of North and   lord of   two lands,   Autocrator,
South,

Rā   se   neb χāu   Kiseres ānχ t'etta Ptaḥ Ȧuset meri
Sun's son,   lord of crowns.   Cæsar (Augustus), living for ever,
    of Ptaḥ and Isis beloved.

276. Suten net neb taiu   Auteqreṭer   Rā se   neb χāu
    Autocrator,   son of the Sun,   lord of
    diadems,

Tebaris Kiseres ānχ t'etta.
Tiberius Cæsar living for ever.

277.

Ḥeq ḥequ Autekreṭer Ptaḥ Auset-meri   son of the
King of kings, Autocrator, of Ptaḥ and Isis beloved,   Sun.

Qais Kaiseres Kermeniqis.
Gaius (Caligula) Cæsar Germanicus.

278.

Suten net   neb   taiu   Auteqreṭer Kiseres
                                    Autocrator Cæsar,

Rā sė neb   χāu   Qlutes Ṭibaresa.
Sun's son, lord of crowns,   Claudius Tiberius.

279.

neb taiu Ḥeq ḥequ-setep-en-Auset meri Ptaḥ
King of North and   lord of   Ruler of rulers, chosen one of Isis,
    South,   two lands,   beloved of Ptah.

se Rā   neb χāu   Autekreṭer Anráni.
Sun's son, lord of crowns,   (Autocrator Nero).

280

Merqes Auθunes (Marcus Otho).

Sun's son,   lord of   Kiseres netχ Autukreter.
              crowns,   Cæsar . . . . Autocrator.

281. Vitellius (wanting).

282.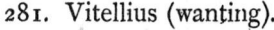

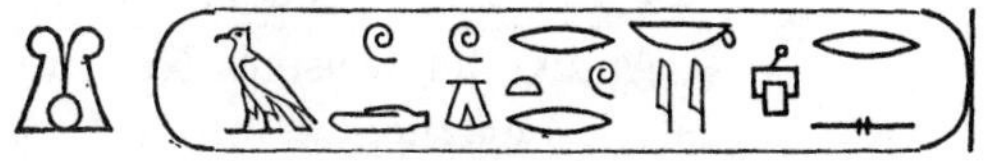

Suten net (?)   Autukretur Kisares
Autocrator Cæsar

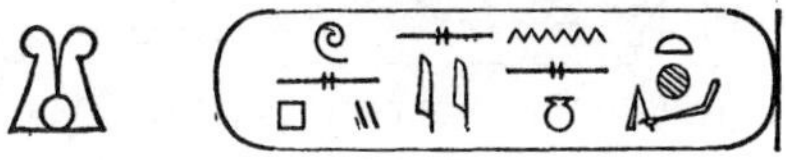

Suten net (?)   Uspisines netχ
Vespasianus . . . . .

283. 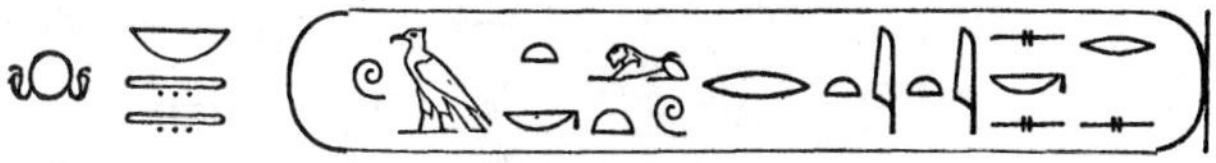 Autekretur Tetis Keseres
Autocrator Titus Cæsar,

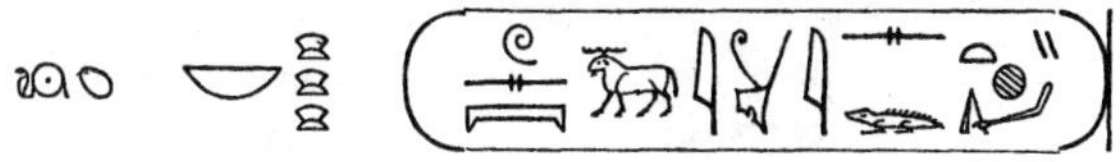

Sun's son,   lord of   Uspesines netχ
crowns,   Vespasianus . . . .

284. 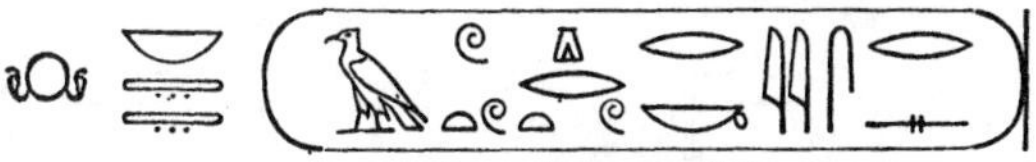 Autukretur Kiseres
Autocrator Cæsar,

Sun's son,   lord of   Tumetines netχ
crowns,   Domitianus . . . .

285. 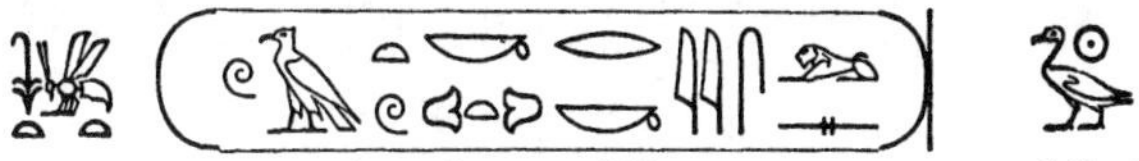 Autukreter Kiseres   son of the Sun,
Autocrator Cæsar,

Neruás netχ
Nerva . . . . .

286.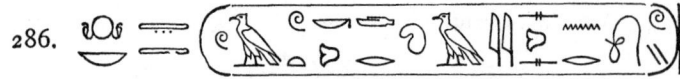

Autukreṭer Kaiseres Neruaui

Autocrator Cæsar Nerva,

the Sun's son, lord of crowns,   Trāianes netχ   Arsut Kermineqsa Ntekiqes.

Trajan . . . . .   (Augustus) Germanicus.   Dacicus.

287.

Autukreter Kiseres Trinus

Autocrator Cæsar Trajan,

the Sun's son, lord of crowns.

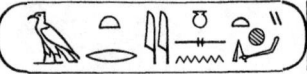

Atrines netχ.

Hadrian . . . . .

288.

Suten ḥemt   Sābinat   Sebestā ānχ t'etta.

Royal wife,   Sabina,   Sebaste living for ever.

289.   King of the North and South, lord of the world,

Autukreter Kiseres Θites Ālis Ātrins

Autocrator Cæsar Titus Aelius Hadrianus,

the Sun's son, lord of crowns.   Āntunines SebesΘesus Baus netiχui.

Antoninus Augustus Pius. . . . . .

290.

Autekreter Kaiseres
Autocrator Cæsar,

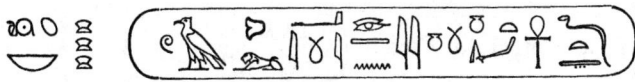

the Sun's son,   Aurelāis Antanines netχ ānχ t'etta
lord of crowns,   Aurelius Antoninus, ... living for ever.

291.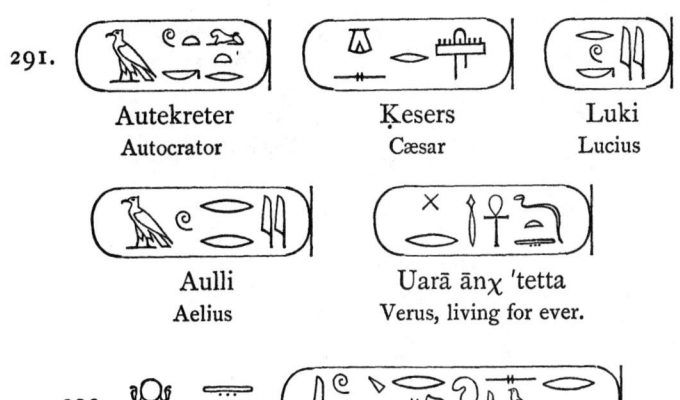

Autekreter   Ḳesers   Luki
Autocrator   Cæsar   Lucius

Aulli   Uarā ānχ 'tetta
Aelius   Verus, living for ever.

292.

Áutekretirs Kisáures
Autocrator Cæsar,

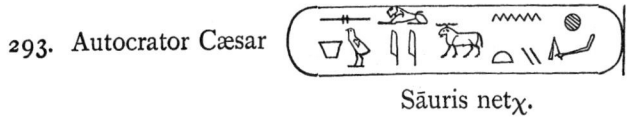

the Sun's son, lord of crowns,   Kāmṭāus Ā-en-ta-nins neteχ.
                         Commodus. Antoninus . . . . .

293. Autocrator Cæsar

Sāuris netχ.
Severus . . . .

294. Autocrator Cæsar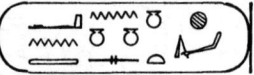

Āntanenes netχ.
Antoninus [Caracalla] . . . . .

295. Autocrator Cæsar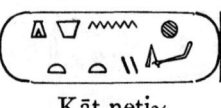

Ḳāt netiχ.
Geta . . . . .

296. Autocrator Cæsar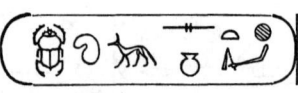

Taksas netχ.
Decius . . . . .

INDEX.

A CATALOG OF SELECTED DOVER
BOOKS IN ALL FIELDS OF INTEREST

CONCERNING THE SPIRITUAL IN ART, Wassily Kandinsky. Pioneering work by father of abstract art. Thoughts on color theory, nature of art. Analysis of earlier masters. 12 illustrations. 80pp. of text. 5⅞ x 8½. 23411-8 Pa. $4.95

ANIMALS: 1,419 Copyright-Free Illustrations of Mammals, Birds, Fish, Insects, etc., Jim Harter (ed.). Clear wood engravings present, in extremely lifelike poses, over 1,000 species of animals. One of the most extensive pictorial sourcebooks of its kind. Captions. Index. 284pp. 9 x 12. 23766-4 Pa. $14.95

CELTIC ART: The Methods of Construction, George Bain. Simple geometric techniques for making Celtic interlacements, spirals, Kells-type initials, animals, humans, etc. Over 500 illustrations. 160pp. 9 x 12. (Available in U.S. only.) 22923-8 Pa. $9.95

AN ATLAS OF ANATOMY FOR ARTISTS, Fritz Schider. Most thorough reference work on art anatomy in the world. Hundreds of illustrations, including selections from works by Vesalius, Leonardo, Goya, Ingres, Michelangelo, others. 593 illustrations. 192pp. 7⅛ x 10¼. 20241-0 Pa. $9.95

CELTIC HAND STROKE-BY-STROKE (Irish Half-Uncial from "The Book of Kells"): An Arthur Baker Calligraphy Manual, Arthur Baker. Complete guide to creating each letter of the alphabet in distinctive Celtic manner. Covers hand position, strokes, pens, inks, paper, more. Illustrated. 48pp. 8¼ x 11. 24336-2 Pa. $3.95

EASY ORIGAMI, John Montroll. Charming collection of 32 projects (hat, cup, pelican, piano, swan, many more) specially designed for the novice origami hobbyist. Clearly illustrated easy-to-follow instructions insure that even beginning papercrafters will achieve successful results. 48pp. 8¼ x 11. 27298-2 Pa. $3.50

THE COMPLETE BOOK OF BIRDHOUSE CONSTRUCTION FOR WOODWORKERS, Scott D. Campbell. Detailed instructions, illustrations, tables. Also data on bird habitat and instinct patterns. Bibliography. 3 tables. 63 illustrations in 15 figures. 48pp. 5¼ x 8½. 24407-5 Pa. $2.50

BLOOMINGDALE'S ILLUSTRATED 1886 CATALOG: Fashions, Dry Goods and Housewares, Bloomingdale Brothers. Famed merchants' extremely rare catalog depicting about 1,700 products: clothing, housewares, firearms, dry goods, jewelry, more. Invaluable for dating, identifying vintage items. Also, copyright-free graphics for artists, designers. Co-published with Henry Ford Museum & Greenfield Village. 160pp. 8¼ x 11. 25780-0 Pa. $10.95

HISTORIC COSTUME IN PICTURES, Braun & Schneider. Over 1,450 costumed figures in clearly detailed engravings–from dawn of civilization to end of 19th century. Captions. Many folk costumes. 256pp. 8⅜ x 11¾. 23150-X Pa. $12.95

THE BEST TALES OF HOFFMANN, E. T. A. Hoffmann. 10 of Hoffmann's most important stories: "Nutcracker and the King of Mice," "The Golden Flowerpot," etc. 458pp. 5⅜ x 8½. 21793-0 Pa. $9.95

FROM FETISH TO GOD IN ANCIENT EGYPT, E. A. Wallis Budge. Rich detailed survey of Egyptian conception of "God" and gods, magic, cult of animals, Osiris, more. Also, superb English translations of hymns and legends. 240 illustrations. 545pp. 5⅜ x 8½. 25803-3 Pa. $13.95

FRENCH STORIES/CONTES FRANÇAIS: A Dual-Language Book, Wallace Fowlie. Ten stories by French masters, Voltaire to Camus: "Micromegas" by Voltaire; "The Atheist's Mass" by Balzac; "Minuet" by de Maupassant; "The Guest" by Camus, six more. Excellent English translations on facing pages. Also French-English vocabulary list, exercises, more. 352pp. 5⅜ x 8½. 26443-2 Pa. $9.95

CHICAGO AT THE TURN OF THE CENTURY IN PHOTOGRAPHS: 122 Historic Views from the Collections of the Chicago Historical Society, Larry A. Viskochil. Rare large-format prints offer detailed views of City Hall, State Street, the Loop, Hull House, Union Station, many other landmarks, circa 1904-1913. Introduction. Captions. Maps. 144pp. 9⅜ x 12¼. 24656-6 Pa. $12.95

OLD BROOKLYN IN EARLY PHOTOGRAPHS, 1865-1929, William Lee Younger. Luna Park, Gravesend race track, construction of Grand Army Plaza, moving of Hotel Brighton, etc. 157 previously unpublished photographs. 165pp. 8⅞ x 11¾. 23587-4 Pa. $13.95

THE MYTHS OF THE NORTH AMERICAN INDIANS, Lewis Spence. Rich anthology of the myths and legends of the Algonquins, Iroquois, Pawnees and Sioux, prefaced by an extensive historical and ethnological commentary. 36 illustrations. 480pp. 5⅜ x 8½. 25967-6 Pa. $10.95

AN ENCYCLOPEDIA OF BATTLES: Accounts of Over 1,560 Battles from 1479 B.C. to the Present, David Eggenberger. Essential details of every major battle in recorded history from the first battle of Megiddo in 1479 B.C. to Grenada in 1984. List of Battle Maps. New Appendix covering the years 1967-1984. Index. 99 illustrations. 544pp. 6½ x 9¼. 24913-1 Pa. $16.95

SAILING ALONE AROUND THE WORLD, Captain Joshua Slocum. First man to sail around the world, alone, in small boat. One of great feats of seamanship told in delightful manner. 67 illustrations. 294pp. 5⅜ x 8½. 20326-3 Pa. $6.95

ANARCHISM AND OTHER ESSAYS, Emma Goldman. Powerful, penetrating, prophetic essays on direct action, role of minorities, prison reform, puritan hypocrisy, violence, etc. 271pp. 5⅜ x 8½. 22484-8 Pa. $7.95

MYTHS OF THE HINDUS AND BUDDHISTS, Ananda K. Coomaraswamy and Sister Nivedita. Great stories of the epics; deeds of Krishna, Shiva, taken from puranas, Vedas, folk tales; etc. 32 illustrations. 400pp. 5⅜ x 8½. 21759-0 Pa. $12.95

THE TRAUMA OF BIRTH, Otto Rank. Rank's controversial thesis that anxiety neurosis is caused by profound psychological trauma which occurs at birth. 256pp. 5⅜ x 8½. 27974-X Pa. $7.95

A THEOLOGICO-POLITICAL TREATISE, Benedict Spinoza. Also contains unfinished Political Treatise. Great classic on religious liberty, theory of government on common consent. R. Elwes translation. Total of 421pp. 5⅜ x 8½. 20249-6 Pa. $10.95

PIANO TUNING, J. Cree Fischer. Clearest, best book for beginner, amateur. Simple repairs, raising dropped notes, tuning by easy method of flattened fifths. No previous skills needed. 4 illustrations. 201pp. 5⅜ x 8½. 23267-0 Pa. $6.95

HINTS TO SINGERS, Lillian Nordica. Selecting the right teacher, developing confidence, overcoming stage fright, and many other important skills receive thoughtful discussion in this indispensible guide, written by a world-famous diva of four decades' experience. 96pp. 5⅜ x 8½. 40094-8 Pa. $4.95

THE COMPLETE NONSENSE OF EDWARD LEAR, Edward Lear. All nonsense limericks, zany alphabets, Owl and Pussycat, songs, nonsense botany, etc., illustrated by Lear. Total of 320pp. 5⅜ x 8½. (AVAILABLE IN U.S. ONLY.) 20167-8 Pa. $7.95

VICTORIAN PARLOUR POETRY: An Annotated Anthology, Michael R. Turner. 117 gems by Longfellow, Tennyson, Browning, many lesser-known poets. "The Village Blacksmith," "Curfew Must Not Ring Tonight," "Only a Baby Small," dozens more, often difficult to find elsewhere. Index of poets, titles, first lines. xxiii + 325pp. 5⅝ x 8¼. 27044-0 Pa. $8.95

DUBLINERS, James Joyce. Fifteen stories offer vivid, tightly focused observations of the lives of Dublin's poorer classes. At least one, "The Dead," is considered a masterpiece. Reprinted complete and unabridged from standard edition. 160pp. 5$\frac{3}{16}$ x 8¼. 26870-5 Pa. $1.00

GREAT WEIRD TALES: 14 Stories by Lovecraft, Blackwood, Machen and Others, S. T. Joshi (ed.). 14 spellbinding tales, including "The Sin Eater," by Fiona McLeod, "The Eye Above the Mantel," by Frank Belknap Long, as well as renowned works by R. H. Barlow, Lord Dunsany, Arthur Machen, W. C. Morrow and eight other masters of the genre. 256pp. 5⅜ x 8½. (Available in U.S. only.) 40436-6 Pa. $8.95

THE BOOK OF THE SACRED MAGIC OF ABRAMELIN THE MAGE, translated by S. MacGregor Mathers. Medieval manuscript of ceremonial magic. Basic document in Aleister Crowley, Golden Dawn groups. 268pp. 5⅜ x 8½. 23211-5 Pa. $9.95

NEW RUSSIAN-ENGLISH AND ENGLISH-RUSSIAN DICTIONARY, M. A. O'Brien. This is a remarkably handy Russian dictionary, containing a surprising amount of information, including over 70,000 entries. 366pp. 4½ x 6⅛. 20208-9 Pa. $10.95

HISTORIC HOMES OF THE AMERICAN PRESIDENTS, Second, Revised Edition, Irvin Haas. A traveler's guide to American Presidential homes, most open to the public, depicting and describing homes occupied by every American President from George Washington to George Bush. With visiting hours, admission charges, travel routes. 175 photographs. Index. 160pp. 8¼ x 11. 26751-2 Pa. $11.95

NEW YORK IN THE FORTIES, Andreas Feininger. 162 brilliant photographs by the well-known photographer, formerly with *Life* magazine. Commuters, shoppers, Times Square at night, much else from city at its peak. Captions by John von Hartz. 181pp. 9¼ x 10¾. 23585-8 Pa. $13.95

INDIAN SIGN LANGUAGE, William Tomkins. Over 525 signs developed by Sioux and other tribes. Written instructions and diagrams. Also 290 pictographs. 111pp. 6⅛ x 9¼. 22029-X Pa. $3.95

THE INFLUENCE OF SEA POWER UPON HISTORY, 1660–1783, A. T. Mahan. Influential classic of naval history and tactics still used as text in war colleges. First paperback edition. 4 maps. 24 battle plans. 640pp. 5⅜ x 8½. 25509-3 Pa. $14.95

THE STORY OF THE TITANIC AS TOLD BY ITS SURVIVORS, Jack Winocour (ed.). What it was really like. Panic, despair, shocking inefficiency, and a little heroism. More thrilling than any fictional account. 26 illustrations. 320pp. 5⅜ x 8½. 20610-6 Pa. $8.95

FAIRY AND FOLK TALES OF THE IRISH PEASANTRY, William Butler Yeats (ed.). Treasury of 64 tales from the twilight world of Celtic myth and legend: "The Soul Cages," "The Kildare Pooka," "King O'Toole and his Goose," many more. Introduction and Notes by W. B. Yeats. 352pp. 5⅜ x 8½. 26941-8 Pa. $8.95

BUDDHIST MAHAYANA TEXTS, E. B. Cowell and others (eds.). Superb, accurate translations of basic documents in Mahayana Buddhism, highly important in history of religions. The Buddha-karita of Asvaghosha, Larger Sukhavativyuha, more. 448pp. 5⅜ x 8½. 25552-2 Pa. $12.95

ONE TWO THREE . . . INFINITY: Facts and Speculations of Science, George Gamow. Great physicist's fascinating, readable overview of contemporary science: number theory, relativity, fourth dimension, entropy, genes, atomic structure, much more. 128 illustrations. Index. 352pp. 5⅜ x 8½. 25664-2 Pa. $9.95

EXPERIMENTATION AND MEASUREMENT, W. J. Youden. Introductory manual explains laws of measurement in simple terms and offers tips for achieving accuracy and minimizing errors. Mathematics of measurement, use of instruments, experimenting with machines. 1994 edition. Foreword. Preface. Introduction. Epilogue. Selected Readings. Glossary. Index. Tables and figures. 128pp. 5³⁄₈ x 8¹⁄₂. 40451-X Pa. $6.95

DALÍ ON MODERN ART: The Cuckolds of Antiquated Modern Art, Salvador Dalí. Influential painter skewers modern art and its practitioners. Outrageous evaluations of Picasso, Cézanne, Turner, more. 15 renderings of paintings discussed. 44 calligraphic decorations by Dalí. 96pp. 5⅜ x 8½. (Available in U.S. only.) 29220-7 Pa. $5.95

ANTIQUE PLAYING CARDS: A Pictorial History, Henry René D'Allemagne. Over 900 elaborate, decorative images from rare playing cards (14th–20th centuries): Bacchus, death, dancing dogs, hunting scenes, royal coats of arms, players cheating, much more. 96pp. 9¼ x 12¼. 29265-7 Pa. $12.95

MAKING FURNITURE MASTERPIECES: 30 Projects with Measured Drawings, Franklin H. Gottshall. Step-by-step instructions, illustrations for constructing handsome, useful pieces, among them a Sheraton desk, Chippendale chair, Spanish desk, Queen Anne table and a William and Mary dressing mirror. 224pp. 8⅛ x 11¼. 29338-6 Pa. $13.95

THE FOSSIL BOOK: A Record of Prehistoric Life, Patricia V. Rich et al. Profusely illustrated definitive guide covers everything from single-celled organisms and dinosaurs to birds and mammals and the interplay between climate and man. Over 1,500 illustrations. 760pp. 7½ x 10⅛. 29371-8 Pa. $29.95

Prices subject to change without notice.

Available at your book dealer or write for free catalog to Dept. GI, Dover Publications, Inc., 31 East 2nd St., Mineola, N.Y. 11501. Dover publishes more than 500 books each year on science, elementary and advanced mathematics, biology, music, art, literary history, social sciences and other areas.